Investigating Workplace Discourse

Investigating Workplace Discourse explores the characteristics of different types of workplace conversation, such as decision-making, training, briefing or making arrangements. Particular attention is also given to interactions with a more social focus, such as small talk or office gossip.

The book provides an overview of a range of approaches to analysing workplace discourse, then argues for a combination of quantitative corpus-based methods, to compare specific linguistic features in different 'genres' (such as decision-making and instructional discourse), and qualitative methods involving a close analysis of individual conversations, to explore such issues as politeness, power, conflict and consensus-building.

A corpus of conversations recorded in a variety of office environments in both the UK and the USA is used throughout to demonstrate the interplay between speakers accomplishing tasks and maintaining relationships in the workplace.

Almut Koester is Lecturer in English Language in the Department of English, University of Birmingham, UK, and author of *The Language of Work* (2004).

The Routledge *Domains of Discourse* series features cutting edge research on specific areas and contexts of spoken language, bringing together the framework and tools for analysis of a discourse.

As our understanding of spoken communication develops, corpus linguistics promises to provide the unifying link between previously compartmentalized areas of spoken language such as media discourse and language pedagogy.

Designed to present research in a clear and accessible form for students and researchers or practitioners, each title in the series is developed around three strands:

- **Content** each title focuses on the subject matter of a particular discourse, e.g. media or business
- **Corpus** each title is based on a collection of relevant spoken texts in its domain of discourse
- **Methodology** each title engages with a number of approaches in language and discourse analysis

Titles in the series

Investigating Workplace Discourse
Almut Koester

Investigating Classroom Discourse
Steve Walsh

Investigating Media Discourse
Anne O'Keeffe

The series editor

Michael McCarthy is Emeritus Professor of Applied Linguistics at the University of Nottingham (UK), Adjunct Professor of Applied Linguistics at the Pennsylvania State University, USA, and Adjunct Professor of Applied Linguistics at the University of Limerick, Ireland. He is co-director of the five-million-word CANCODE spoken English corpus project, sponsored by Cambridge University Press, at the University of Nottingham.

Investigating Workplace Discourse

Almut Koester

P
302
K634
2006
WEB

Routledge
Taylor & Francis Group

LONDON AND NEW YORK

First published 2006
by Routledge
2 Park Square, Milton Park, Abingdon, Oxon OX14 4RN

Simultaneously published in the USA and Canada
by Routledge
270 Madison Ave, New York, NY 10006

Routledge is an imprint of the Taylor & Francis Group, an informa business

© 2006 Almut Koester

Typeset in Perpetua by The Running Head Limited, Cambridge
Printed and bound in Great Britain by The Cromwell Press,
Trowbridge, Wiltshire

All rights reserved. No part of this book may be reprinted or
reproduced or utilized in any form or by any electronic,
mechanical, or other means, now known or hereafter
invented, including photocopying and recording, or in any
information storage or retrieval system, without permission in
writing from the publishers.

British Library Cataloguing in Publication Data
A catalogue record for this book is available from the British Library

Library of Congress Cataloging in Publication Data
Koester, Almut
    Investigating workplace discourse / by Almut Koester
    p.   cm. – (Domains of discourse)
    Includes bibliographical references.
    1. Discourse analysis. 2. Interpersonal relations. I. Title. II. Series
P302.K634 2006
401'.41–dc22
2006007745

ISBN10: 0–415–36470–1 (hbk)
ISBN10: 0–415–36471–X (pbk)

ISBN13: 978–0–415–36470–6 (hbk)
ISBN13: 978–0–415–36471–3 (pbk)

To my parents, Helmut and Gisela Koester

Contents

Notes on data and transcription

Data

Unless otherwise stated, all extracts in the book are the author's own data.

Transcription

For purposes of anonymity, all speakers, company names, organizations and some products are identified by pseudonyms in the transcripts.

The following transcription conventions were used:

,	slightly rising in intonation at end of tone unit
?	high rising intonation at end of tone unit
.	falling intonation at end of tone unit
!	animated intonation
…	noticeable pause or break within a turn of less than one second
—	sound abruptly cut off, e.g., false start
italics	emphatic stress
:	colon following vowel indicates elongated vowel sound
::	extra colon indicates longer elongation
↑	a step up in pitch (higher key) (the notion of 'key' is based on Brazil 1997)
↓	a shift down in pitch (lower key)
( )	parentheses around tone units spoken *sotto voce* (low key intonation)
/ /	words between slashes show uncertain transcription
/?/	indicates inaudible utterances: one ? for each syllable
⌐	overlapping or simultaneous speech
⌐ ⌐	words in these brackets are utterances interjected by a speaker within another speaker's turn
=	latching: no perceptible inter-turn pause
[ ]	words in these brackets indicate non-linguistic information, e.g. pauses of 1 second or longer (the number of seconds is indicated), speakers' gestures or actions;

[…]   ellipsis marks between square brackets indicates that the speaker's turn
        continues, that the extract starts in the middle of a speaker turn, or
        that some turns have been omitted

.hh   inhalation (intake of breath)

hhh   aspiration (releasing of breath)

t   tongue click

'Heheheh' indicates laughter, for each syllable laughed a 'heh' is transcribed

<u>underlining</u> indicates key features in a data extract

Acknowledgements

I am indebted to the many people who have helped me with the research that went into this book. First and foremost to Michael McCarthy, for his invaluable support, guidance, inspiration and encouragement in carrying out the original research, and in writing this book. Also to Ron Carter, who has given intellectual, practical and moral support with many aspects of the research.

This project would not have been possible without the people who enabled me to collect my data. Very great thanks therefore go to those who put me in touch with the organizations where I collected my data, and to those working in the organizations, who acted as my helpers and informants, in particular to Ulrich Koester, Sharron Pritchard, Jeanne McCarten and Rob Machalek. I also owe a great debt to those who were kind enough to let me record their conversations and interview them: Dave, John, Ron, Mary C., Mary V., Kathy, Elka and Amy, who will not be named in full to preserve their anonymity, as well as to all the others whose voices are on my tapes. I am very grateful to the organizations who allowed me to make recordings and spend time in their offices. I would also like to thank Cambridge University Press for transcribing a portion of my data and allowing me to access the Cambridge and Nottingham Corpus of Discourse in English (CANCODE), while a part-time member of staff at the University of Nottingham (1998–2001), and the Cambridge International Corpus.

I am also extremely grateful to Michael Handford and Rosamund Moon for advice with specific aspects of the research and to Jane Restorick for help with statistics. A particularly big thank you to Ian McMaster for his help and support through the years, especially in giving me opportunities to apply many aspects of my research findings to different areas of language teaching. It has been wonderful to have feedback and support from fellow writers Anne O'Keeffe and Steve Walsh.

Many other people have provided inspiration, ideas, feedback and help of various kinds:

- my fellow PhD students at the University of Nottingham and in Limerick: Svenja Adolphs, Leticia Frossard, Martha Jones, Fiona Farr, Mario Saraceni,

Melinda Tan, Julia Harrison, Xiaoling Zhang, Popi Hatzikosta, Ahmed Melie-bary, Salwa Nugali, Danny Badran, Christiana Gregoriou, as well as other members of the MEL group

- teachers and members of staff in the School of English Studies: Norbert Schmitt, Peter Stockwell, John McRae, Margaret Berry, Zoltan Dörnyei, Valerie Durow, Ann Collins and Roseanne Richardson.

Finally, I want to express my great appreciation for the support and encouragement of my family: to my parents, Helmut and Gisela Koester, to my aunt Elisabeth Harrassowitz, and above all to my husband, Terry Pritchard.

Some of the research results reported in this book, as well as some of the data samples, have been previously published in 'The role of idioms in negotiating workplace encounters', in H. Trappes-Lomax (ed.), *Change and Continuity in Applied Linguistics: Selected Papers from the Annual Meeting of the British Association for Applied Linguistics held at the University of Edinburgh, September 1999*, Clevedon: Multilingual Matters (2000); 'Getting things done and getting along in the office', in M.Coulthard, J. Cotterill and F. Rock (eds), *Dialogue Analysis VII: Working with Dialogue: Selected Papers from the 7th IADA Conference, Birmingham 1999*, Tübingen: Max Niemeyer Verlag GmbH (2000): 197–207; 'The performance of speech acts in workplace conversations and the teaching of communicative functions', *System* 30, 2 (2002): 167–84; *The Language of Work*, London: Routledge (2004). Many thanks to Elsevier for allowing me to reprint parts of 'Relational sequences in workplace genres', *Journal of Pragmatics* 36 (2004) in Chapter 7 of this book.

1 Workplace discourse

An overview

1.1 Introduction

This book is concerned with the analysis of naturally occurring talk in workplace environments, such as the following extracts from longer conversations:

Example 1.1

1	Dave	[...] Basically I've used their o:ld. price list,
2	Val	Right,
3	Dave	And ... I've made a few changes.
4	Val	Yeah,
5	Dave	An' then there's the cover.
6	Val	Right,
7	Dave	So that— ↓ I got sent down a few things, I got that up this morning, Uh ... This ... She wanted to know, if we've done this before, I went through the ... file, it didn't look like it had. [...]

Example 1.2

1	Chris	Um I'm— I'm going white water rafting next— next weekend.
2	Joe	*Really!*
3	Chris	⌊So hopefully if I don't die, I'll be back ... the Monday after that
4	Joe	⌊Hahahahahah haha
5	Joe	You— Would you please wear a— a life jacket you know
6	Chris	⌊Hahahahahahahah

Example 1.3

1	Carol	Be nice if there was some place where you could print it out and the date would show up every time, ... ↓ But anyway ...
2	Beth	↑ Oh it's right *here* Carol. Revised. Seven, one, ninety-seven.

 3 Carol   ⌊(/automatic/)
 4 Carol ↑ Oh.
 5 Beth   ⌊That's the last time I worked on it.
 6 Carol .hh ↑ Oh you *do* have that.
 7 Beth   ⌊That– Oh yeah. Yeah. It's very small.
 8 Carol   ⌊Does that update
        itself … uh automatically?
 9 Beth   ⌊Yes it does. I don't have to touch it.
10 Carol Okay. Good. That's exactly what I wanna do.
11 Beth   So that's what you want? Like a snapshot thing.
12 Carol   ⌊Yeah.
13 Beth   Okay.
14 Carol ⌊Right. Okay. .hh So. ↑ Boy it's tiny up there,
15 Beth   I know, hehehe You need a big magnifying glass. [chuckles]
        (from the Cambridge International Corpus © Cambridge University Press)

We can easily recognize Example 1.1 as taking place at work, as the speakers are obviously focusing on a particular task. In the second extract, on the other hand, the conversation addresses topics outside work (activities at the weekend) and looks like a typical example of small talk. The only indication that this conversation takes place at work is the reference to Monday (when the speakers will be back in the office after the weekend).

In the third example, the speakers are again engaged in a workplace task; however it is different from Example 1.1 in a number of ways. In Example 1.1, the discourse is fairly one-sided in that one speaker does most of the talking, while the other merely produces back-channels such as *right* to show understanding. In contrast to this, Example 1.3 seems much more interactive, as both speakers contribute more or less equally to the discourse. Another difference is that while the speakers in Example 1.1 remain task-focused throughout, in Example 1.3, the comments in turns 14 and 15 (about the size of the item on the computer screen) are not actually necessary in order to accomplish the task. These turns share some features with the small talk extract in Example 1.2, such as laughter and expressions of interest or surprise (*Really! Boy it's tiny up there*). The function of these two turns seems to be to express subjective evaluations and show solidarity with the interlocutor, rather than get the job done.

These examples demonstrate some of the variation found in workplace conversations. First of all they show that people engage in a range of workplace tasks, for instance in the first extract a speaker briefs a co-worker about a job, and in the third example the two participants discuss how they can set up a particular procedure. While there is considerable variation in the types of spoken interaction occurring across different workplaces, many interactions have similar goals, and can therefore be said to be instances of the same 'genre'. The genre in Example 1.1 could thus be described as 'briefing', and in Example 1.3 the speakers seem to be involved in some kind of decision-making. This book attempts to show that genre is a significant factor influencing the linguistic choices made by speakers, and it will explore key differences between some of the most common spoken workplace genres.

The above extracts also show that discourse participants may be more or less task-focused in their interactions with one another at work: in Example 1.1, the speakers remain task-focused throughout, while Example 1.2 consists entirely of small talk; Example 1.3 again deals with a workplace task, but contains some elements of relational talk. Clearly then, a comprehensive exploration of workplace discourse should take account of such variation in task-orientation. Particular attention will be paid in the following chapters to investigating the way in which linguistic choices reflect not only speakers' goals in getting a job done, but also their attention to relational aspects of the encounter. The aim of this book is therefore to examine the linguistic and interactive devices which people working together use jointly to accomplish a variety of workplace tasks, as well as to build, maintain and negotiate workplace relationships.

1.2 Institutional, professional and workplace discourse

Workplace talk occurs in a wide range of settings from talk between co-workers, as in the examples above, to interactions in service encounters or health-care settings, to international business communication. It will not be possible to cover all these types of interaction in any kind of detail, but this chapter attempts to provide an overview of previous research in this area and of the kind of discourse that has been investigated. But first we need to examine what is distinctive about workplace discourse, and why it warrants special investigation.

1.2.1 The characteristics of institutional talk

The term 'institutional talk' is frequently used in the literature to refer to interactions in all kinds of workplace setting. Institutional talk differs from ordinary conversation in a number of ways (Drew and Heritage 1992: 3–65, Schegloff 1992a, Heritage 1997). According to Drew and Heritage (1992: 22), the distinctiveness of institutional discourse is reflected in three dimensions of interaction:

1 *Goal orientation*: 'an orientation by at least one of the participants to some core goal, task or identity ... conventionally associated with the institution.'
2 '*Special and particular constraints* on what one or both of the participants will treat as allowable contributions to the business at hand.'

3   '*Inferential frameworks and procedures* that are particular to specific institutional contexts.'

Participants' goal orientation is reflected in a number of features of workplace talk, for example in the recurrence of particular types of discursive activity which can be associated with specific workplace practices, such as instruction-giving, decision-making, briefing. Institutional encounters may also have an overall structural organization consisting of a number of phases, each of which plays a particular role in terms of the overall goal of the encounter. It is noticeable that task-oriented talk tends to be more structured than talk in which participants are not focused on a workplace task. Such conversations often begin with the initiator announcing the purpose of the encounter, e.g.:

Uh … just wanted to tell you about my … conversation with ↑Tony.

Such explicit signalling of discourse goals is less common in casual conversation, where speakers do not have such clear transactional goals, and a specific reason for engaging in talk is not needed. Because task-oriented workplace conversations are often highly structured, they lend themselves particularly well to genre analysis, which has been applied to a variety of institutional contexts (see Chapters 2 and 3).

Constraints on what can be said or done can be manifested in a number of different ways. In some institutional settings (e.g., the courtroom, the classroom) specialized turn-taking systems are in operation; but even in less formal settings where this is not the case (e.g., in most interactions between co-workers), participants' orientation to the institutional context may be displayed in the details of talk (Hutchby and Wooffitt 1998). According to Heritage (1997), institutional interaction often involves the reduction of the range of interactional practices compared to ordinary conversation. For example, in many professional–lay interactions (e.g., doctor–patient), it is the professional who tends to ask the questions, although no official turn-taking rules exist.

The institutional context and the constraints it imposes can also be reflected in lexical choice, most obviously when technical or professional jargon is used. But the link between lexical choice and the institutional context can also be more subtle, for example using *we* instead of *I* and thereby speaking as a member of an organization, or through a variety of 'institutional euphemisms' (Drew and Heritage 1992: 3–65, Heritage 1997). Recent corpus-based research on spoken Business English (McCarthy and Handford 2004) confirms that such institutional discourse is indeed distinct from casual conversation in terms of the relative frequencies of many lexico-grammatical items.

The distinctive inferential frameworks of specific institutional contexts can be reflected, for example, in turn design and adjacency pair structure, that is the action a turn is designed to perform and the way in which it is responded to (Heritage 1997). Adjacency pairs have been identified in conversation analysis as the basic unit of interaction, consisting of a first pair part, which sets up the expectation (or 'conditional relevance') for a matching second pair part to be produced by the addressee (see Levinson 1983: 284–370). In the following extract from a conversation in the sales office of a small US business, an adjacency pair is produced by the president, Chris, and his sales manager, Joe:

Example 1.4

Chris	Haven't seen much in the way of *sales* the last half of the week.
Joe	.hh Well, a lot of the media, the– the orders have been *very* difficult getting out. Stuff is– is jammed.

Joe responds defensively to Chris's initiating comment that sales have been low, and attempts to explain this situation in terms of problems that have arisen. It is because of the institutional context and the roles the speakers play within it (Joe, as the sales manager, is expected to ensure that sales are kept at a certain level) that Chris's comment is heard as a kind of accusation against which Joe tries to defend himself. Chris's comment in this example has consequences well beyond the sequence and influences the rest of the conversation, in which Joe gives details of the problems the sales team has been having.

1.2.2 Institutional roles and identities

Another way in which institutional talk differs from ordinary conversation, according to Heritage (1997), is that institutional interactions are often asymmetrical (although casual conversation is only symmetrical at a certain level of idealization). Institutional roles may be linked to certain discursive rights and obligations, for example in terms of initiating and controlling interactions, asking questions, and so forth. In lay–professional encounters, there is often asymmetry of knowledge about the goals and procedures of the interaction: for the professional the encounter is often routine, whereas for the lay-person it may be new, and s/he may be unaware of the professional's objectives. In such encounters, access to expert knowledge is often unequal. At the same time as professionals possess expert knowledge which their lay clients do not have, they are also often reluctant to commit themselves (and thereby their institution) to firm positions, and thereby display what Heritage (1997: 177) refers to as 'epistemological caution'.

   In professional and workplace interactions, participants therefore take on particular institutional roles which are often asymmetrical (e.g., doctor–patient, teacher–student, employer–employee). But it cannot simply be assumed that these institutional roles are always relevant to the talk in which speakers are engaged. As Greatbatch and Dingwall (1998) show, one can distinguish between social identities (parent, spouse, manager, teacher) and discourse identities (speaker–addressee, questioner–answerer, inviter–invitee), which refer to actions performed by the discourse participants through talk. Speakers may make relevant their institutional identities through the discourse identities they take up (e.g., in Example 1.4 above the institutional identities of company president and sales manager are invoked), but they may also invoke other social identities.

Roles and identities are therefore not predetermined and fixed, but actively negotiated through talk (ten Have 1991, Holmes *et al.* 1999, Roberts and Sarangi 1999a). In addition, speakers usually invoke multiple identities in the course of one encounter, which may be more or less symmetrical or asymmetrical (Gavruseva 1995, Holmes *et al.* 1999). The primacy of discursive roles for the analysis of talk is a recurring theme throughout this book.

1.2.3 Overview of previous research

There is by now a well-established tradition of discourse studies in institutional and workplace environments. Drew and Heritage's edited volume *Talk at Work* (1992) brings together research carried out in the tradition of conversation analysis on spoken discourse in a range of institutional settings, including health-care delivery, legal proceedings, news and job interviews. In a more recent edited volume on workplace talk, Sarangi and Roberts (1999) take an interdisciplinary approach, but cover a similar range of contexts: medical and legal settings are again well represented; discourse in management and industry is also investigated.

In another collection of papers, Gunnarsson *et al.* (1997) examine *The Construction of Professional Discourse* and include research on both spoken and written discourse (legal documents and scientific writing are examples of the latter). While the terms 'institutional' and 'professional' are often used interchangeably, 'professional discourse' often seems to refer to written discourse; for example Bhatia's (1993) edited volume *Analysing Genre: Language Use in Professional Settings* deals exclusively with written texts (business, academic and legal genres). Sarangi and Roberts (1999), however, propose a different kind of distinction, using 'institutional' to refer to discourse practices as part of an organization, and 'professional' for the discourse used by professional practitioners.

Discourse in medical and health-care settings has received particular attention, especially by sociologists working with conversation analysis or ethnography (Cicourel 1987 and 1999, Heath 1992, Heritage and Sefi 1992, Maynard 1992, ten Have 1995, P. Atkinson 1999). Medical discourse has also been examined from a sociolinguistic perspective using frame analysis (Tannen and Wallat 1987/1993,

J. Coupland *et al.* 1994), and an early study takes a discourse analytical approach to doctor–patient interactions (Coulthard and Ashby 1976). Legal discourse has also been extensively investigated by sociologists (J.M. Atkinson and Drew 1979, Maynard 1989, J.M. Atkinson 1992, Drew 1992, Greatbatch and Dingwall 1997 and 1999). Linguists have also taken an interest in the legal arena, and have examined legal language or 'forensic discourse' (Gibbons 1994, Kniffka 1996, Cotterill 2000, Coulthard 2000). Related to institutional discourse is public discourse in the media, i.e. radio, television and the press, which has been investigated using a number of approaches: conversation analysis (e.g., Hutchby 1996), critical discourse analysis (e.g., Fairclough 1995a) and, more recently corpus-based approaches (O'Keeffe 2006).

Besides media discourse (see Fairclough 1995a), a number of other types of institutional discourse have been examined from the point of view of language and power, using the tools of critical discourse analysis (CDA). A variety of institutional contexts are examined in Thornborrow's (2001) book *Power Talk*, including police interviews and media discourse, while Mayr (2004) sheds light on a specialized and socially marginalized institutional environment in analysing prison discourse. Relationships between employers and employees and managers and subordinates are also subject to critical examination in workplaces such as call centres (Cameron 2000) or government departments (Holmes *et al.* 1999, Holmes 2000a, Holmes 2000b, Holmes and Stubbe 2003).

Customer–client interactions in service encounters have also been investigated quite extensively (Mitchell 1957/1975, Merritt 1976, N. Coupland 1983, Ventola 1983 and 1987, Hasan 1985, Iacobucci 1990, McCarthy 2000), especially by linguists working with genre analysis (see also Chapters 2 and 3). Classroom language is another type of institutional discourse to receive attention (e.g., Edwards and Westgate 1994, Johnson 1995), and has been investigated using a number of different approaches, for example the exchange structure model of discourse analysis developed at the University of Birmingham (Sinclair and Coulthard 1975, Coulthard and Montgomery 1981, Jarvis and Robinson 1997), critical discourse analysis (Kumaravadivelu 1999) and systemic functional linguistics (Christie 2002). In a recent volume, Walsh (2006) brings together a number of different approaches, based on a data-driven model.

Research has also been carried out on business communication; for example Boden (1994) examines the role of talk within business organizations. Structured events, such as meetings and negotiations, have received particular attention; for instance Firth (1995a) brings together a variety of studies on the discourse of negotiation. Most of these use conversation analytical methods (e.g., Bilmes 1995, Button and Sharrok 1995), as do Francis's (1986), Firth's (1995b) and Neu's (1998) articles on negotiation; while Lampi (1986) takes a linguistic approach to analysing the language of business negotiations. A variety of different types of meeting have been investigated: Bargiela-Chiappini and Harris (1997a) describe the discourse of corporate meetings, Handford (2004) and McCarthy and Handford (2004) examine data from 'internal' and 'external' meetings (among other types of business interaction), while Holmes and Stubbe (2003) look at both formal and informal meetings within organizations. Hewings and Nickerson's (1999) edited volume examines both spoken and written business discourse from a pedagogical perspective (the teaching of Business English), while Bargiela-Chiappini and Nickerson (1999) focus exclusively on written business discourse, such as business letters, faxes and email. McCarthy and Handford (2004) investigate spoken business discourse using a corpus.

One area of language use to receive a great deal of attention in recent years is cross-cultural and multicultural business communication, for example in a volume of collected papers (Bargiela-Chiappini and Harris 1997b) on the language of international business situations. Other studies of cross-cultural and multicultural interactions in a variety of business situations include analyses of the language of meetings (Yamada 1990, Bargiela-Chiappini and Harris 1995 and 1997a, Bilbow 1997, Spencer-Oatey and Xing 1998, Rogerson-Revell 1999 and Poncini 2002 and 2004), the language of negotiations (Garcez 1993, Marriott 1995), telephone conversations (Halmari 1983) and service encounters (Aston 1995). Related to studies of cross-cultural communication are those investigating differences in business situations between the communication strategies of men and women (Tannen 1994 and 1998) and native and non-native speakers (Dow 1999, Williams 1988, Oertli 1991).

It is not surprising that research on business communication has been concerned mainly with relatively formal and structured events such as meetings and negotiations. Such encounters have clear beginnings and endings as well as internal structures in the form of separate phases. They therefore lend themselves to formal analysis, and the fact that everyday labels exist for these events indicates that they are generally recognized to constitute distinct genres.

But a great deal of face-to-face business or office communication takes place outside such structured events, for example workplace conversations involving ad hoc interactions such as making arrangements, briefing, giving instructions, decision-making or simply socializing. Whereas casual conversation has been studied extensively, such informal oral office communication has received less attention. Nevertheless a number of studies do examine less formal types of office communication, such as spontaneous manager–employee interactions (Gavruseva 1995, Holmes *et al.* 1999, Holmes 2000a, Holmes and Stubbe 2003); or interaction between co-workers involved in a variety of workplace tasks, for example problem-solving (Willing 1992) or learning new technology (Linde 1997). Some of the research on negotiating also deals with unplanned problem-solving arising in the course of workplace encounters (e.g., Boden 1995 or Wagner 1995).

As illustrated in Example 1.2 at the beginning of the chapter, co-workers also engage in casual conversation that does not centre around a workplace task. In recent years discourse analysts have also begun to examine such interactions. Small talk has been investigated in a variety of service encounters (Ylänne-McEwen 1996, N. Coupland and Ylänne-McEwen 2000, Kuiper and Flindall 2000, McCarthy 2000) and in health-care contexts (J. Coupland *et al.* 1994, Ragan 2000); and Eggins and Slade (1997), Holmes (2000b) and Holmes and Stubbe (2003) look at casual conversation among co-workers. Focusing attention on more casual types of interaction in the workplace entails re-examining the distinctive characteristics (described in Section 1.2.1) that institutional discourse is said to display in contrast to casual conversation between friends. If, for example, talk among co-workers, or between service providers and customers, is not always goal-oriented, the boundaries between casual conversation and institutional talk become blurred. These issues will be addressed in some detail in the following chapters.

The above overview shows that there exists already a wealth of studies on a wide range of institutional discourse. However, previous studies, especially earlier ones, have tended to focus on the 'institutional' and task-oriented nature of such discourse, while paying less attention to relationally oriented features of talk. Although small talk and issues such as politeness and relationship-building in workplace talk are now receiving more attention, there is still much scope for further research. In addition, many studies have been carried out within specific approaches, for example conversation analysis, ethnography or CDA. There is now a need for more integrated approaches, and indeed a move in this direction is apparent (e.g., Sarangi and Roberts 1999, Holmes and Stubbe 2003). This book aims to contribute towards filling these gaps, and will propose that corpus linguistics and genre analysis, approaches which have not been widely applied to the analysis of spoken workplace discourse, provide particularly useful methods for exploring linguistic variation in institutional and professional talk.

1.3 Outline of the book

While addressing issues that should be relevant to most workplace contexts, this book will focus mainly on interactions between co-workers in office environments. It draws on a corpus of naturally occurring office conversations recorded in a variety of workplaces and geographical environments in the USA and the UK. These include university departments, editorial offices of a publisher, and small to medium-sized businesses in areas such as printing, advertising, the paper trade and food retailing.

This chapter has provided an introduction to the topic and aims of the book, and an overview of previous research on institutional and professional talk, including the different workplace contexts which have been investigated. The key differences between institutional talk and 'ordinary conversation' have been identified.

In the next chapter, a range of approaches to analysing workplace discourse will be surveyed. These approaches will be critically reviewed, and the main advantages and disadvantages of each highlighted. It will be suggested that an integrated approach using both quantitative and qualitative methods is most suitable, as this provides complementary perspectives on the data analysed, thus resulting in a richer and more comprehensive description. Genre analysis, in combination with corpus-based and discourse analytical methods, will be put forward as particularly suitable for the analysis of workplace discourse.

The aim of Chapter 3 is to provide an overview and illustrative examples of some of the most commonly occurring spoken workplace genres, such as decision-making, negotiating and procedural/instructional discourse. As workplace interactions are usually oriented towards clear transactional outcomes, a goals-based approach is used to identify a number of broadly defined genres that can occur across a range of workplace environments. The chapter will include sample analyses of selected genres, highlighting the variation that exists.

Chapter 4 presents a framework for analysing the interpersonal dimension of workplace talk. It suggests that evidence of relational goals can be found at various 'levels' of discourse from longer stretches of small talk down to individual turns or even lexical items. An overview is then provided of a range of lexico-grammatical features which frequently perform interpersonal functions, including modal items, hedges, vague language and idioms.

Chapter 5 presents a corpus-based comparison across a variety of workplace genres of the linguistic features identified in Chapter 4. The purpose of this chapter is to demonstrate the application of corpus linguistic methods to the analysis of workplace data in general, and comparison of genres in particular.

Chapter 6 examines some of the discursive and linguistic strategies used by co-workers to negotiate consensus and manage conflict. An analysis of selected encounters investigates some of the following issues: politeness and solidarity strategies in different genres, institutional and discursive asymmetry and the negotiation of discursive roles and identities, and the characteristics of conflictual versus consensual discourse.

Chapter 7 takes up the framework introduced in Chapter 4 and aims to provide a comprehensive account of relational talk in workplace interactions. The various types of relational talk identified in Chapter 4 are described in detail with illustrative examples. Relational talk is compared in the different genres; and a close analysis of various encounters reveals the occurrence, placement and function of relational talk within transactional discourse.

Finally, Chapter 8 summarizes and brings together the issues raised in the book, and concludes with directions for future research and areas of practical application.

2 Approaches to analysing workplace discourse

2.1 Introduction

A range of approaches, originating within a variety of disciplines – sociology, anthropology and linguistics – have been used to study talk in institutional and workplace settings. These approaches will not be reviewed in detail here, as this has been done elsewhere; for example Sarangi and Roberts (1999) provide an excellent critical discussion of different approaches to analysing workplace discourse. This chapter touches on some of the key issues involved in collecting and analysing workplace talk, and shows how different approaches deal with these issues and what they can reveal about the data. One central issue is the role of context, therefore the chapter will begin by examining different views and treatments of context and how these are linked to methodology. Next quantitative and qualitative approaches to analysing naturally occurring talk will be compared, and the advantages and disadvantages of each highlighted. Finally, it will be suggested that the notion of genre is useful in examining workplace discourse, as it allows for an integrated approach using both quantitative and qualitative methods and a range of discourse analytical approaches.

2.2 The role of context

2.2.1 Some methodological issues

One of the distinguishing features of institutional talk is that it is often difficult at first for an outsider to understand what people are talking about. The topics and procedures discussed, as well as a great deal of vocabulary, are unfamiliar and specific to the work of the organization or branch of business. The lay researcher often lacks the relevant background information or context to make sense of the discourse.

But defining what constitutes 'context', and therefore what kind of background knowledge is relevant, is no simple task. It can be defined narrowly, as the actual physical (and institutional) setting, or more broadly in terms of the larger socio-cultural context of the speaker–hearer world, which provides a backdrop to the encounter. Another view of context is that it is *created* through verbal or non-verbal interaction (see Duranti and Goodwin 1992, Pomerantz 1998). As Sarangi and Roberts (1999: 25–33) show, the different approaches to analysing workplace discourse vary considerably in terms of how they define and deal with context.

Two very different definitions of context, linked to different methodological approaches, have been put forward in sociologically oriented investigations of institutional talk. Within ethnography, the importance of gathering information about the institutional context and the background knowledge of the participants is stressed (e.g., Cicourel 1987), and thus a very broad view of context is taken. Ethnographic methods involve observation of workplace interactions, collecting documentary evidence and interviews with practitioners, which aim to reveal participants' views of their workplace practices. Ethnography is often combined with the analysis of audio- or video-recorded interactions, involving a triangulation of data, for example by eliciting participants' interpretations of recorded interactions.

Conversation analysis (CA), which is one of the dominant methods used in analysing workplace talk, takes quite a different approach to context. Conversation analysts argue that such an 'external' definition of context is problematic, as there are 'indefinitely many potentially relevant aspects of context' (Schegloff 1992b: 197). They therefore propose a talk-intrinsic definition of context, where talk is seen as creating its own context. Context is defined as dynamically created and expressed in and through interaction; and only by examining the details of talk is it possible to see which aspects of the socio-cultural context are oriented to by the participants (Mandelbaum 1990/91, Schegloff 1992a, 1992b, Heritage 1997, Silverman 1999). Conversation analysts emphasize that it cannot simply be assumed that all features of the institutional context will be relevant to an interaction within the institutional setting, but that evidence for its 'institutionality' must be found in the talk itself: 'it is through interaction that institutional imperatives originating from outside the interaction are evidenced and made real and enforceable for the participants' (Heritage 1997: 163).

A very obvious case in which the institutional context does not seem to be oriented to by the discourse participants is the case of small talk at work; especially if the talk is about topics outside the workplace, such as in the extract in Example 1.2, where two co-workers discuss the forthcoming weekend. As noted in discussing the extract, there are very few clues in the talk itself that it takes place at work, or, to put it in CA terms, there is no evidence in the talk of participants orienting to institutional concerns.

Ethnographers, on the other hand, argue that by limiting the analysis only to verbal interactions, the researcher may be missing essential background information that is relevant to the interpretation of any given stretch of institutional discourse:

Verbal interaction is related to the task at hand. Language and other social practices are interdependent. Knowing something about the ethnographic setting, the perception of and characteristics attributed to others, and broader and local social organizational conditions becomes imperative for an understanding of linguistic and nonlinguistic aspects of communicative events.

(Cicourel 1987: 218)

This point can be illustrated with the following example from a workplace conversation between two colleagues, Dave and Val, who work for a small printing firm:

Example 2.1

1	Dave	⌊And she said something about Christmas brochures, this was on Friday, I can't remember what it was, ↑ Is she waiting for a quote on *that* still?
2	Val	Christmas brochures … ↑ Uhm …
3	Dave	Ah! … Oh I see,
4	Val	Is it– ↑ Are these the ones that we're doing. That they want–
5	Dave	to go in, ↑ Oh did they want a *separate* quote on that, I suppose, =
6	Val	= Which. Which ones. Which *ones*.
7	Dave	You know the … four page things? Have you not seen it. It's the same style but from Malcolm Hennessy. No it's not Malcolm Hennessy, it's Delaney.
8	Val	⌊Delaney
9	Dave	Christmas … So it would be … I have to refer to her again, ↑'Cause *they* wanna come through *you* really, 'cause *you* haven't got a clue what you're *doing*.
10	Val	No.
11	Dave	Did you wanna s– … just get in touch–?
12	Val	⌊I mean can– I can deal with *that* now, I can work– I can do a price, Except I'll find out whether i– whether⌊Dave: Yeah.⌋ she was mistaken, whether she was expecting it to *be* two colour.
13	Dave	⌊Yeah.
14	Dave	And these … if I give you um … um … what I've done for the … Christmas … thing⌊Val: Yeah⌋ now, an' then you get– you … talk to her.

Clearly, it is difficult to make sense of this extract without some knowledge of the immediate context, the specific job Val and Dave are discussing, the nature of the company and the respective roles of the speakers within it. Knowing that the conversation takes place in a printing firm, we can assume the speakers are discussing some kind of printing job, but it is also essential to know who is responsible for what in relation to this job. Dave is in fact the firm's artist, who does all the design work, and Val is the office administrator, whose duties include putting together quotations for customers. It is also helpful to know that *Delaney* is the name of the firm they are doing the job for, and that the *she* referred to several times in the extract is the woman they deal with at the customer's firm. Although there is not much technical vocabulary in this particular extract, it is important to understand that the issue of the number of colours to be used in the brochure (turn 12: *two colour*) makes a difference to the price quotation. Knowing about the physical context is important as well, as Dave is actually showing Val some work he has done. In fact it is a typical characteristic of workplace discourse that documents in the physical environment are often the object of discussion, and therefore an integral part of the interaction. Finally, the nature of the relationship between the speakers also has an impact on how we interpret the discourse: it is useful to know that Val and Dave are on the same level within the company, that they have a friendly relationship, and that therefore Dave's remark in turn 9 (*'cause you haven't got a clue what you're doing*) is not perceived by Val as hostile or threatening.

Other approaches to analysing workplace interactions also vary in the way they view context. Interactional sociolinguistics (IS) also takes a talk-intrinsic view of context, but is particularly interested in the way in which participants individually interpret the discourse and in the inferences they draw. Gumperz (1992: 230) refers to this process as 'contextualization', which he defines as 'speakers' and listeners' use of verbal and nonverbal signs to relate what is said at any one time and in any one place to knowledge acquired through past experience'. Interactional sociolinguists are particularly interested in interactions between people from different cultural, social or ethnic backgrounds and the extent to which inferential procedures are shared or not. Thus, although IS analysis involves examining the details of talk in interaction, the aim is to address broader issues of the inferential frameworks operating within different cultural and social groups; indeed IS method also involves carrying out ethnographic research (see Gumperz 1999).

Gumperz (ibid.) gives the example of two interviews conducted by the same interviewer in a job centre, one with a native of the region and the other with an applicant who has a South Asian background. Although the interviewer asks roughly the same questions in each interview, the applicants differ considerably in the way they answer. Gumperz explains these differences in terms of the different inferences drawn by the participants based on their respective cultural backgrounds, and shows how this results in the applicant of South Asian origin being disadvantaged, although no overt prejudice is involved.

A social constructionist approach to workplace interactions takes a similar view of context, considering both the wider social context and the talk-intrinsic context as essential in the interpretation of the discourse. These two types of context are seen as mutually reflexive, and social and institutional identities as subject to negotiation through interaction (Holmes *et al.* 1999, Holmes and Stubbe 2003). Holmes and Stubbe, for example, show how managers may either assert or down-play their power in interactions with subordinates. A dynamic, rather than a static view is thus taken of social and institutional contexts.

The widest view of context is taken within critical discourse analysis (CDA), which attempts to link specific discursive practices with ideological frameworks (Fairclough 1992, Sarangi and Roberts 1999: 32–3). Critical discourse analysts also take an overtly critical stance in relation to their object of study, aiming to 'provide an account of the role of language, language use, discourse or commu-nicative events in the (re)production of dominance and inequality' (van Dijk 1993: 279). While detailed analysis of talk and texts are also carried out in CDA, the categories of analysis are derived from social theory and philosophy. This contrasts with CA method, which claims to use categories which the discourse participants themselves orient to.

Another reason critical discourse analysts deem it is important to look beyond the individual institutional contexts for their interpretation is the increasing 'hybridity' of talk in different domains of social activity (Cameron 2000: 21–3). Fairclough (1992: 204–5) argues that there is an increasing tendency in institu-tional discourse towards what he calls 'conversationalization', that is the adoption of less formal styles of communication in institutional environments, which fre-quently obscure the existing power structures. This can be illustrated with an example (ibid: 138–49) in which he compares two doctor–patient encounters: one 'standard' medical interview, where the doctor's control of the interaction is overt and obvious, and another interview which is more conversational, and where the doctor thus uses more indirect methods of control.

2.2.2 Summary: the role of context

The above discussion has highlighted the differences and similarities in the way the various approaches used in analysing workplace and institutional talk view the notion of context. While certain methods, such as ethnography and conver-sation analysis, diverge considerably in what they consider to be relevant aspects of context for the purposes of analysis; others, i.e. interactional sociolinguistics and social constructionist approaches, consider that both talk-extrinsic and talk-intrinsic context needs to be taken into account

A number of researchers have proposed that a combination of ethnography and conversation analysis is the best approach to analysing interaction in institutional environments (Cicourel 1987, Maynard 1989). Sarangi and Roberts (1999: 1–57)

argue for a 'thick description' which includes fine-grained linguistic analysis and ethnographic description as well as the larger political and ideological context. Similar to the social constructionist view of context described above, is the dynamic view proposed by Goodwin and Duranti (1992: 31), involving linguistic as well as non-linguistic dimensions:

> Instead of viewing context as a set of variables that statically surround strips of talk, context and talk are now argued to stand in a mutually reflexive relationship ... with talk, and the interpretative work it generates, shaping context as much as context shapes talk.

We have already seen that, as a lay researcher in an unfamiliar institutional environment, it is often quite difficult to make sense of institutional interactions without the help of informants and without any knowledge of institutional structures and workplace practices. It is therefore essential to carry out at least a certain amount of ethnographic research in order to gain insight into the 'local communicative ecology' (Gumperz 1999: 465). As Cicourel (1987) points out, understanding a particular communicative event from the perspective of the participants (which is the stated aim of conversation analysis) may depend on having access to the knowledge and background assumptions with which the participants operate.

Nevertheless, conversation analysts warn against taking a 'bucket' view of context, as it is sometimes called, i.e. simply to assume that external contexts will constrain any given interaction. Some approaches to institutional or professional discourse, for example the Hallidayan approach to genre analysis (which will be discussed in more detail below), seem to view context as having a deterministic influence on language. Hasan (1985) sees the 'contextual configuration', made up of field, tenor and mode, as being predictive of the generic structure of a text. But if one takes a talk-intrinsic view of context, the relevance of the institutional context must be demonstrated through what speakers actually say, and is not assumed to determine a priori what they *will* say. This is especially important with workplace interactions that vary considerably in terms of how task-oriented they are, as illustrated with the three extracts from workplace conversations discussed at the beginning of Chapter 1.

2.3 Quantitative and qualitative approaches

Most studies of workplace talk have been carried out using one or a combination of the qualitative approaches described above, which all involve some detailed analysis of talk-in-interaction, that is some form of discourse analysis. While the sequential and interactional features of talk can only be discovered using a qualitative approach, the investigation of workplace data can also benefit from the use of quantitative methods provided by a corpus linguistic approach. For example, in order to compare high-frequency items across a range of encounters, quantitative corpus linguistic methods are extremely useful, indeed indispensable. It will be argued here that corpus-based methods and discourse analysis can be usefully combined to analyse the same data set, as they provide different but mutually complementary perspectives, resulting in a more complete description of the data.

While corpus-based methods pick up on recurring features over a wide set of data, discourse analysis focuses in detail on individual texts.

2.3.1 *Corpus linguistic methods*

Corpus linguistic methods have traditionally been used to investigate very large computerized collections of written and spoken texts, such as the Bank of English, with hundreds of millions of words, or the British National Corpus (BNC) containing 100 million words. Early studies used large general corpora to carry out lexicographical research which led to the production of dictionaries. More recently specialized corpora have been compiled in order to examine texts belonging to a particular register or genre, for example newspapers or academic discourse (see Hunston 2002, and McEnery and Wilson 1996 for a description of existing corpora). With such specialized corpora, which tend to be smaller than general corpora, there has been a move to combining corpus-based methods with discourse analysis. An example of this is work done using the Cambridge and Nottingham Corpus of Discourse in English (CANCODE), which consists of five million words of naturally occurring informal conversations of British English (e.g., McCarthy 1998, McCarthy and Carter 2000, Adolphs and Carter 2003, Carter and McCarthy 2004). A corpus of spoken business encounters, the Cambridge and Nottingham Business English Corpus (CANBEC) has now been compiled at the University of Nottingham (see McCarthy and Handford 2004), and although a few corpus-based studies have been carried out (see Bargiela-Chiappini and Harris 1997a and Nelson 2000), corpus-based research into spoken workplace and institutional discourse is still rare. For spoken academic English, the Michigan Corpus of Academic Spoken English (MICASE) and British Academic Spoken English Corpus (BASE) are accessible on-line. While the BNC contains 1.3 million words of 'business events such as sales demonstrations, trades union meetings, consultations, interviews' (see BNC 2005), there is to date no openly available corpus composed exclusively of business or workplace talk.

Using corpus-based methods means that analysis involving quantification, which would be extremely onerous or even impossible to do manually, can be done very quickly and easily. As Hunston (2002: 3) points out, corpus access software enables the user to rearrange and process the information in the corpus in ways that allow particular types of observation and provide 'a new perspective on the familiar' (ibid.). The frequency of individual words or phrases can be examined, and compared across sub-corpora, for example in different genres or institutional contexts. Concordancing programmes show all the instances of the same lexical item in concordance lines (which provide a minimal context), thus giving some indication of how and for what purposes these items are used, as well as revealing any frequent phraseological patterns. For example, simply counting the occurrences of the word *just* in a corpus of workplace talk does not tell us all that much, as it is multi-functional, and can be used as a time adverb, a hedge, an intensifier or as a synonym for *only*. However, by looking at this word in concordance lines, the different functions can be identified, and the information classified accordingly. In a small corpus of office conversations (ABOT, see below), such an examination of *just* revealed that it was used most frequently as a hedge, as illustrated in the following sample of concordance lines:

Example 2.2

well we ought to	**just**	get it sorted hadn't we
we'll	**just**	keep a note of 'em
so you should	**just**	... continue with the same workings
then you would	**just**	put in ... over here just put in ...
so why don't you	**just**	hold onto it until
um last week I guess it was Monday she	**just**	wanted to check her mail
Okay I	**just**	wanted to get like a focus on it
So I ...	**just**	wanted to come an' tell you

The last three lines also show the emergence of a phraseological pattern or 'chunk' associated with *just*: *just wanted to*. Refining the search even more, and examining the use of *just* as a hedge in a sub-corpus of discourse involving instruction-giving shows that this adverb seems to have the function of making the task described appear easy to carry out, e.g.:

Example 2.3

- But ... you can just say you do: ... uhm ... white– sheet size is one twenty by one eighty, ...
- and you just say well that took me about four hours to deliver it

Widely available corpus software tools can also show the most frequent collocates of a word. For example, the words occurring most frequently immediately
before *just* in the ABOT corpus are, perhaps not surprisingly, *I* and *you*; but what
is less predictable is the fact that *I* is more than twice as frequent as *you*. Corpus
tools thus permit a particular perspective on the data which cannot be achieved
via qualitative analysis (see Hunston 2002: 3–13 for a more detailed description
of these methods).

Most studies of workplace interaction are by definition small-scale, as they
usually involve the investigation of a particular organization or one type of interaction, for example business meetings. Therefore, it is reasonable to ask whether
reliable results can be obtained by using corpus linguistic methods with such small
corpora. Although the advantage of corpus-based methods is that they can handle
very large amounts of text, size is not everything when it comes to the reliability of the results that can be obtained from a corpus. It must be borne in mind
that even a large corpus represents only a sample of all language use. An equally
important consideration is whether the corpus is representative, i.e. whether it
is balanced and adequately represents the population and range of text types (see
Biber 1993, McEnery and Wilson 1996, Biber *et al.* 1999: 27–8, Hunston 2002).

In addition, the corpus size needed in order to have a reliable sample depends
on what is investigated. If high-frequency items (e.g., grammatical items) are analysed, then a relatively small corpus may be adequate, whereas for lower-frequency
features (e.g., some lexical items) a larger corpus is necessary. Biber (1990) shows
that even corpus samples of 1,000 words are large enough to yield reliable results
when examining grammatical items such as pronouns or tenses. Cutting (1999
and 2000) has shown that a modest corpus of approximately 25,000 words yields
powerful insights into the use of high-frequency grammatical items. Furthermore, McCarthy (1998) notes that for high-frequency items, larger corpora (even
only 1 million words) may yield too much information for qualitative analysis, and
necessitate taking a sub-sample. One advantage of investigating high-frequency
items in a small corpus is that *all* occurrences of an item can be examined, rather
than merely a sample.

For some studies the issue of representativeness may not arise. While having
a representative sample is important in examining a particular genre or type of
workplace interaction, a case study of one particular institution obviously does
not aim to be representative. In this case, corpus-based methods simply enable
the researcher to investigate certain aspects of the data rapidly and efficiently, for
example identifying frequent lexical items, common phrases and collocations.

It is an obvious but nevertheless important point to remember that a corpus
will only be able to tell you something about the data that are actually in the
corpus. Thus generalizations based on the results from a small corpus, for example
about workplace discourse in general, must be made with caution; and it can be

useful to check the results against larger corpora for greater reliability, and for researchers using similar data to compare their results.

2.3.2 Qualitative approaches

While valuable insights can be gained using corpus-based methods, quantification has the drawback that it necessitates an 'either–or' classification which results in a certain idealization of the data, and in the loss of finer distinctions (see McEnery and Wilson 1996: 62–3). Also, quantification involves a close-up perspective on similar details from disparate parts of the corpus, but does not show the moment-by-moment dynamics or the overall development of an encounter or stretch of talk. Nor of course can it tell us anything about the non-verbal or social context, such as the relationship between the participants, unless this is specifically coded in some form in the corpus (a huge and demanding task) or in an allied database. In order to examine these aspects of the discourse, a qualitative approach is needed.

Conversation analysis (CA), which focuses on the interactive and sequential details of talk, is particularly well suited for analysing the dynamics of spoken interaction. Conversation analysts have identified some general structures and characteristics of talk-in-interaction, such as turn-taking organization, adjacency pairs, preference organization. As CA focuses on the organization of talk, and avoids imposing an analyst's interpretation of the discourse, it has sometimes been criticized for being too mechanistic. Interactional sociolinguistics also examines the minutiae of talk, but adds a further dimension, linking surface-level phenomena to participants' goals and inferences (see Gumperz 1992, 1999).

Critical discourse analysis (CDA) has also been used to analyse workplace discourse (e.g., Fairclough 1992: 137–68, Eggins and Slade 1997, Holmes *et al.* 1999, 2000b). As discussed in Chapter 1, institutional roles are often linked to asymmetries in terms of power and control, and as CDA addresses the discourse dimensions of power, this should be a particularly useful approach to analysing institutional talk. However, because of the explicit socio-political stance taken by critical discourse analysts (see van Dijk 1993), such analyses could run the risk of assuming that issues of power deriving from institutional roles are always relevant to a particular interaction.

Using CDA also raises an ethical issue for the ethnographer. A great deal of CDA has focused on written discourse, and therefore has been removed from the actual discourse participants. However, when using an ethnographic approach to collect spoken workplace data, taking an overtly critical stance towards the more powerful members of an institution can be problematic (see Roberts and Sarangi 1999b: 393–6). Obtaining permission to gain access to an organization, and subsequently gathering information, involve building a relationship of trust with the members of the organization with whom one is dealing (who usually wield a certain degree of power); and such a relationship is not compatible with an adversarial stance.

This does not mean that issues of power cannot be addressed in the analysis of the data. Indeed, in spite of some of the criticisms levelled at CA (see above), Hutchby and Wooffitt (1998: 204–5) claim that CA provides the tools for examining issues of power as they are oriented to by the participants in the discourse. Holmes and Stubbe's (2003) study of *Power and Politeness in the Workplace*, which takes a social-constructionist approach, demonstrates that it is possible to combine ethnographic work with an examination of power. But rather than taking an oppositional stance, the results of the study were fed back into the organization with a view to providing practical help with aspects of workplace communication relevant to the participants themselves. Roberts and Sarangi (1999b: 393–6) also advocate a critical but collaborative approach that will have practical outcomes for the institution studied, rather than an oppositional one as in CDA, or even a detached one of simply doing research 'on' the organization, as in most studies of institutional discourse.

Institutional and professional discourse has also been examined from the point of view of genre analysis (e.g., Bhatia 1993, Bargiela-Chiappini and Harris 1995, 1997a), and this approach is particularly useful for identifying the global structures and phases of different types of interaction. Workplace interactions are often specific to certain professions or institutions. Genre analysis, which aims to identify the specific characteristics of different types of talk or texts, is therefore particularly suitable for the analysis of workplace discourse. It is also an approach which is capable of bringing together some of the different qualitative methods discussed above, as the notion of genre is drawn on in a number of different disciplines, including social constructionism (e.g., Miller 1984) and linguistics (e.g., Hasan 1985, Martin 1989). Furthermore, it allows for a 'thick description' of data, as genre analysis lends itself to various levels of analysis, and also takes into account the social context of interaction. These issues will be discussed in more detail in the next section.

2.4 Genre analysis

2.4.1 What is genre?

Genre analysis attempts to account for regularity of language use in a cultural context; nevertheless, the notion of genre is by no means easy to pin down exactly. Definitions of genre abound in the literature, for example:

- *'relatively stable types* of utterances' 'in each sphere in which language is used' (Bakhtin 1986: 60, original italics)
- 'a culturally significant way of meaning' (Christie 1986: 222)

- 'a class of communicative events, the members of which share some set of communicative purposes. ... [The] rationale shapes the schematic structure of the discourse and influences and constrains choices of content and style' (Swales 1990: 58)
- 'a socially ratified way of using language in connection with a particular type of social activity' (Fairclough 1995b: 14).

While Christie's and Fairclough's definitions emphasize the socio-cultural aspect of genre, Bakhtin's and Swales's also see genres as having some formal or structural characteristics. The defining feature of genre for Swales, however, is shared communicative purpose.

There is some disagreement between the different schools and traditions whether a genre should or can be defined and described in terms of its structure. In the Hallidayan approach to genre, based on systemic functional linguistics, the 'generic structure potential' is supposed to account for all the structural variation of a genre (see below). Biber (1988), Paltridge (1996) and Bhatia (1993), however, distinguish between genre, which is determined by communicative purpose, and text type, which refers to linguistic and structural form. Bhatia (ibid.: 45–75) shows how two different text types, sales promotional letters and letters of application, are actually both examples of promotional genres, due to their similar communicative purpose. Social constructionists, on the other hand, emphasize the dynamic and evolving nature of genres, and are therefore not particularly interested in their formal characteristics; preferring to focus on the way in which discourse communities express and construct socio-cultural norms and values through the genres they use (Freedman and Medway 1994 and Hyon 1996). Approaches which seek to describe the structural characteristics of genres have also been criticized for not taking into account the fact that genres evolve and change (Miller 1984, Threadgold 1989).

The view taken here is that formal linguistic characteristics *are* important aspects of genre, however they should not be considered as the defining features of a genre, which should be communicative purpose, as set out by Swales. Common communicative purpose, therefore, is what identifies any two speech events as belonging to the same genre. However, as genre is a socially defined category, this necessarily results in conventionalized formal and linguistic features. Particular lexico-grammatical features or textual patterns may therefore become conventionally associated with particular genres; for example decision-making conversations usually follow a problem-solution pattern, as we shall see in the next chapter. Such features characterize, but they do not determine genre. Taking this view of genre allows for the possibility of generic variation – there can be different ways of 'doing' the same genre – and it also takes into account the fact that genre is dynamic and subject to change (see Bakhtin 1986, Threadgold 1989).

Obviously, some genres are more structured and conventionalized than others. Looking at the different ways of using language which have been described as genres in the literature, one finds a great deal of variation in terms of how institutionalized these are. Thus jury summations (Bettyruth 1988), business meetings (Bargiela-Chiappini and Harris 1995, 1997a) or MSc dissertations (Dudley-Evans 1994) are obviously highly institutionalized types of speech and writing and have specific structures and conventions. Other types of discourse that have been described generically, such as narrative (Labov 1972[1]), observation–comment (Martin and Rothery 1986), or gossip (Eggins and Slade 1997) do not have an official status as the ones just mentioned, and are less tied to setting and participants, as they can occur across a range of different settings.

2.4.2 Methods of genre analysis

This section examines some of the issues and methods involved in describing genres. A central concern in all descriptions of genre is how to account for both stability and variation in genre. While members of a discourse community would not be able to recognize or perform a genre unless there were a certain degree of predictability, examination of real data shows that a great deal of variation exists within the same genre.

But to begin with the predictability of a genre; it is noticeable that certain actions or 'rhetorical moves' recur, often in the same order, across different speech events or texts of the same type. While some of these moves (Swales 1990, Bhatia 1993) or 'elements of genre' (Hasan 1985) seem to occur consistently across the different texts or speech events, others only occur in some. A distinction is therefore usually made between 'obligatory' moves or elements, and 'optional' moves. For instance, in service encounters, according to Hasan (1985), elements such as sales request and sales compliance are obligatory, whereas others like greetings and sales enquiry, are optional. Differences between real instances of the same genre are thus accounted for by this distinction between obligatory and optional moves, as well as by allowing for variation in the order of certain moves, and repetition of moves or 'move cycles' (e.g., Dudley-Evans 1994).

But even models that allow for such variation may prove inadequate when applied to real data. Ventola (1987), for example, in examining travel agency data, found that some of Hasan's (1985) obligatory elements for service encounters were often missing. For this reason, some genre analysts (e.g., Mitchell 1957/1975, Eggins and Slade 1997) have suggested that the moves or elements of structure of a genre should be seen as abstractions: 'A generic structure description is therefore an account of the ideal type. It is not to be interpreted as a fixed or rigid schema: it is a description of the underlying abstract structure which participants orient to' (Eggins and Slade 1997: 227–311).

Nevertheless, Eggins and Slade argue that certain types of talk are not amenable to generic analysis: highly interactive segments of the discourse which do not fit into a linear progression through the stages of a genre. They therefore distinguish between 'chunks', which have a global or macro-structure, and 'chat' segments, which are managed locally on a turn-by-turn basis (ibid: 230).

This problem encountered by Eggins and Slade, of discourse not following expected linear patterns, is one the discourse analyst inevitably comes up against as soon as the data do not consist of highly formulaic, ritualized instances of language. Work done by Gail Jefferson (1988) in the field of conversation analysis on the sequential organization of 'troubles-talk' provides some useful insights here. By analysing a corpus of talk in which people talked about 'troubles' (usually health problems), Jefferson was able to propose a tightly organized sequence with a number of stages that any 'troubles-talk' could potentially go through. However, she found that a complete sequence is never realized, and suggests that the 'roughness' she observed in the actual production of troubles-telling sequences might be a feature of longer sequences in general. She points out that the types of sequences 'which tightly run off in template order are the small conversational machinery, many of which have been described as highly "ritualized"' (Jefferson 1988: 439).

Jefferson's work suggests that it may be problematic to assume that speakers follow 'global scripts' in longer stretches of discourse. The work done by Jefferson and many others (e.g., Pomerantz, Sacks, Schegloff) within the field of conversation analysis has shown time and again the importance of looking at the local, turn-by-turn management of discourse in order to account for its relevant features. Conversation analysts are not concerned with describing genres, but some discourse analysts working with the notion of genre have also advocated using a 'bottom-up', rather than a 'top-down' approach which assumes global generic structures. Aston (1988: 128) proposes that speakers used 'smaller schematic structural units', such as adjacency pairs, in service encounter data he analysed, rather than 'global scripts'.

As a number of genre analysts have pointed out, it is important to take into account both global and local features of genre (Bhatia 1993, Dudley-Evans 1994, McCarthy 1998). Bhatia (1993) proposes a three-level analysis for highly institutionalized written genres (such as academic research articles):

Level 1: Analysis of lexico-grammatical features
Level 2: Analysis of text-patterning or textualization
Level 3: Structural interpretation of the text structure

Bhatia stresses that this involves a holistic, rather than an atomistic analysis, as the three levels of analysis are interrelated. McCarthy (1998) advocates a similar multi-layered approach to spoken genre: by comparing extracts from different genres in the five-million-word CANCODE Corpus, McCarthy (1998) demonstrates that higher-order features, such as goal-type and context, can be linked to lower-order features of grammar and lexis.

Adopting such an integrated, multi-level method of analysis does not, however, simplify the task of the genre analyst. McCarthy's work (ibid.) shows that the boundary between related genres is by no means clear-cut, but that there is a gradation which can be traced according to variability along different dimensions (e.g., the degree of shared knowledge, the relationship between the participants). This gives some indication of the complexity of real language in use and the problems inherent in trying to classify it in terms of genre. Biber's (1988) work on large-scale corpora, in which he examined variation between and within different written and spoken genres, also reflects this complexity.

In spite of the contradictions and problems inherent in trying to establish what exactly genres are and how they can be described, the notion of genre is nevertheless a useful one to work with. Clearly, people engage in a range of verbal activities which can be distinguished from one another; and the fact that we have lay terms for many of these activities (chat, discussion, story, etc.) indicates that such distinctions are also socially recognized. And as genre is defined by communicative purpose, it should provide a useful approach to analysing workplace encounters, which are usually oriented towards specific goals and outcomes.

Taking into account global as well as local features of the discourse, as well as the social context in which it is embedded, allows for a 'thick' description of the communicative event, as advocated by Bhatia (1993) and Sarangi and Roberts (1999). While, as the preceding discussion shows, defining genres in terms of a linear progression of specific obligatory stages is problematic, it is not difficult to find evidence (as we shall see) of speakers orienting to higher-level phases as part of the accomplishment of certain tasks. But it is important to remember that such phases always exist at a certain level of abstraction. As conversation analysts have shown, the actual 'machinery' of talk is made up of turn-by-turn interactive units; that is, the actual construction of conversation is local and jointly produced. This means that global generic structures are subject to interruption, incompletion, variation and even subversion, depending on the exigencies of the moment and on the individual goals and concerns of the speakers involved.

2.5 Goals, frames and genre

If genre is defined by communicative goal or purpose, then as analysts we need some way of trying to identify what discourse participants' goals are from the evidence of the data. Two approaches to analysing discourse provide some useful theoretical orientations and methodological tools here: communication goals studies and interactional sociolinguistics.

2.5.1 Transactional and relational goals

The discussion so far has perhaps seemed to imply that discourse participants always have a clear, unitary goal in any interaction. But as communication goals studies have shown, speakers usually have *multiple* goals (see Tracy and N. Coupland 1990), and at least two distinct types of goal can be distinguished: those, on the one hand, that have to do with accomplishing a task or outcome, and those that guide the way in which people relate to and present themselves to one another. These two distinct types of goal will be referred to as 'transactional' (or task) goals and 'relational' goals. In addition to these two types of goal, Ylänne-McEwen (1996) distinguishes 'identity goals', based on her analysis of interactions in travel agencies. Lampi (1986) also adopts a three-way distinction: in analysing business negotiations, she distinguishes between 'task-orientation', 'interaction-orientation' and 'self-orientation'. Identity goals can be seen as linked to either a transactional *or* a relational orientation (or both), as speakers can make relevant either their institutional roles and identities (when orienting to transactional goals) or some other identity, which may be relevant in terms of a relational goal (see Chapter 1).

In different types of discourse, speakers may orient primarily towards relational or transactional goals. Thus many types of casual conversation do not involve the accomplishment of a specific task, but rather the cementing of social or personal relationships through the building up of shared worlds. Speakers' goals in such conversations, which Malinowski (1923) refers to as 'phatic communion', are mainly relational.

In many types of institutional or workplace discourse, on the other hand, the speakers may be primarily concerned with getting things done, therefore with transactional goals. This is particularly true in service encounters between strangers, where there is no relationship to maintain. The literature on institutional talk has stressed the predominance of task goals in such talk (e.g., Drew and Heritage 1992), as discussed in Chapter 1. However, taking a multiple goals approach to discourse means acknowledging that, in most types of discourse, speakers orient to both transactional and relational goals, although one type of goal might be dominant. Recent research has shown the importance of relational goals in transactional settings as diverse as the travel business, government offices, telephone companies and health care (N. Coupland and Ylänne-McEwen 2000, Iacobucci 1990, Ragan 2000, Holmes and Stubbe 2003). Chapter 4 will explore in more detail methods of incorporating relational aspects of talk into the study of workplace discourse.

2.5.2 Contextualization cues and frames

Trying to identify speakers' goals is, however, not unproblematic, as it is not possible to 'get inside' speakers' heads and access their intentions directly. As Tracy and N. Coupland (1990) point out, speakers use discourse as a resource to display and infer goals. A useful approach which addresses the problem of how to relate speakers' goals and intentions to surface discourse features was developed within interactional sociolinguistics. According to Gumperz (1982, 1992), speakers and listeners use 'contextualization cues' to signal and make inferences about communicative goals. Contextualization cues are defined as 'any feature of linguistic form that contributes to the signalling of contextual presuppositions' (1982: 131).

Contextualization cues can be signalled through any aspect of linguistic or paralinguistic behaviour, from prosody to lexical forms, as well as through choice of code or style. They channel interpretations through conventionalized co-occurrence expectations between content and surface features, and when participants do not share these expectations (e.g., in cross-cultural interaction) miscommunication can occur (see Section 2.2 above). Contextualization cues also operate at different discourse levels: they are used to make local assessments, for example regarding individual speech acts, and they also enter into the inferential process at the global level, where they guide interpretations of what the 'activity' is that speakers are engaged in (Gumperz 1992). At this global level, contextualization cues are therefore indicative of generic activity, and, as Gumperz (ibid.) points out, converge with Goffman's (1974) notion of 'frame': the definition which participants give to the current social activity.

The notion of frame is further developed by Tannen (1993b) and Tannen and Wallat (1987/1993). Frames have some similarity with notions of 'schemas' (Rumelhart 1975) or 'scripts' (Schank and Abelson 1977), which also have to do with structures of expectations participants have about a verbal event based on previous experience. However, as Tannen and Wallat point out, schemas consist of participants' expectations based on prior knowledge or experience, whereas frames are dynamic and interactional: they are defined as the participants' sense of what they are doing – what activity they are engaged in. Therefore while schemas are essentially individual, cognitive phenomena, frames, as interactional phenomena, are necessarily social, and can therefore be linked to genre.

According to Tannen (1993b), evidence for participants' frames can be found in a variety of surface linguistic forms, for example negative statements, as they indicate that an expectation has not been met, or modals, because they reflect speakers' judgements. One very obvious evidence of frames is in metalinguistic comments made by speakers to refer to the discursive activity they are engaged in. Speakers frequently preface workplace conversations or stretches of talk with introductory statements such as:

- I have a quick question for you. I *hope* it's a quick question
- I don't know if you've *heard*, but if you haven't, it's confidential
- I got a suggestion … by the way with this.

What all these openers have in common is that the speakers say something about the upcoming discourse, thereby giving the addressee some idea of what they want to talk about. *I have a quick question* ... shows that the speaker is going to make some kind of query; *I don't know if you've heard* ... indicates the speaker has some news to tell (and *it's confidential* is suggestive of gossip); and finally, with *I got a suggestion* ... the speaker indicates how he wishes his upcoming discourse to be understood (as a suggestion or advice). Such phenomena have been identified as 'pre-sequences' in conversation analysis: turns or sequences which prefigure an upcoming action, for example pre-closings, pre-invitations or pre-announcements (see Levinson 1983: 345–64).

Detailed analyses of many encounters in the ABOT Corpus (see below) revealed that speakers frequently used initial meta-statements, such as the ones shown above, to signal the genre or type of communicative activity they wished to engage in, thereby invoking certain frames for whole conversations or stretches of conversation. That such meta-statements can set up expectations for the whole discourse is to some extent a result of their conversation-initial or sequence-initial placement. As Schegloff and Sacks have pointed out, what comes first in a conversation is significant: 'to make a topic "first topic" may provide for its analysability (by co-participants) as "the reason for" the conversation'(1973: 300–1). McCarthy (1998: 33–4) refers to the same phenomenon, the signalling of upcoming generic activity, as 'expectations', and points out a number of other linguistic devices, for example discourse markers, which can perform such a function. Such meta-statements and other linguistic choices made by speakers therefore provide evidence of speakers' goals or what genre they see themselves as 'doing'.

The next chapter examines in more detail how linguistic evidence of frames, such as meta-statements and lexico-grammatical choices, provide clues to generic activity in terms of the participants' transactional discourse goals in accomplishing workplace tasks. Frames and relational goals will be discussed in Chapter 4. These topics will be explored using a small corpus of audio-recorded workplace interactions from a variety of offices in the United States and the UK, which will be referred to as the Corpus of American and British Office Talk (ABOT).

2.6 The ABOT Corpus

The data for the project were collected between October 1996 and September 1997 in eight offices in Britain and the United States. The British data are from the South of England (Kent) and the Midlands, and the American offices are located in Boston, New York City and Minneapolis. The reason for including both British and American data was not for comparative purposes, but in order to broaden the scope of the study and investigate the nature of office talk in two of the main varieties of native-speaker English. Rather than investigate one particular type of workplace environment, as most studies of institutional talk have done, the aim was to collect data from a range of offices and to identify types of spoken interaction or genre which occurred across all these settings. In order to ensure consistency between the two data sets, similar office settings were chosen in each country.

The data were collected from three different types of office in Britain and the USA: university offices, editorial offices of a publishing company, and companies in the private (non-publishing) sector, as detailed below.[2]

1   University data
British: Departmental office for undergraduate administration and teaching
American: Graduate school office for post-graduate administration and teaching

2   Publishing data
British: editorial office for English Language Teaching (ELT)
American: editorial office for ELT

3   Business data
British:
Paper supplier: branch office selling (mainly on the telephone) to wholesalers and printers
Printer: specializing in printing labels. Recordings made in the office, which dealt with orders for printing jobs
American:
Advertising: selling specialist advertising to businesses (mainly on the telephone) in the form of postcards
Food retailer: the back office of a co-operative selling organic food

The university and publishing data from Britain and the USA are very closely matched: both sets of university data are from an academic department (although the discipline and level of teaching are different), while the publishing data are from the same publisher with offices in both Britain and North America, and the same type of editorial office (ELT). It proved impossible to find strictly matching settings for private businesses in the two countries due to the difficulties in obtaining permission to make recordings. Data were therefore collected from a variety of companies, which admittedly differ in terms of their business activity and size. The printer and the American advertising company are both small family businesses or partnerships, whereas the paper supplier is a small branch office of a larger company, and the food retailer is co-operatively owned. The companies also deal with different products and services; however, all are involved with sales of some kind, and most conversations recorded are between co-workers (rather than with customers).

An ethnographic method was used to collect the data, with the researcher spending one to several days in each office observing, recording conversations, speaking to employees and taking notes. The recordings of spontaneous conversations were supplemented by field notes made during many of the encounters and in consultations with informants, and by interviews conducted with employees. In addition to providing background information about the interviewees' jobs and positions in the organization, these questions were designed to elicit participants' accounts of specific features of the interactions, particularly the range of activity types or genres in which the speakers engaged and relational aspects of the discourse (relationship to co-workers, formality, small talk, etc.). The content of the corpus is described in more detail in the next chapter.

2.7 Conclusion

This chapter has provided an overview of different approaches and methods to analysing workplace discourse, and has shown that these different methodologies imply different views of what constitutes relevant 'context' for the study of workplace interactions. It was suggested that a genre-based approach, with its emphasis on goal-orientation, is particularly suitable for the analysis of workplace discourse, and that it is useful to combine qualitative with quantitative, corpus-based methods in order to describe the data as fully as possible. We explored the complex notion of speakers' goals, and discussed some discourse analytical methods that seem useful in trying to identify discourse participants' transactional and relational goals. Finally, the ABOT Corpus, a small-scale corpus of American and British office talk, was described, and this corpus will be used for illustrative purposes throughout the book, alongside references to workplace data from other studies.

In the next chapter, we turn to the examination of specific workplace genres, in particular decision-making and procedural/directive talk. Chapter 3 will thus focus on transactional goals and the accomplishment of workplace tasks.

3 Pursuing transactional goals

Spoken workplace genres

3.1 Introduction

In the last chapter, genre analysis was put forward as an approach that is particularly well-suited to the analysis of workplace discourse, and a detailed discussion of genre analysis was provided. It was also suggested that the best method to identify genres in spoken discourse is to look for surface linguistic clues to the discourse participants' goals (both transactional and relational). This chapter provides an overview and illustrative examples of some of the most commonly occurring spoken workplace genres, focusing on the way in which speakers signal and negotiate genre in the pursuit of transactional goals. The ABOT Corpus, introduced in Chapter 2, will be used for this purpose, and research on other workplace data will also be drawn on where appropriate.

3.2 Description of the corpus

On the one hand, genre analysis can be used to identify specialized genres which are specific to certain professions or institutions. Devitt's (1991) study of the written genres used by tax accountants is a good example of such an application of genre analysis. The ABOT Corpus, on the other hand, comprises spoken interactions in a wide variety of workplace contexts, albeit all 'white collar' (see Chapter 2), and therefore the aim was to identify genres which can occur across a range of workplace environments. Thus the genres identified are necessarily of a fairly general nature, and of course more specialized 'sub-genres' of these general categories may exist within any given institution or profession. But the advantage of a fairly general system of classification is that it can be applied to other workplace contexts and to other studies of spoken workplace interactions.

The ABOT Corpus consists of just under 34,000 words of text transcribed from about 30 hours of audio-recorded data, approximately half from the American data and half from the British data. As the aim of the study was to examine particular features of workplace talk across a range of genres, the extracts chosen for transcription and inclusion in the corpus are examples of generic activity recurring throughout the different offices in which data were collected.

The types of interaction included in the corpus can be located on a continuum from quite formal workplace situations, such as meetings with a set agenda, to informal chit-chat which might take place between colleagues, but does not actually deal with workplace tasks. The majority are two-party encounters between co-workers which are task-oriented, but still fairly informal. This means that they were mostly ad hoc conversations which were not arranged in advance, or if they were, did not have an official agenda. In addition, talk which is not task-oriented (i.e. small talk, gossip) was included in the corpus.

In order to make comparisons between genres, the conversations transcribed first had to be classified in some way. First, a distinction was made between those encounters or stretches of talk in which participants focused on a workplace task and those in which they did not: these were labelled 'transactional' and 'non-transactional' respectively. Within transactional discourse, a broad distinction can be made between two types of interaction based on the discursive roles of the participants. There are those encounters in which one of the speakers clearly plays a dominant role, in so far as s/he imparts information the other participant does not possess, instructs/directs the other participant in some action to be taken, or requests some action from the interlocutor. This type of discourse is referred to as 'unidirectional' (following McCarthy 1998: 1–25). Other encounters can be classified as 'collaborative', as both (all) participants contribute more or less equally towards accomplishing the goal of the encounter (although there may still be some asymmetry in both the institutional and the discursive roles).

Next the transcribed data were sub-divided in terms of the overall goal of the encounter or stretch of talk into distinct genres. Within unidirectional discourse, five genres are distinguished:

1   briefing
2   service encounters
3   procedural and directive discourse
4   requesting action/permission/goods (or favour-seeking)
5   reporting.

Both briefing and service encounters involve information provision: briefing occurs between co-workers, whereas service encounters are, for example, secretary–student/ supplier–customer interactions. The four encounters in this category (three from university offices and one supplier–customer meeting from the British business data) are the only interactions in the corpus not between co-workers.

In the category of collaborative discourse, three genres are identified:

1   making arrangements
2   decision-making
3   discussing and evaluating.

A further type of collaborative talk consists of longer stretches of discourse which involve moving out of the encounter. This type of talk is transitional (really just an extended closing sequence), and therefore does not constitute a genre in its own right; however as two such extended sequences occur, they are classified separately from the other genres and given the label 'liminal talk'.

The corpus classification is therefore based on task orientation (transactional versus non-transactional), discourse roles (unidirectional or collaborative) and the goal of the encounter. Other types of classification would have been possible; for example a distinction could have been made between discourse which is activity-focused (e.g., decision-making, planning, directive discourse) and idea or information-focused discourse (information provision, discussing and evaluating), as was done, for example, for the CANCODE Corpus (see Carter *et al.* 1997 and McCarthy 1998). It is obviously possible to divide up the world of discourse in a number of ways, and whatever classification is chosen will have implications for the results found.

Non-transactional discourse, in which participants are not involved in a work-place task, falls into two categories. The generic category 'reporting' includes only conversations in which what is reported relates specifically to a workplace task (e.g., reporting actions taken to solve a problem), but not other conversations, in which events in the office or in the professional field at large are talked about (e.g., talking about a burglary in the office, gossiping about a co-worker). Such conversations do not involve getting work done, but simpy chatting *about* work, and therefore can be described as office gossip. Finally, there are conversations or stretches of talk which do not involve workplace topics or tasks at all, which are labelled as 'small talk'. These conversations involve talk about the weather, the weekend, health, family, etc., or various forms of joking and teasing.

Below is a summary of the corpus showing the number of words for each sub-corpus and genre.

A	**Unidirectional discourse**	**14,717**
	Briefing	3,524
	Service encounters	2,424
	Procedural and directive discourse	5,195
	Requesting	1,250
	Reporting	2,324

B	**Collaborative discourse**	**14,386**
	Arrangements	2,812
	Decision-making	8,782
	Discussing and evaluating	1,865
	Liminal talk	927
C	**Non-transactional discourse**	**4,633**
	Office gossip	1,955
	Small talk	2,678

The amount of data in the two transactional sub-corpora, unidirectional and col-laborative discourse, is almost the same; however, as the above list shows, the amount transcribed for each of the individual genres varies considerably. Although it would be preferable for comparative purposes to have the same number of words in each sub-corpus, this discrepancy in size between the sub-corpora reflects the fact that some activities (e.g., decision-making) are particularly frequent in these kinds of workplace environment. This gives a more accurate picture of the nature of office discourse than would have been achieved by having an equal number of words per genre. In addition, some encounters were longer than others, for example decision-making conversations tended to be longer than those involving making arrangements. On the whole, it was considered preferable to transcribe entire conversations, in order to preserve generic units (only in a few instances of very long encounters were extracts transcribed). Statistical comparisons across genres are nevertheless still possible by using a measure of 'normalized' word fre-quency, as described in Chapter 5 (see also Biber *et al.* 1999: 25–6).

These fairly general types of genre identified in the ABOT Corpus are not restricted to office discourse, but occur in many different settings, both profes-sional and private. Some of these genres have been analysed within other contexts, e.g., oral narrative (Labov 1972), which reporting, office gossip and small talk largely consist of, or (written) procedural discourse (Martin 1989). Others, such as making arrangements or requesting, are less well described. This classification shows the range of genres which the speakers employed in the course of their daily work. Although the corpus, with less than 34,000 words, is small, the fact that these genres recurred across different office settings is an indication that they perform an important function in the accomplishment of many workplace tasks (see Chapter 2 for a discussion of corpus size).

Many of the interactions involving a variety of genres could be described as meetings (and indeed were often referred to as such by the participants). There is only one formal multi-party meeting in the corpus, but many more informal meetings between two or three people. Meetings have been extensively exam-ined in the literature on workplace discourse, focusing mostly on multi-party meetings with a formal agenda and a chair (e.g., Bargiela-Chiappini and Harris 1997a, Rogerson-Revell 1999, Poncini 2002 and 2004); but some research has also examined more informal, ad hoc meetings with as few as two participants (e.g., Boden 1995, Holmes and Stubbe 2003). However the term 'meeting' is not particularly useful as a genre label, as meetings can have a variety of goals. Holmes and Stubbe's (2003) Language in the Workplace corpus comprises 80 meetings (both formal and informal) involving 2–18 participants with a range of transactional goals. Holmes and Stubbe (pp. 63–4) group these into three categories according to 'their overt primary "business" goals and expected outcomes' (p. 63):

- planning or prospective/forward-oriented meeting, e.g., making decisions, requesting permission
- reporting or retrospective/backward-oriented meeting, e.g., reporting, updating
- task-oriented or problem-solving/present-oriented meeting, e.g., problem-solving, collaborative task completion.

Each of the above categories encompasses a variety of specific genres, a number of which are dealt with in the ABOT Corpus, although the principles of classification are different.

As shown in the last chapter, meta-statements and other linguistic choices made by speakers provide evidence of speakers' goals or discourse 'frames', i.e. what genre they see themselves as 'doing'. Examples from the corpus will be used to demonstrate the way in which such linguistic evidence of frames provide clues to the genre being performed. Data from the two most frequently occurring genres in the corpus will be analysed: decision-making, with 8,782 words and 11 separate encounters or generically separate stretches of talk, and procedural/directive discourse, with 5,195 words and nine conversations or parts of conversations. These two genres make up 26 and 15 per cent of the corpus respectively, and thus account for the largest proportion of talk in each of the two macro-genres – collaborative and unidirectional discourse. The main structural features and other characteristics of these genres will be highlighted mainly with reference to the ABOT Corpus, supplemented with examples from research on other workplace data.

3.3 Decision-making

Over a quarter of the corpus consists of talk which is oriented towards making a decision on some work-related issue. Decision-making always focuses on a problem of some kind which needs to be resolved. Generally this involves participants deciding which course of action to take in a specific situation, therefore decision-making is essentially an action-oriented genre. It is not surprising that this genre should play a central role in office discourse, since decisions need to be taken on day-to-day business activities, and problematic decisions often necessitate talk with co-workers. McCarthy and Handford (2004) and Willing (1992) also identified problem-solving as a key activity in business meetings and the workplace talk of white-collar professionals.

Decision-making or problem-solving is a genre for which a sequence of distinct phases can be identified. Willing (ibid.) describes the phases as:

1   defining/describing
2   deepening comprehension/interpreting
3   devising/deciding.

Hundsnurscher (1986) also describes problem-solving discourse (*Planungsgespräche*) in terms of a three-phase structure:

1   identifying the problem (*Problemfixierung*)
2   problem-solving (*Problemlösungsphase*)
3   agreeing on a course of action (*Handlungsvereinbarung*).

'Deciphering handwriting'

In the corpus, decision-making conversations often begin with the identification of some kind of problem. In data from the back office of an American food co-operative, one such conversation begins with the bookkeeper, Ann, asking her co-workers, who share the same office space:

Example 3.1

1   Ann   Anyone wanna <u>decipher</u> some handwriting?

The word *decipher* signals a decision-making frame, as it indicates the existence of a problem (Ann cannot read a handwritten word) which needs to be solved (she needs to know what the word is). The formulation of this initial turn as a question (a request or offer) is an indication of the interactive nature of this genre – it is produced collaboratively. As Gumperz (1982: 167) notes 'the signalling of speech activities is not a matter of unilateral action but rather of speaker–listener coordination'. Here Ann is looking for someone to engage in decision-making with her, and her bid to 'do' decision-making is taken up by Greta, who sits next to her, and responds:

Example 3.2

2   Greta   I will. I will.

The word which Ann and Greta try to decipher is on a handwritten list of items, on which co-workers in the 'deli' section of the co-op's shop must write down any items they take from the shop for cooking. In the remaining 35 turns of this conversation, the speakers orient to the decision-making frame initiated in the first turn (turn numbers in the extracts are from the full transcript). Both speakers put forward guesses or make suggestions as to what they think the word or individual letters could be, for example:

Example 3.3

11   Greta   It <u>looks like</u> S-H.O-W-Y. showy.
12   Ann   ⌊Mhm
13   Ann   or *soury*. ... soury.
14   Ann   (sou:r <u>I think</u> that's a G)
15   Greta   *Where*.
16   Ann   /Grewry/
17   Greta   The first one?
18   Ann   Mhm,
19   Greta   Mm. ↓ No. it's /a-/ <u>Let's see</u>. I'm usually really good at this. ↑ Oh <u>I think</u> it's a– S.

The verbs used by both speakers (*looks like*, *I think*, *let's see*) involve hypothesizing, and are therefore evidence of their engagement in the decision-making or problem-solving process.[1] According to Willing (1992), hypotheses or suppositions about possibility often occur in the 'deepening comprehension/interpreting' phase of problem-solving. Their responses involve accepting or rejecting each other's proposals – for example in turn 19 above Greta disagrees that the first letter is a G – and also evaluating each other's suggestions:

Example 3.4

24   Greta   Mm begins with an S, an' ends with a Y.
25   Ann   ⌊Heheh
26   Ann   That's good.

In the end they seem to agree that the word is 'sherry'.

Not surprisingly, many decision-making conversations follow a problem-solution pattern, a textual pattern identified by Hoey (1983, 1994) with the following phases:

situation → problem → response/solution → evaluation

According to Hoey, the phases of a problem-solution pattern are often signalled lexically through the use of certain key words. Decision-making discourse in the corpus frequently involves the use of some of the signal words identified by Hoey for the different phases of the pattern:

- problem: *problem, difficult*
- response/solution: *response, result, figure out*
- evaluation: *work, good.*

McCarthy (1998: 41–5) identified problem-solution patterns in decision-making conversations from both familiar and professional contexts in the CANCODE Corpus and notes that such conversations can have an episodic structure consisting of a series of problem-solution patterns. Holmes and Stubbe (2003: 68–71) identified two different types of problem-solving pattern in meetings: a linear pattern, where each problem is dealt with before moving on to the next, and a spiral pattern, where a point may recur several times, with further discussion. They found that the pattern followed correlated both with the overall function of the meeting and the relationship between the participants, in other words with both transactional and relational factors. In examples from their data, problem-signalling words are also evident, for example in a meeting in which an employee, Barbara, seeks guidance from her manager, Ruth:

Example 3.5

1 Barb: hey Ruth
2 Ruth: yeah
3 Barb: I've got a little problem
4   I've finally looked at these questions and …
5   I've discovered a few difficulties …

(Holmes and Stubbe 2003: 66)[2]

As this is the opening phase of the encounter, the words *problem* and *difficulties* provide a clear frame for the interaction, similar to the one found at the beginning of the decision-making conversation on deciphering handwriting discussed above (Example 3.1).

However, problem-solution patterns can also occur in other genres besides decision-making. The pattern was first identified by Hoey in expository prose, and McCarthy and Carter (1994) show that this textual pattern is also used in other written genres (e.g., advertising, journalism). In the ABOT Corpus, problem-solution patterns can also be found in discussing and evaluating (problems are talked *about*), reporting (problems are reported) or requesting (the reason for the request is presented as a problem). What distinguishes decision-making conversations is that participants collaboratively and actively engage with an unsolved problem by entering into the decision-making process. This does not mean, however, that the problem is necessarily resolved in that encounter (or even resolved at all); therefore the problem-solution pattern may be incomplete.

'Green envelope'

A good example of a decision-making conversation which follows a complete problem-solution pattern, and in which speakers often use signal words, is from the British business data. The two speakers, Greg, a sales rep, and Paul, the office manager and Greg's superior, work in the sales office of a paper supplier. Unlike 'Deciphering handwriting', this conversation does not immediately begin with the statement of a problem. Here it takes longer for a problem to be clearly identified:

Example 3.6

1　Greg　Who's the one that does the Strange Range. Index innit? (/that do
　　　　those/)
2　Paul　Yeah what you after.
3　Greg　That's what I'm after, trying /to get/ the Pantone colour.
4　Paul　hh Ri:ght, ... So you nee:d ...
5　Greg　But no d– forget the Pantone bit now, because the company–
6　Paul　　　　　　　　　　　　　　　　　　　　⌊end of this week!
7　Greg　Yeah. The company I got it from last time, *do* do it, but– they got to
　　　　make it, and it won't be till November.
8　Paul　S– yeah.
9　Greg　Yeah. So basically I've just got to get ... a: green envelope, pocket
　　　　preferably gummed,

The conversation begins with a simple query on the part of Greg in turn 1, but Paul enquires into the reason for his question (turn 2), and eventually elicits the information (turn 9) that Greg needs to get a green envelope for a customer. There is some indication in this initial part of the conversation that Greg has a problem, for example his use of the verb *trying* in turn 3 and the information in turn 7 that the company he used last time will not be able to do the job this time. But his use of *just* in turn 9 seems to indicate that he sees his task as relatively straightforward (or else he may be reluctant to show that he has a problem). However, when Paul becomes aware of the deadline (which he probably sees on a document Greg shows him), his animated tone in turn 6 (*end of this week!*), expressing surprise or alarm, is a clear indication there is a problem. He then overtly 'problematizes' the situation in turn 15, by saying:

Example 3.7

15 Paul   Well there's not many people that'll make you a green envelope,
              number one,

After this, the speakers, especially Paul (the speaker in all the examples below), use a large number of problem-signalling words and phrases, so the discourse has clearly entered a problem-phase:

Example 3.8

17   I mean if you want something at the end of this week, he's gonna
            struggle,
21   [...] the only one you're gonna get's a C5.
25   Yeah the green's the one that's gonna be a killer.

This is a good example of how genre is emergent and negotiated: the identification of a problem which necessitates a joint decision arises in the course of this conversation. Once the problem has been clearly identified, Paul and Greg start to generate some ideas for a possible solution and thus move into the response phase from around turn 32:

Example 3.9

32 Paul   [...] Unless you can persua::de someone like ... C.S. Roth to make
              it?
33 Greg   ⌊Is—
34 Greg   Could do, what sort of send him the paper,
35 Paul   ⌊for next week?
36 Greg   ↑That's a point yeah because—
              [...]
41 Paul   I'm surprised Sanders and White can't— we— with a— a— Have you
              asked 'em if they could send it out to be made.
42 Greg   ↑Oh well they could send me the paper,

There is a progression from more tentative suggestions (e.g., using *could*) to more assertive ones, for example with the use of an imperative:

Example 3.10

45 Paul   Well <u>speak</u> to C.S. Roth. […]

What was initially a suggestion finally becomes the proposed solution, with the use of a confident *will* and *gonna* in turns 53 and 54 and positive evaluation in 55 (*dead easy*):

Example 3.11

53 Paul   Yeah I mean … C.S. Roth'<u>ll</u> <u>be able</u> to make it,
54 Greg   ⌐↑Yeah 'cause i– uh i– uh I was <u>gonna</u> do that.
55 Paul   'cause they can make the C5s. [1] <u>Dead easy</u>.

This conversation shows how speakers jointly negotiate the various phases of decision-making, and how these phases are signalled at the lexical level, for example through certain modal verbs or through 'signal words' typical for a problem-solution pattern. This conversation also shows that some decision-making discourse can be more 'collaborative' than others. Although Greg initiates the conversation (expecting perhaps only a simple response), it is Paul who controls the direction the discourse takes. Greg certainly also plays an active role in the decision-making, as the above examples show, for example he evaluates and comments on Paul's proposals (Examples 3.9 and 3.11). But it is Paul who identifies the presence of a problem and proposes most of the solutions. This can probably be explained by his more senior position (he is Greg's boss) and his greater experience, as he has been in the company longer, and thus knows the work much better than Greg does.

3.3.1 Negotiating

One specific type of decision-making encounter that should be mentioned in a discussion of workplace genres is negotiating, as it has received a great deal of attention in the literature on workplace and business discourse. It is generally considered to be a clearly structured and staged type of activity, for example, Graham (1983) proposes a four-stage model, based on investigations of Japanese and American business negotiations: (1) non-task sounding, (2) task-related information exchange (3) persuasion and (4) concessions and agreement. However, Charles and Charles (1999), in examining sales negotiations in small to medium-sized British companies, found that these stages were not usually neatly separated, but that 'our negotiators seemed to hold themselves in that second task-related information exchange stage, merging that with persuasion, re-cycling pieces of non-task sounding, and pushing the final stage away from them' (p. 74). Nor did they find overt, conflictual bargaining, but negotiators strategically used 'tactical summaries' to nudge the negotiation in a direction favourable to their own position. An example from their data is shown below.

Example 3.12[3]

1	B:	what you sent on this fifty ton trial is ... really gone quite well/the other aspect though that is important to us is what it meant in terms of potentially good —mainly in terms of surface finish on a finished shaft.
2	S:	yeah
3	B:	and ... uhhh ... the/the quality of the finished product / ... / as George and you I'm sure know this is ... a notoriously difficult thing to actually
4	S:	{yeah
5	B:	measure} ... because it's very subjective [but
6	S2:	Mm}
7	B:	I would say that frankly ... err ... we haven't seen any problems ... and if I was asked to make an a ... assessment I would say that what we have seen has been slightly better than what we normally get
8	S:	uhuh
9	B:	So ... technically I'd say that err ... /everything is ...
10	S:	we've got a product
11	B:	we've got a product ... yeah

(Charles and Charles 1999: 75–6; turn numbers have been added)[4]

By saying *we've got a product* in turn 10, the seller interprets the buyer's assessment of the product as positive, although this may not be exactly what the buyer had intended. Nevertheless, the buyer agrees in turn 11, and an agreement is therefore reached without any overt bargaining. Thus in this interaction, and other sales negotiations examined by Charles and Charles, the participants deliberately seem to avoid explicit signalling of the phases of the genre, unlike in the decision-making encounters analysed above. This extract however also exhibits some typical characteristics of decision-making discourse: the tactical summary is preceded by a series of evaluations of the product by the buyer, e.g., *gone quite well* (turn 1), *notoriously difficult thing* (turn 3). As illustrated in the extracts from the ABOT Corpus discussed above, evaluation is a central component of decision-making in general (see also Chapter 5).

The ABOT Corpus does not contain any formal sales negotiations; however, as Boden (1995) points out, negotiation also occurs in everyday business interactions, in which at least two participants with some divergent (but also some shared) goals try to arrive at a mutually satisfactory agreement. Such informal types of negotiation will be examined in Chapter 6. For a more detailed examination of formal business and industrial negotiations, the reader is referred to the extensive literature on this subject (e.g., Francis 1986, Lampi 1986, Garcez 1993, Firth 1995a and b).

3.4 Procedural/directive discourse

Procedural and directive discourse, the second most frequently occurring genre in the corpus, involves a discursively dominant speaker telling an addressee *how* to do something or *what* to do. Procedural discourse has been described principally in terms of written monologue, for example it is one of a number of factual written genres described by Martin (1989). In examining the structure of monologue, Longacre (1983) identifies four 'discourse types': narration, procedural, expository, behavioural. These are general rhetorical categories and, depending on factors such as verb tense and whether there is an agent or not, they yield more specific genres, for example: story, 'how-to-do-it', scientific paper, eulogy. But applying this model to dialogic discourse is problematic. Procedural discourse is described as 'agentless', but obviously in procedural dialogue there is an agent (an instruction-giver). According to Longacre, the intent or goal of these discourse types or genres can be paraphrased as a performative verb, for example procedural discourse as 'I prescribe', expository prose as 'I explain' and hortatory (a behavioural genre) as 'I propose, suggest, urge, command'. Again, this type of division is problematic for spoken procedural discourse, as speech acts from all three of these discourse types can occur here: prescribing, explaining and commanding.

As a dialogic interactively constructed genre, spoken procedural discourse can therefore not be described in exactly the same terms as written procedural discourse. *Describing* how to do something, *explaining* the procedure and *telling* the addressee to do it are not speech acts which can necessarily be neatly separated from one another, as they may all be used to achieve the same communicative goal.

Nevertheless, two basic sub-genres can be identified within the conversational extracts classified as procedural/directive. A number of conversations involve giving general instructions on how to go about a certain task or procedure; in two instances this involves a more senior person (in both cases the addressee's boss) training a new colleague. Such conversations therefore bear some basic resemblance to written procedural discourse, which Martin (1989) describes as a sequence of general events (whereas narrative involves specific events). Other encounters involve instructions or directives in a specific instance: what to do now, in the near future or even, in one case, what should have been done. Such interactions tend to have more elements of 'hortatory' discourse.

Directives are obviously essential speech acts in all types of procedural discourse, and in its most basic form, the generic structure consists of one or a series of directives. But actual instances of instruction-giving are often more complex. For example, Pufahl Bax (1986) found that directives in spoken office discourse tend to be preceded by pre-sequences which check the ability of the addressee to carry out the directive; and Delin (1998) shows that directives, narratives and 'markers' alternate in the language of instructors in step-aerobics workouts. The strategies used by instruction-givers in the corpus to 'do' procedural discourse will be examined in more detail in Chapters 5 and 6. The following examples simply show how a procedural/directive discourse frame is instantiated and negotiated by the discourse participants via the use of surface-level contextualization cues.

Evaluation procedure

The first example of procedural discourse is from an American company selling postcard advertising. The encounter involves a meeting (which had been pre-arranged) between the president of the company, Chris, and Mike, the circulation manager (responsible for the company's publications), to discuss setting up a method of evaluating Mike's performance. Mike has drawn up a proposal and is discussing it with Chris.

Mike is supposed to keep a 'log' with which he will effectively evaluate his own performance. The criterion they are discussing here is how quickly Mike responds to requests. After a phatic exchange to open the encounter, Mike makes explicit reference to the transactional goal of the encounter:

Example 3.13

1   Mike   Twelve o'clock already [as he's walking in]
2   Chris   Isn't it amazing?
          [Mike sits down]
3   Mike   Okay. [2] <u>You— you want me to</u> make a log. To— to— it'll measure ... how well I'm doing /pre-counting. recounts/ an' getting the list out to /??/ how <u>do you want</u> that to show up over here.
          [4]
4   Chris   As an average ... number of hours ... between ... uh:m ... request and delivery.
          [3]
5   Mike   (Hm)
          [3]
6   Chris   ↑ An' it's an' it's kind of a— ↓ you know you <u>don't have to</u> like write down the minute that you— got the request and the minute that you

got– it done, an' <u>you just say</u> well that took me about four hours ↓ to /
deliver it/. [1] /??? four/

7 Mike So what if the request comes … uh … by e-mail at the end of a day, on
Monday, and I don't even see it until …

8 Chris I don't know how were you– how were you gonna keep this before.

9 Mike (Uh that's a good point) Okay. So I'll … so I'll just– ignore time …
between … me leaving and– heheh an' me coming in. [3] ↓Okay.

By saying *you want me to* and asking *do you want … ?*, Mike clearly signals that he
expects instructions or directives from his boss. This 'bid' to engage in directive
discourse is taken up by Chris, as he then tells Mike how he should keep his log
(turn 4); when Mike does not immediately acknowledge this instruction (which is
followed by an unusually long silence), he gives more details in turn 6.

The linguistic strategies used by Chris to give directives are quite different
from those used in the decision-making conversations analysed above (Examples
3.1–3.11). In these conversations, modals and other devices were used for hypothesizing, making suggestions, expressing opinions and evaluations (e.g., epistemic
modals like *could*, *think*, and evaluative lexis and idioms). Here Chris first produces an unmodalized, moodless utterance (turn 4), and then a deontic modal,
don't have to (expressing lack of obligation), as well as a 'you' imperative hedged
with *just* – *you just say* (turn 6), thus clearly indicating that he is giving directives
rather than suggesting. Later in the conversation he uses more deontic modals
(expressing obligation):

Example 3.14

↑ An' it's <u>gotta</u> be … a– a– but what you <u>need to</u> do is set your *dates* ↓ for
when it's <u>gotta</u> be done.[…]

All these devices (deontic modals, imperatives) indicate a directive/instructional
frame, but notice also that Chris's directives in turn 6 are delivered with a great
deal of hedging: he uses an interactive device, *you know*, and the modal adverbs *just*
and *like*. The use of such hedging devices in procedural discourse will be returned
to later in the book (especially Chapters 5 and 6).

Mike's responses to Chris are also consonant with a procedural/directive discourse frame. In the two decision-making conversations, both speakers make
suggestions, and accept/reject and evaluate the other's proposals. Mike, however,
does not treat what Chris says as a suggestion that he is free to accept or reject.
He either asks for more information, as in turn 7, or he acknowledges that he has
understood, as in turn 9:

7   So what if the request comes ... uh ... by e-mail at the end of a day [...]
9   [...] Okay. So I'll ... so I'll just– ignore time ... between ... me leaving
      and– heheh an' me coming in.

The possibility of rejecting Chris's directives does not seem to be an issue for
Mike here; his main concern is to ensure that he has understood the directives
correctly. This is reflected in how he formulates his responses. He not only
acknowledges that he has understood, but often repeats or rephrases the instruction, for example:

Example 3.15

51   Mike   [...]↑ Well, uh– so– so what do you want over here for these. if it's
            pass fail ... or not applicable.
52   Chris .hh Then you would just put in ... over here just put in ... um ... just
            that
53   Mike   ⌊Either
            I did it or I didn't do it,
54   Chris Yeah. PF ...
55   Mike   Okay.
56   Chris or NA
57   Mike   Okay, ↓ Did it, didn't do it, doesn't apply. Okay.

Mike's *did it, didn't do it, doesn't apply* is a reformulation of Chris's *PF or NA* (i.e.
pass, fail or not applicable), and a partial repetition of his own words in turn 53.
Heritage and Watson (1979) call such phenomena 'formulations': when speakers
provide the 'gist' or 'upshot' of the conversation (or part of the conversation) thus
far. A major function of formulations is for speakers to check their understanding, precisely what Mike is doing here. His initial meta-statement (*you want me to
make a log*) is in fact also a formulation: he begins the conversation by summarizing what he thinks he is expected to do.

   Such formulations are not, however, necessarily present in all directive discourse. In other encounters in the corpus, instructions are sometimes simply
acknowledged with a minimal response (*right* or *yeah*). In this encounter, Chris and
Mike are in the process of setting up a new procedure (whereas in many other cases
the procedure is routine); it is therefore paramount that both parties understand
the procedure, especially Mike, as it will be the basis on which he is evaluated.

   The linguistic choices made by the speakers (e.g., the use of deontic modals)
and the types of adjacency pair that occur (e.g., directive – acknowledgement +
formulation, in Example 3.15 above) show that this interaction occurs within a
different discourse frame from the previous decision-making conversations. But

in spite of being unidirectional in terms of interactive roles, procedural/directive discourse is nevertheless a collaboratively constructed genre. Here, as in a number of other examples of instruction-giving in the corpus, it is the instruction-receiver who elicits directives. As shown in Example 3.13 above, it is Mike who initiates this generic activity through his opening meta-statement (*you want me to make a log*), and he also reframes the activity as directive discourse after an interruption involving a third person, using the same modal verb *want* (see Example 3.15 above):

> ↑ Well, uh— so— so <u>what do you want</u> over here for these. if it's pass fail … or not applicable.

Furthermore, Chris's hedged reformulation of his instructions in turn 6 (Example 3.14 above) shows that he is 'fine-tuning' his directives to his interlocutor's response (or lack of response in this particular instance).

3.5 Fuzzy boundaries between genres

These analyses show that the two genres dealt with above are in many ways diametrically opposed: decision-making involves collaborative negotiation of a problem, whereas procedural discourse is concerned with the unidirectional communication of instructions or directives. Nevertheless, a number of encounters or stretches of interaction seem to be on the borderline between these two genres.

3.5.1 Advice-giving

One conversation in the corpus classified as directive discourse is an example of a distinct sub-genre: advice-giving. Support for considering advice-giving as a sub-genre of procedural/directive discourse can be found in Tsui's (1994) classification of 'discourse acts' based on naturally occurring data, where advice is classified as a sub-category of directives. As with 'classic' directives (what Tsui calls 'mandatives'), the advice-giver tries to get the addressee to carry out a particular action, but, as Tsui points out, the addressee need not necessarily comply (unlike with mandatives, where compliance is assumed). This means that advice-giving discourse is different in a number of ways from other directive discourse, as the analysis below demonstrates.

'Conversation stoppers'

The advice-giving extract is from the same American company as the last conversation ('Evaluation procedure'), and one of the speakers is again the company president, Chris. Here he speaks to his sales manager, Joe, about a list of 'conversation stoppers' which Joe compiled and gave Chris to look at earlier in the day. This is a list of ways in which sales reps should *not* begin their conversations with prospective customers; the first few lines are shown in Figure 3.1.

Discussing these conversation stoppers is the last of a series of work-related issues which Joe and Chris discuss during a longer meeting in Chris's office, and it is introduced quite deliberately by Chris via a metalinguistic statement:

Example 3.16

4   Chris: Uh ... I got a <u>suggestion</u> ... by the way with this,
5   Joe: Okay,
6   Chris: Two things ...

By using the performative noun *suggestion*, Chris clearly signals an advice-giving frame for what he is going to say next. Joe shows his acceptance to engage in this genre in the next turn, by saying *okay*. Chris then goes on to propose a number of changes to the list of 'conversation stoppers' and suggests how Joe could use it in training his sales force. The beginning of the conversation (after a brief interruption during which Chris speaks on his intercom) is shown below:

Example 3.17

21   Chris   [referring to list of 'conversation stoppers'] Uh ... <u>I don't know</u> why this is ... large.[5] Isn't this the same as all the rest of these? It's just another ... example?
22   Joe   Yeah. It <u>should</u> be, [1.5] Yeah that's just another example.

Figure 3.1 'Conversation stoppers'

A conversation stopper is a question or a statement that limits or shuts down the conversation.

Here are a few examples of conversation stoppers:
- Did you get the new media kit?
- Have you had a chance to look over the info I sent you?
- What do you think of the media kit I sent?

You don't mail nationally, do you? (could be any other qualifying question)

23	Chris	⌈I was thinking this
		also ... the: 'I was wondering' approach?[6] Hehehehehehehehehehe
24	Joe	⌊Yeah 'I was
		wondering' Heh yeah I like that, okay,
25	Chris	U:hm ... an' a– an' maybe just a note at the end here, that says to the
		person ↑ Ask yourself is this question ... a: an indirect invitation for
		the prospect to end the conversation ⌊Joe: Yeah⌋ because ... I mean if
		they really answered that honestly, almost all of these are.
26	Joe	Yeah. That's right.
27	Chris	So. An' you might include– what I had here was some conversation
		starters or approa– you know,
28	Joe	.hh Okay I hadn't even thought about that yet.
29	Chris	⌊??
30	Joe	But good I'm glad you have a ... ↓ a note on that

Unlike in the previous extract analysed ('Evaluation procedure'), where Chris frequently uses deontic modality and imperatives to gives directives, here he uses mainly epistemic modal items: *I don't know, I was thinking, maybe, you might*. This reflects the generic difference between the two extracts: by using indirect and tentatively worded formulations, Chris indicates that he is giving advice, not issuing orders. Only one suggestion is delivered more forcefully later in the conversation:

Example 3.18

| 35 | Chris | They gotta be ... they gotta be involved in it. It won't– it won't work |
| | | as a lecture. |

Most of these suggestions therefore look quite similar to suggestions made by speakers in decision-making conversations. Nevertheless there is an important difference: suggestions in decision-making discourse can be made by either participant and their goal is the negotiation of a joint decision. Suggestions in advice-giving, on the other hand, are only made by the advice-giver (which is why this genre can be considered unidirectional) and their goal is to get the addressee to carry out some action.

Joe's responses are also quite different from Mike's in 'Evaluation procedure' (Examples 3.13–3.15 above), which involve simple acknowledgements, queries or formulations. Joe not only acknowledges that he has understood (*okay, yeah*), but frequently evaluates the advice: *I like that* (turn 24), *good I'm glad* ... (turn 30). Again there are similarities here with decision-making responses, which often involve evaluation. Joe's responses are consonant with an advice-giving frame, where the addressee has the option of either accepting or rejecting the advice.

It is interesting, therefore, that Joe overwhelmingly accepts Chris's suggestion. This corroborates Mandala's (1998) findings in a corpus of advice-giving sequences that institutional advice tends to be accepted, which can probably be attributed to the unequal power relationship in situations like this (it is obviously easier to accept one's boss's advice than to reject it). Although Chris, the boss, seems to take pains to word his advice so as to give Joe the option of rejection, Joe, as the subordinate may not in fact be as free to reject the advice as it may appear (or as might be the case between equal partners). This contrasts with Heritage and Sefi's (1992) study of advice-giving in another type of institutional context: a corpus of recorded conversations between health visitors and mothers of new-born babies. Heritage and Sefi (1992) found that advice given by the health visitors was overwhelmingly resisted by the mothers, as it was perceived as challenging the mothers' competence. These examples illustrate some of the ways in which the participants' perceived institutional roles may have an effect on discourse structure, although it is argued throughout the book that institutional parameters do not necessarily determine discourse roles.

Like the previous conversations, 'Deciphering handwriting' and 'Evaluation procedure', 'Conversation stoppers' is an example of an interaction in which the transactional goal is signalled quite clearly at the outset via an initial metastatement which indicates the genre expected in the upcoming discourse. The above analysis of how advice-giving is 'played out' in the initiation and response of the participants shows that this sub-genre of directive discourse differs in a number of ways from other procedural/directive discourse, and shares a number of features with the genre of decision-making. This is one example of how the borderline between genres can be fuzzy. The distinction between collaborative and unidirectional discourse is not always a sharp one, but should be seen as a cline along which some interactions are more collaborative or unidirectional than others.

3.6 Conclusion

These examples show that boundaries between genres are fluid, and that it is not always easy to determine exactly what kind of activity the speakers are engaged in. However, examining the discourse for contextualization cues provided by the speakers themselves of their communicative goals at least means that decisions about genre classification are based as much as possible on participants' discourse frames and not on categories imposed by the discourse analyst. Evidence of frames can be found in all aspects of the discourse. This analysis has concentrated on metalinguistic signals, modal items or lexical items indicating a problem-solution pattern, but interactive features, such as turn construction and length, can also be important indications of genre.

The above analyses of conversations from the two main genres in the corpus, decision-making and procedural/directive discourse, have attempted to demonstrate that a detailed examination of individual interactions can provide evidence of the speakers' transactional discourse goals, and therefore of the genre in which they are engaged.

But an analysis of genre in terms of speakers' transactional goals only provides half the picture; relational goals must also be taken into account in examining workplace interaction. The next chapter will address the question of how relational aspects of discourse can be integrated into a description of workplace discourse, and examines the types of linguistic feature that might provide evidence for speakers' orientation to relational goals.

4 Relational goals

A framework for analysing interpersonal
dimensions of workplace talk

4.1 Introduction

This chapter considers the role of relational goals within commonly occurring workplace genres, and proposes a framework for analysing the interpersonal dimension
of workplace talk.

Traditionally, transactional and relational goals were seen as entirely separate
and as characterizing two different kinds of talk. The term 'phatic communion'
was coined by Malinowski (1923/1972), who defined phatic talk as 'language
used in free, aimless, social intercourse in which ties of union are created by a
mere exchange of words' (1972: 149, 151). Malinowski thus distinguishes phatic
communion, as 'purposeless', from other types of talk which are more obviously
purposeful (see Coupland 2000: 1–25). Schneider (1989) makes a similar distinction between 'instrumental' or 'purpose-oriented' talk (*zweckorientiert*) and
'phatic communication'. While arguing that the latter has been neglected in linguistic enquiry, he sees these as two entirely separate types of talk.

But positing such a dichotomy between transactional and relational talk represents an over-simplification of most communicative situations. As discussed in
Chapter 2, speakers usually orient to both transactional and relational goals in most
types of discourse. Ragan (2000) argues that this is in fact a false dichotomy, as in
some types of work (e.g., the women's health-care interactions she investigated),
sociable talk constitutes an integral part of the task. In addition, seeing the building
or maintenance of relationships as a goal in itself implies that even purely 'phatic'
communication cannot be considered to be 'purposeless'. We need to develop
much finer distinctions than the traditional instrumental/phatic dichotomy.

4.2 Workplace and business relationships

It is a fairly obvious point that people who work together do not merely trans-
act business, but also interact as individuals or in groups, and thereby build some
kind of relationship. As a number of studies have shown (Charles 1996, Ylänne-
McEwen 1996, Holmes and Stubbe 2003), the nature of the relationship can
influence workplace and business interactions in a number of ways. For example,

Charles (1996) found that the discourse of business negotiations varied markedly and consistently depending on whether negotiators had an 'old' or a 'new' relationship. But not only does the relationship have an influence on discourse, it is mainly *through talk* that relationships are built; language therefore contributes to relationship-building in significant ways. Poncini (2002) examined some of the specific linguistic strategies used by participants in multicultural meetings to build relationships and a sense of group identity. She found that the use of linguistic features as diverse as personal pronouns, specialized lexis and evaluative language all contributed to building group identity and cohesion, as they performed a variety of functions such as facilitating participation in meetings, claiming common ground or showing co-operation and reciprocity. Example 4.1 below from Poncini's data of an Italian company's meeting with its international distributors illustrates such a use of evaluative language. Here one of the company representatives uses evaluative lexis (in bold) in order to build a positive image of the company, Alta (not the company's real name), which makes products for skiing and other outdoor sports:

Example 4.1[1]

uh Edo yesterday explained to you that (+) our **success** (.) the **success** of *Alta* (+) has grown together (+) parallel (.) to the **success** of our athletes (++)**the the best example in this case is Rossi** (++) ((well known Italian skier)) where Rossi began to **win** (+) uh he **won** (.) thanks (.) to (.) *Alta* (.) to products of *Alta* (.) also— not only (.) of course ((smiles, almost laughs))

(Poncini 2002: 361)[2]

Poncini suggests that in this and other examples from her data 'the company speaker uses evaluation strategically to create a shared image of the company, its products, ... activities and strategy so that the image comes to represent what is highly valued by the group' (ibid.).

Clearly, then, relational goals and relationship-building pervade all aspects of workplace interaction, even talk that is fully focused on a workplace task, as in Example 4.1 above. Nevertheless, it is possible to identify talk, or stretches of talk, that show a stronger orientation towards either transactional or relational goals; for example a clear switch from work talk to small talk. A genre-based approach, which starts from the notion of goal orientation, is a useful starting point for exploring these issues.

4.3 Relational goals and genre

First, it is important to recognize that relational exchanges and sequences can occur within genres with clear transactional goals, such as service encounters.

Minimally, this would involve greeting and leave-taking to initiate and close encounters, but server and customer may also engage in small talk (e.g., about the weather) in the course of the service transaction. In her study of service encounters, Ventola (1987) recognizes the presence of relational side-sequences in her data; however, she considers these to be instances of genre-switching or genre-embedding. Thus if small talk occurs within a service encounter, this is considered to constitute a temporary switch out of the genre of service encounters into a different genre (that of casual conversation).

Taking Ventola's reasoning to its logical conclusion, such an approach would only see the transactional stages as defining and characterizing a particular genre. But is it really satisfactory to view relational sequences as irrelevant to genre? Some genres typically involve a great deal of non-transactional talk, for example McCarthy (2000) found that less than 10 per cent of talk between hairdressers and their customers was task-focused. Only identifying the transactional elements in this type of encounter would leave a large portion of the data unaccounted for.

Furthermore, as we have already seen, a number of studies on spoken workplace discourse have shown that 'business talk' and 'small talk' cannot be neatly separated (Cheepen 2000, Holmes 2000b, McCarthy 2000, Holmes and Stubbe 2003). Holmes (2000b: 38) proposes a continuum of task-orientation for workplace talk, with core business talk at one end and phatic communion at the other:

core business talk — work-related talk — social talk — phatic communion

Core business talk is 'on-topic' in terms of the transactional goal of the particular encounter, whereas work-related talk departs from this goal, but still focuses on issues relevant to the work in general. At the relational end of the continuum, phatic communion is topically unrelated to the workplace, whereas social talk addresses some aspect of the workplace context, although relational goals are foregrounded. In the ABOT Corpus, such a gradation from transactional to relational goal orientation is reflected in the distinction made, on the one hand, between transactional and non-transactional genres, and, within the latter category, between two types of non-transactional talk: small talk and office gossip. Small talk addresses topics outside the workplace, and office gossip is off-topic in terms of the transactional goal of the encounter, but does involve workplace topics (see Chapter 3).

4.4 Types of relational talk

In analysing data from a hairdressing salon and a driving lesson, McCarthy (2000: 104) identified similar degrees of task-orientation within these two types of service encounter. He proposes a distinction between four types of talk, which can all occur within the same encounter:

1   phatic exchanges (greetings, partings)
2   transactional talk (requests, enquiries, instructions)
3   transactional-plus-relational talk (non-obligatory task evaluations and other comments)
4   relational talk (small talk, anecdotes, wider topics of mutual interest).

Only the second type, transactional talk, focuses exclusively on task goals, whereas the other three involve some degree of relational orientation. McCarthy argues that an adequate description of these genres must include all four types of talk. The third category, transactional-plus-relational is particularly interesting in terms of genre: it may be that many of the 'non-obligatory' elements of structure identified in traditional descriptions of genre (e.g., Hasan 1985) involve such an intermingling of transactional and relational goals.

In the ABOT Corpus, evidence of relational goals can be found in various types of talk. First there are entire conversations, classified as small talk or office gossip, which primarily have a relational focus. Some interactions with a clear transactional focus on a workplace task also have relational episodes embedded within them. We also find examples of McCarthy's 'transactional-plus-relational' talk – non-obligatory relational elements linked to the task at hand – which will be referred to as 'relational sequences' or 'relational turns'. Finally, evidence of speakers orienting to relational goals could also at times be seen in talk which was central to accomplishing a workplace task. The way in which speakers designed their turns and the lexical choices made (e.g., choosing a more indirect way of expressing themselves over a more direct alternative) often showed their orientation to the relational dimension of the interaction (e.g., Example 4.1 above). It will be argued that certain types of lexico-grammatical choice frequently reflect speakers' relational goals (see Section 4.6 below). Such items will be referred to as 'interpersonal markers', and include devices such as modal verbs, vague language and idioms. Evidence of relational goals can therefore be found at the following levels of discourse, from entire conversations down to individual words:

1   non-transactional conversations: office gossip and small talk
2   phatic communion: small talk at the beginning or end of transactional encounters
3   relational episodes: small talk or office gossip occurring during the performance of a transactional task
4   relational sequences and turns: non-obligatory task-related talk with a relational focus

5   interpersonal markers: modal items, vague language, hedges and intensifiers, idioms and metaphors.

These different types of relational talk (or aspects of talk reflecting relational goals) are described in more detail below, and illustrated with examples from the ABOT Corpus.

4.4.1 Non-transactional conversations

The distinction between the two types of non-transactional conversation and stretches of talk, office gossip and small talk, is based not on the structure of the talk, but solely on the topic: office gossip is not task-oriented, but involves talk about some aspect of the workplace, whereas small talk addresses topics outside the workplace. More fine-grained distinctions in terms of genre could obviously be made within these two categories. Eggins and Slade (1997: 265) provide a useful classification of casual talk at work (recorded during coffee breaks), e.g., different types of story-telling genre, observation–comment, gossip, each with its own generic structure. In the ABOT Corpus, similar sub-genres can be identified within office gossip and small talk, including narratives, joke-telling, observation–comment, gossip and teasing. Narratives occur particularly frequently, as a great deal of small talk and office gossip involves the telling of personal or workplace anecdotes, as illustrated by these extracts from longer conversations:

Example 4.2 Small talk

  1 Kate   I've got a bad back
  2 Sally   Oh Kate!
  3 Mary   ⌊Have you?
  4 Kate   ⌊I moved furniture … Friday night, I – helped my friends at [name of town] Saturday afternoon, they're selling, and yesterday I helped a friend move into a flat and … I've–
  5 Mary   stiffened up
  6 Sally   You alright.
  7 Kate   Yeah no it's … ago– yesterday I couldn't bend down and just before I left, the phone rang, and it was Cindy, Corin, had got a new picnic hamper, he'd been and he'd– the knives, he'd just nearly sliced his finger off.
  8 Sally   *.Hhh!*
  9 Kate   So there was a mad dash up to [name of hospital], and … um …
10 Mary   Oh my God!
11 Kate   And … I mean this child's, hand, it was … just bleeding and so I had

Alice, so I took *her* with me for the move, George looked at her, an'—
[…]

Example 4.3 *Office gossip*

1 Liz   We were saying though, that it won't be long before there *are* cameras,
        because Careers was broken into again over the weekend
2 Vicky Och. It wasn't!
3 Liz   *Second* time in a fortnight.
4 Susan Yeah
5 Vicky The computers were stolen.
6 Liz   ↑ *No, cash.* An' they even *locked.* the *doors.* be*hind* them.

4.4.2 *Phatic communion*

I use Malinowski's term 'phatic communion' following Laver (1975) to refer specifically to ritualized relational talk in the opening and closing phases of an encounter. As has been observed by conversation and discourse analysts (e.g., Schegloff and Sacks 1973, Ventola 1979) the opening and closing segments of conversations are highly structured, often involving, among other elements, ritual phatic exchanges, for example:

Example 4.4

1 Liz   ↑ Morning Danny
2 Dan   ↑ Hello, how are you?
3 Liz   ↑ Fine, thank you, how are you?
4 Dan   ↑ Yeah all right, yeah,
5 Liz   ↑ Good,

In spite of its ritualistic nature, Laver (1975: 233) stresses that phatic communion cannot be seen as trivial, but that it performs an important function in human interaction 'in that the cumulative consensus about a relationship reached as the result of repeated encounters between the two participants constitutes the essence of that relationship'. The following opening phase of a transactional encounter from the ABOT Corpus demonstrates this point very nicely:

Example 4.5

1 Gene   Hello Helga,
2 Helga Hi.

3   Gene   Thank you for your card.
4   Helga   Oh. Happy new year.
5   Gene   I'm thinking of … writing out something with … a– a family
              newsletter to bring to you, with uh– but most o' the news you already
              know. ↑ You know about our new grandson?
6   Helga   Yes. That's uh really wonderful. ↑ How old is he now?
7   Gene   Well uh about … three weeks old, Hehehe
8   Helga   That's nice.

In this brief opening sequence the participants make reference to the extent of their relationship: they are well-enough acquainted to send each other cards, Helga knows about Gene's family (i.e. *most o' the news you already know*), and this degree of intimacy entitles her also to know about the new grandson. By demonstrating this degree of intimacy to one another and adding to it, they consolidate the relationship for the current and future encounters.

4.4.3 Relational episodes

Relational episodes are instances of small talk or office gossip occurring in the middle of, and temporarily interrupting, transactional talk. As discussed above, considering such episodes as instances of genre-switching, with no relevance for the task being performed, seems unsatisfactory. The question *why* speakers should choose to engage in relational talk in the middle of performing a workplace task will be addressed in Chapter 7.

4.4.4 Relational sequences and turns

Relational sequences or turns are different from relational episodes, as they do not actually involve a switch out of transactional talk, but consist of remarks that are task-related, but do not actually contribute to getting the job done. An example of this was shown at the beginning of this book (Example 1.3). Here a brief extract from the conversation is reproduced to illustrate the occurrence of a relational sequence (underlined):

Example 4.6

1   Beth   So that's what you want? Like a snapshot thing.
2   Carol   ⌊Yeah.
3   Beth   Okay.
4   Carol   ⌊Right. Okay. .hh So. <u>Boy it's tiny up there!</u>
5   Beth   <u>I know, hehehe You need a big magnifying glass. [chuckles]</u>

The comments made by Carol and Beth in turns 4 and 5 (about the font size of an item on a document) are relevant to the current task they are involved in, but not actually necessary. Rather they seem to have an evaluative function closely linked to the speakers' relational and identity goals. Carol seems to want to justify the fact that she did not notice the item on the document (the date) earlier, and Beth affiliates with her through her humorous comment. Relational sequences typically consist of such task evaluations, often involving joking and humour. Relational sequences are particularly interesting for workplace discourse, as they are more closely associated with transactional genres than the other kinds of relational talk discussed so far; and therefore a substantial part of Chapter 7 is devoted to the analysis of relational sequences in the ABOT Corpus.

4.4.5 Interpersonal markers

Even when none of the types of relational talk described above occurs, participants nevertheless orient to relational as well as transactional goals in workplace interactions. Evidence for this can be found at the lexico-grammatical level in a variety of linguistic features, for example the kind of evaluative lexis seen in Example 4.1 above. Such words or expressions which predominantly have an interpersonal function are referred to in this book as 'interpersonal markers'. Consider the underlined words in the following example from a conversation in a publishing company, in which an assistant editor explains to a senior editor how to order a free copy of a book:

Example 4.7

Oh it's <u>really</u>– it's <u>really</u> easy to do it. <u>I mean</u> :hh <u>actually</u>, <u>I think</u> if you <u>just</u> wanna send them to a friend <u>or something</u>, you <u>could</u> order them through the gratis order form.

Although the underlined words and expressions represent an assortment of different types of item: adverbs (*really*, *actually*, *just*), (modal) verbs (*mean*, *think*, *could*) and a vague expression (*or something*), they all have a number of things in common. First of all, they are not absolutely necessary in order to get the message across, and could have been left out. We could also say that they all in some way either intensify (*really*, *just*) or tone down the utterance (*I mean*, *actually*, *I think*, *or something*, *could*). They thus allow the speaker to qualify her utterance in a number of ways. If they had been left out, the utterance would have sounded much more blunt and less chatty and friendly.

The use of these interpersonal markers shows that the speaker is taking account of her relationship with her colleague, even when fully focused on a workplace task, here explaining a procedure. A more detailed overview of the kinds of item included in the category of interpersonal markers will be given at the end of this chapter.

4.4.6 *Summary of relational features of talk*

The framework proposed above provides a tool for systematically examining relational features of workplace discourse at all levels. It can be used for the study of relational talk within a particular organization, or as a component of specific workplace genres. For instance, one might want to investigate whether phatic communion, relational sequences or particular interpersonal markers occur frequently in the performance of certain genres. These topics will be taken up in more detail in subsequent chapters. But, of course it is not just the extent and form of relational features of talk that are of interest, but, more importantly, the functions these perform within workplace discourse.

4.5 The functions of relational talk

It has been a recurrent theme throughout this book that one must take into account speakers' relational goals when attempting to describe workplace discourse. But how exactly can speakers' relational goals be characterized, and what kind of things are people trying to achieve when they use language with a relational orientation?

Manifestations of relational goals often involve the notion of 'politeness', or 'face-work', for which extensive frameworks have been developed within sociolinguistics, principally by Goffman (1967 and 1972) and Brown and Levinson (1978/1987). 'Face' is an individual's 'positive social value' (Goffman 1972: 319); and face-work thus involves maintaining one's own and other participants' face in the course of an interaction, and avoiding or correcting threats to face that arise. Brown and Levinson (1978/1987) distinguish between positive and negative politeness. Both types of politeness involve maintaining – or redressing threats to – positive and negative face, where positive face is defined as the addressee's 'perennial desire that his wants ... should be thought of as desirable' (p. 101), and negative face as the addressee's 'want to have his freedom of action unhindered and his attention unimpeded' (p. 129).

Many instances of a relational orientation involve either positive or negative politeness. Holmes (2000a) shows that speakers often use self-deprecatory humour as a means of protecting their own positive face (thereby pre-empting criticism). The following example shows a new trainee, Meg, using humour in this way to excuse the fact she has forgotten something she has already been told:

Example 4.8

1	Meg	Yeah. an' I immediately forgot everything you told me about–
2	Ann	⌊That's okay.
3	Meg	[chuckles]
4	Ann	I'll show you.

In Chapter 2 we saw that speakers frequently use meta-statements at the beginning of workplace conversations to signal their transactional goals. Such
meta-statements often involve the use of negative politeness strategies, as in this
example of an employee addressing her manager:

Example 4.9

I've got a couple more queries actually Mary, then I'll leave you to get on.

In this meta-statement, the speaker does more than simply communicate her transactional goal (getting answers to her queries), but she simultaneously conveys the
message that she does not want to impose too much on Mary's (her boss's) time.
She uses a vague quantifier, which shows that she does not have many queries (*a
couple*), a hedge (*actually*), and indicates that she will not be long (*then I'll leave you
to get on*), thereby minimizing the imposition on the addressee's time. She is in
fact making extensive use of negative politeness which, according to Brown and
Levinson (1978/1987), has the function of minimizing the imposition caused by
a face-threatening act.

The use of hedges and vague language (*just, about*, etc.) and other distancing
devices that contribute to negative politeness, such as epistemic modals (*could*) and
use of the past tense (*wanted, I was wondering*), are also common in other examples
from the ABOT Corpus where speakers initiate new generic activity and explicitly refer to their discourse goals using meta-statements:

Example 4.10

- Uh … <u>just wanted</u> to tell you about my … conversation with ↑Tony.
- I have a <u>quick</u> question for you. I *hope* it's a <u>quick</u> question.
- Uh ↑<u>Just wanted</u> to come and chat to you <u>a little</u> about the company.

In all these examples, the use of negative politeness shows speakers are attending to the relational aspect of the interaction, even in explicitly framing their task
goals. It is likely that negative politeness is particularly common in such opening
statements, as initiating an encounter or a new phase of the conversation constitutes an imposition on the addressee's freedom of action. This provides evidence

that speakers have multiple goals, simultaneously attending to transactional as well as relational concerns.

When discourse participants can be seen to make efforts to preserve – or ward off threats to – their own or others' positive or negative face, they are clearly orienting to relational goals. Whereas negative politeness, according to Brown and Levinson (1978/1987) always involves redressive action to face-threatening acts, positive politeness can have a more general function of showing appreciation for the others' wants. One common positive politeness strategy, according to Brown and Levinson, is to claim common ground. The following example of such a strategy occurs in the course of an encounter in which two co-workers make arrangements (see Example 7.9). In commenting on an action one participant has just taken, the other one says:

Example 4.11

Yeah we're thinking together on that.

While one function of such a comment may be to reinforce the addressee's (and the speaker's own) self-esteem, it is not clear that the notion of face adequately accounts for all reasons why speakers might want to invoke common ground. Other reasons might be building a positive relationship or creating a pleasant atmosphere or even a feeling of intimacy. Expressions of solidarity, as in Example 4.11 above, go beyond politeness, and are indicative of an affective dimension of relational goals (as will be explored in more detail in Section 4.6.3 below). A distinction will therefore be made between two general types of relational orientation, involving either politeness or the expression of solidarity, as detailed below:

1 **Politeness**: We shall use this term to cover instances of Brown and Levinson's positive and negative politeness which are concerned with redressing or avoiding face-threatening acts. Negative politeness therefore involves such discursive acts as apologizing and expressing deference, whereas examples of positive politeness include hedging opinions, mitigating criticism and self-deprecation. Linguistic politeness strategies mainly involve indirectness and distancing devices used to soften and hedge propositions.

2 **Solidarity**: This refers to the affective dimension of interpersonal relations, and involves the expression of mutuality and common ground. Solidarity strategies include claiming common ground or showing interest, approval, sympathy, etc., as well as the use of in-group language and colloquialisms.

Of course, not all interaction is co-operative, and building a positive relationship may not always be the discourse participants' goal. In discourse which is conflict-ual and argumentative, the speakers' relational orientation can often be described in opposite terms from those detailed above: rather than use politeness strategies, speakers may express themselves bluntly and directly, and instead of emphasizing common ground, they may highlight differences and separateness. The character-istics of conflictual and argumentative discourse will be examined in Chapter 6.

4.6 The lexico-grammatical level: approaches to linguistic manifestations of relational goals

As we have seen, even in stretches of discourse which clearly have a transactional function, the use of interpersonal markers, such as modal verbs and adverbial hedges, indicate that speakers are simultaneously orienting to relational goals. As such lexico-grammatical items have been described within a number of approaches using a variety of labels and definitions, it is worth providing an over-view of these descriptions and the types of item included.

Examining linguistic manifestations of relational goals can be situated within an area of linguistic enquiry which focuses on interpersonal meanings. Halliday (1978) uses the term 'interpersonal' to refer to one of the three macro-functions of lan-guage: 'ideational', 'interpersonal' and 'textual'. The interpersonal function of language is defined as 'expressing relations among participants in the situation, and the speaker's own intrusion into it'(p. 46).

Interpersonal aspects of language are therefore those which express the sub-jective views and assessments of the discourse participants, rather than the informational or ideational content of the message. According to Halliday, the clause embodies all three functions at once, with the interpersonal function being expressed by such grammatical structures as mood, modality and person. All lan-guage therefore has an interpersonal dimension, and the interpersonal function of language represents one type of meaning in the meaning system of language.

In terms of speakers' goals, which are of course pre-linguistic, we can say that the linguistic system provides resources for pursuing discourse goals. Regardless of whether discourse participants are focusing on transactional goals (getting the job done) or relational goals (building and maintaining the relationship with their interlocutor), some kind of interpersonal meaning is always expressed. However, as we shall see, interpersonal linguistic choices provide a particularly important resource when speakers are focusing on relational goals.

Another perspective on this comes from Hunston and Thompson (2000), a volume which brings together, under the cover term 'evaluation', a wide range of approaches to the interpersonal dimension of language. In their introduction to the volume, Hunston and Thompson (p. 6) identify three main functions per-formed by evaluation:

1   to express the speakers'/writer's opinion and the underlying value system
2   to construct and maintain relations between the discourse participants
3   to organize the discourse.

Only the second function concerns relational goals. Therefore while building and maintaining relational goals are not the only functions of evaluation or interpersonal meaning in language, they represent a major resource for speakers in pursuing these goals.

In the ensuing discussion, we shall explore the range of linguistic features which express interpersonal meanings, and suggest how a link can be established between interpersonal meanings and relational goals.

4.6.1 Expressing commitment and detachment

Modality

Modality provides a good starting point for an investigation of interpersonal meanings in general, and relational goals in particular. This is a complex area of language theory and language use, but modality can be very broadly defined as the expression of the speaker's stance towards the propositional content of an utterance, and thus involves the expression of interpersonal rather than ideational meanings. In the literature two main types of modality are usually recognized: epistemic modality, which is concerned with degrees of commitment to the truth of a proposition, and deontic modality, which deals with degrees of obligation or necessity to perform acts (Lyons 1977). Therefore, according to Lyons, modality is centrally concerned with possibility and necessity, but other notions, such as intention, prediction, volition, ability and inclination are also dealt with in the literature (see Lyons 1977, Palmer 1979/1990, Coates 1983, Halliday 1985/1994). The different types of modality, and how modal items can be classified, will be considered in more detail in Chapter 5.

The investigation of modality is often limited to modal verbs (*may*, *must*, *will*, etc.), e.g., Palmer's 1979/1990 study, but there are obviously many other ways of expressing modal meanings besides through the use of modal verbs. Holmes (1983), for example, also looks at certain lexical verbs (e.g., *think*), modal adjectives (e.g., *certain*), modal adverbs (e.g., *maybe*) and nouns (e.g., *possibility*). Stubbs in his seminal (1986) article, in which he makes a call for a systematic investigation of a 'modal grammar of English', discusses a whole host of linguistic features: in addition to the modal items dealt with by Holmes, he also touches upon vague language, tense and voice, among other things. Although he does not actually define modality, Stubbs's description of what the object of investigation should be is very broad in scope:

ways in which language is used in communication to express personal beliefs and adopt positions, to express agreement and disagreement with others, to make personal and social allegiances, contracts, and commitments, or alternatively to disassociate the speaker from points of view, and to remain vague or uncommitted.

(Stubbs 1986: 1)

Hedges and intensifiers

The expression of commitment and detachment, as Stubbs shows, is central to modality. Another way of expressing either commitment or detachment to a proposition is by using adverbs such as *sort of*, *just*, *really*, *a bit*, to modify a proposition or lexical item. These either function as hedges, in which case they express detachment from the item that is modified, e.g.:

It's <u>a bit</u> confusing,

or they function as intensifiers, thereby emphasizing the speaker's commitment to what they are saying, e.g.:

It's <u>just</u> dreadful.

In many descriptions such hedges are included in the same category as other modal items (often under the general label of 'hedge'), for example Biber *et al.* (1999: 557) classify hedges such as *sort of* together with modal adverbs (e.g., *possibly*, *certainly*) in the category of 'stance adverbs'. However, Prince *et al.* (1982: 85–6) distinguish between 'approximators', where the propositional content of the modified item (the 'blueness' in the example below) is hedged, e.g.:

His feet were <u>sort of</u> blue,

and 'shields' (i.e. modals), which express marked speaker commitment to the truth of a proposition, but where the propositional content itself (the 'blueness') is not affected, e.g.:

<u>I think</u> his feet were blue.

Such a distinction is also made in the present volume, where hedges (what Prince *et al.* call 'approximators') and intensifiers are examined separately from epistemic and deontic modality. However, this distinction, based on semantic criteria, is not always relevant in practice, and, as we shall see, hedges and intensifiers often have functions very similar to those of modal verbs and adverbs.

Vague language

Closely related to hedges are devices which introduce vagueness to a proposition: vague approximators (*around, about*), vague ways of referring to entities (*stuff, thing*) and categories (*or something, and things like that*). In some descriptions (Prince *et al.* 1982, Biber *et al.* 1999), vague approximators are included in the category of hedges. In the classification used here, hedges which downtone or weaken a proposition are examined separately from vague language, which makes an expression less specific or precise (*about, or something*, etc.), but, again, in practice these semantic distinctions may not be relevant. As indicated above, Stubbs (1986), in his discussion of 'a modal grammar', also mentions vague language as one of the devices speakers use to express detachment.

Speakers may use vague language for a number of different purposes: Channell (1994: 194) lists ten possible communicative functions of vague language. All these uses fall broadly into one of two categories: (1) those that are related to the information state of the participants and therefore serve the transactional function of language, and (2) uses that have to do with the relational aspect of the interaction, including self-protection, power, politeness and informality.

Such a range of functions, covering transactional and relational purposes, can also be found in the way speakers use modals and hedges. Stubbs (1986: 1) mentions politeness as one 'obvious reason' why speakers might avoid direct or clear expressions; and both Holmes (1983) and Willing (1997) address this multifunctionality of modals: they can convey either epistemic meanings – the speaker's attitude towards the utterance or relational meanings – the speaker's attitude towards the addressee.

4.6.2 Language and affect

So far the interpersonal features discussed have involved mainly notions of commitment and detachment, which, in terms of relational goals, can be linked most readily to politeness functions. However, as Hunston and Thompson (2000: 1–27) show, this is only one aspect of what they call 'evaluation': speakers also may express judgements and opinions of goodness/desirability. Such interpersonal meanings relate to speakers' and writers' attitudes and feelings, and therefore frequently involve a relational orientation towards solidarity. Compared to the notions of commitment and detachment expressed, for example, through modality, this affective dimension of language has been relatively neglected, as Hunston and Thompson (20–1) point out. Nevertheless, interpersonal features of language relating to affect have been addressed by a number of linguists and discourse analysts within a range of approaches.

One aspect of the affective expression of language is covered by the term 'involvement' first used by Chafe (1982) to characterize one of the ways in which spontaneous speech is different from writing (although he does not use the term 'affect'). Some of the ways in which, according to Chafe, involvement is manifested in speech are simply products of the face-to-face interactivity of speech (for instance the frequent use of first and second person reference), but others seem to have an affective dimension as well. For example 'emphatic particles' (intensifiers) are said to express 'enthusiastic involvement' in what is being said (p. 7), and vague expressions and hedges 'may also express a desire for experiential involvement' (p. 48).

Tannen (1989) borrows the term 'involvement' from Chafe in her examination of 'involvement strategies' in spoken discourse. Her definition of involvement clearly involves affect: 'an internal, even emotional connection individuals feel which binds them to other people as well as to places, things, activities, ideas, memories, and words' (p. 12). Involvement strategies are defined as linguistic strategies which create involvement through sound or sense patterns. They include a range of linguistic and discursive phenomena; for instance sound strategies include rhythm and repetition, and examples of sense strategies are indirectness, tropes, constructed dialogue and narrative. Indirectness often involves many of the linguistic features discussed above in relation to politeness, such as epistemic modals, hedges and vague language. But Tannen points out that face-saving is only one reason for using this strategy; speakers may also be indirect 'to achieve the sense of rapport that comes from being understood without saying what one means' (p. 23). Indirectness may therefore also involve affect (see also Chafe on hedges and vague expressions above).

Biber and Finegan (1989) also deal with language and affect in their corpus study of styles of stance. 'Stance' is defined as: 'the lexical and grammatical expression of attitudes, feelings, judgements, or commitment concerning the propositional content of a message' (p. 93). According to Biber and Finegan, stance involves two main types of expression of attitude: affect – the expression of personal attitudes and emotions and 'evidentiality', which refers to the speaker's attitude towards knowledge (see also Chafe 1986), and therefore covers basically the same semantic area as epistemic modality. The lexical and grammatical markers of affect they investigate involve explicit expressions of feelings, e.g., *I'm shocked, I enjoy*, whereas evidentiality markers express degrees of doubt and certainty, e.g., modal verbs, modal adverbs, hedges, and so forth.

4.6.3 Evaluative language

One of the major functions of interpersonal linguistic devices is evaluation. In one sense, all interpersonal language is evaluative; as we have seen, Hunston and Thompson (2000: 1–27) use 'evaluation' as a cover term for the expression of interpersonal meanings, or what Biber and Finegan (1989) call stance. Here I will use the term evaluation in a more restricted sense to refer to speakers' and writers' judgements of goodness or desirability. This is similar to what Martin (2000) calls appraisal, which includes the sub-categories appreciation, affect and judgement.

Evaluation belongs to the domain of 'affective stance' (as defined by Biber and Finegan 1989) and is often encoded lexically via adjectives, adverbs, nouns and verbs. The expression of judgements and personal attitudes frequently involves the use of evaluative adjectives, as in the following extract from the ABOT Corpus showing speakers talking about a French dairy product, *crème fraîche*:

Example 4.12

1   Don   Crème fraîche. yeah.
2   Helga (Right.) ↑ *Oh!* ↓(Crème fraîche.) =
3   Andy   It's <u>great</u> =
4   Helga = *That* is the <u>*best*</u>.

Using the evaluative adjectives *great* and *best* provides the participants the opportunity to show their appreciation of and involvement with the talk of their interlocutors. Goodwin and Goodwin (1992), who examine the interactive construction of assessment, note that affect and involvement are central to the performance of assessments. McCarthy and Carter (2000) and McCarthy (2003) show that evaluative adjectives, such as *great* or *excellent*, are often used as 'non-minimal response tokens' to show 'engagement and interactional bonding'. Evaluation (or assessment) therefore often has a relational function. As mentioned above in Section 4.4, relational sequences (non-obligatory sequences of transactional talk) often also involve evaluation.

Evaluative adjectives are of course not the only linguistic devices used by speakers for evaluation. Idioms frequently have an evaluative function, as pointed out by a number of researchers who have investigated idioms (Moon 1992 and 1998, Strässler 1982), for example:

Example 4.13

- I think *that's* hangin' over all of our heads
- it's like pulling teeth

As examined in Chapter 6, idioms often provide speakers with the opportunity for performing indirect, 'off-record' evaluations.

Powell (1992) in her corpus-based study of informal lexis shows that informal lexical items, especially idioms, can also be evaluative. Powell also identifies three other functions for informal lexis: intensity and expressivity, which are clearly affective, and vagueness, which can also have an affective dimension (see also Chafe 1982 and Tannen 1989). Hyperbole is another area of lexical usage which frequently performs an evaluative function (McCarthy and Carter 2004). Modal verbs and modal lexical verbs which express the speaker's opinion are other devices which express assessments, e.g.:

Example 4.14

- I <u>would</u> go for the varnished one myself
- I <u>think</u> it's a good idea

These will be dealt with in some detail in the analysis of modality in Chapter 5.

Not all evaluative language, however, has a relational function. In many workplace tasks, evaluation is an integral part of the accomplishment of the task. For example, evaluating different proposed courses of action is an essential component of decision-making activities (from which the two examples in 4.14 above are taken). Linde (1997) shows that evaluation plays a central role in workplace talk in which co-workers are learning to use new technology. Evaluation can therefore play a role in terms of either transactional or relational goals, depending on whether evaluating is an obligatory element of the genre or not.

4.6.4 Summary

This discussion has provided an overview of a range of linguistic approaches dealing with interpersonal aspects of language use which are therefore relevant for an examination of discourse participants' relational goals. While a confusing variety of labels has been used in the literature to characterize interpersonal meanings (modality, evaluation, appraisal, stance, involvement), an overview of the different approaches shows there are common themes, and allows us to identify a number of functions which interpersonal devices can perform, including the expression of commitment/detachment, judgements, opinions and feelings. As previous studies have shown, a whole range of linguistic devices, which I refer to as 'interpersonal markers', from grammatical items, such as modal verbs and adverbs, to lexical nouns and adjectives can be used to express interpersonal meanings. While, as we have seen, interpersonal markers can have either a transactional or a relational function, they represent a particularly rich resource for pursuing relational goals.

In the discussion above, different types of interpersonal marker have been dealt with separately, but they can of course be used in conjunction with one another. The following example from the ABOT Corpus (see Example 7.10) shows a clustering of different interpersonal markers within a turn, in which the speaker suggests arranging a meeting:

Example 4.15

↑I <u>was wondering</u> if … you an' I <u>could</u> *possibly* this week, at <u>about</u> eleven o'clock on Thursday morning, reinforce each other half an hour on– <u>just</u> to look through …

Here a modal verb (*could*) is post-modified by a modal adverb (*possibly*) and within the same utterance a vague approximator (*about*) is used as well as a hedge (*just*). The whole request is introduced by an 'unreal past' construction (*I was wondering*) which can have a similar function to modality, as a distancing is achieved through the metaphor of temporal remoteness (Lyons 1977 and Stubbs 1986).

The clustering of these markers reinforces the negative politeness evident in the speaker's suggestion for a meeting and, more generally, seems to be strongly indicative of the foregrounding of relational goals. Such a foregrounding is achieved through the co-occurrence of a number of features, as Gumperz (1992) points out in his discussion of how contextualization cues are recognized:

> Foregrounding processes … do not rest on any one single cue. Rather, assessments depend on co-occurrence judgments … that simultaneously evaluate a variety of different cues.
>
> (Gumperz 1992: 232)

Relational goals are therefore foregrounded in particular parts of the discourse through the clustering of interpersonal markers within the same turn or interactional sequence. Sinclair (1987, cited in Hunston and Thompson 2000) observes that evaluation in speech and writing tends to occur at boundary points in the discourse. Example 4.15 above occurs at such a boundary point: here the speaker signals a new generic activity in the encounter – arranging a meeting. On the one hand, this involves the signalling of a transactional goal, but the clustering of interpersonal markers provides evidence that he is also paying particular attention to relational goals, involving mainly negative politeness (see Examples 4.9 and 4.10 above).

The focus in this discussion on interpersonal markers – i.e. on discrete lexical items with an interpersonal function – has perhaps created the impression that interpersonal meaning is expressed solely through such devices. This is of course not the case: interpersonal meanings not only are expressed through individual lexical items, but also can be encoded grammatically, for example through tense (Labov 1972, Lyons 1977, Stubbs 1986), through prosodic and paralinguistic features, and through interactive devices such as echoing, co-operative turn-construction, latching and non-intrusive overlaps. The 'involvement strategies' identified by Tannen (1989) include a number of these devices, as well as extended discursive units such as constructed dialogue and narrative.

Nor can it be assumed that interpersonal markers have fixed, stable meanings. As Carter (1987: 76–8) points out, evaluative meanings are often negotiated in naturally occurring discourse processes. Channell (2000) makes a similar point in showing that the evaluative meanings of certain lexical items are not semantically encoded, but only become apparent by examining the discourse contexts of these items in large corpora. It is because many of these items have vague and variable meanings that they provide a valuable resource for negotiating relational goals, for which indirectness and vagueness are often preferred.

4.7 Conclusion

This chapter has proposed a framework for investigating participants' relational goals in workplace interactions. It was suggested that linguistic evidence for relational goals can be found on five 'levels of discourse': non-transactional conversations (office gossip and small talk), phatic communion, relational episodes, relational sequences/turns and interpersonal markers; and illustrative examples at these different levels were shown. This framework will be drawn on in subsequent chapters in order to explore these relatively neglected aspects of workplace discourse in more detail. The next chapter provides a corpus-based comparison of interpersonal markers in a range of workplace genres, exploring both their transactional and relational functions.

5 A corpus-based comparison of workplace genres

5.1 Introduction

A range of spoken genres frequently occurs across different workplace environments, as shown in Chapter 3, in which methods of describing and classifying such genres were proposed. While Chapter 3 focused on the overall structure and staging of such commonly occurring genres as decision-making and procedural discourse, in this chapter we turn to the investigation and comparison of selected lexico-grammatical features in different workplace genres. In order to compare discrete linguistic items across a range of workplace conversations, corpus-based methods, as described in Chapter 2, provide some extremely useful tools. The chapter thus also serves to illustrate, using the ABOT Corpus, how workplace genres can be analysed and compared using corpus linguistic methods, which have hitherto not been used extensively in studies of workplace talk.

5.1.1 Interpersonal markers

The previous chapter provided an overview of a range of linguistic devices, labelled 'interpersonal markers', which can be used to express interpersonal meanings. As we have seen, interpersonal markers can have either a transactional or a relational function, but they represent a particularly rich resource for pursuing relational goals. In order to further investigate the relatively neglected interpersonal dimension of workplace interaction, this chapter investigates a selection of interpersonal markers in the ABOT Corpus and compares their frequency and use in the different genres found in the corpus. The following types of interpersonal marker were selected for comparison:

1   modal verbs (e.g., *can*, *will*, *should*, *think*)
2   hedges (e.g., *just*, *a bit*, *sort of*) and intensifiers (e.g., *really*, *very*)
3   vague language (e.g., *about*, *stuff*, *or something*)
4   idioms and metaphors (e.g., *hanging over our heads*, *par for the course*).

As elaborated in Chapter 4, all these lexico-grammatical features could be described as having modal meanings, as they can all express speaker stance. However, for the sake of clarity, the use of the term 'modality' here only refers to items that actually express degrees of speaker commitment and a range of modal meanings, i.e. possibility, necessity, volition, ability, etc.: modal verbs (e.g., *could*, *must*), modal lexical verbs (e.g., *think*, *want*), modal adjectives (e.g., *certain*, *necessary*), modal adverbs (e.g., *maybe*, *definitely*) and modal nouns (e.g., *possibility*, *opinion*).

In their investigation of styles of stance in different genres, Biber and Finegan (1989) found relatively few overt expressions of affect (i.e. lexical items expressing feelings, e.g., *enjoy*, *amazing*, *sadly*, etc.) in informal conversation. They found that stance was most frequently marked with hedges, 'emphatics' (called 'intensifiers' here) and modal verbs and adverbs. A similar tendency can be found in the ABOT Corpus, where modals were by far the largest category, followed by hedges and intensifiers, with fewer lexicalized markers of stance. The largest category of explicit markers of affect was evaluative adjectives and adverbs (e.g., *amazing*, *pleased*, *maddening*), with just under 300 tokens. Only a few other kinds of lexical item (verbs and nouns) expressing affect, such as *like*, *love*, *feel*, were found in the corpus. Only about 15 different types were identified, and most occurred only once or twice.

One reason for this infrequency of overt markers of affect may be that the data involve workplace talk; a context in which speakers may avoid personal and emotive language. However, most of the conversations investigated by Biber and Finegan were private rather than public, an indication that markers of affect are not necessarily more frequent in non-workplace contexts. In Biber and Finegan's corpus, the only texts which made extensive use of affect markers were personal letters; and they conclude that face-to-face conversations may simply be too face-threatening (because of the physical proximity) for overt expressions of feelings and opinions. They remark that affect may nevertheless be expressed more indirectly in conversations through the involvement created, for example, by using hedges and intensifiers.

Modal verbs

Modal items were the most frequent of the lexico-grammatical markers investigated in the corpus, and as this category is so large, the analysis is restricted to the 11 most frequent modal items, which are all modal or modal-lexical verbs (in order of frequency): *will*, *can*, *want (to)*, *know*, *think*, *going to/gonna*, *have (got) to*, *would*, *could*, *need (to)*, *should*. These most frequent modal items alone totalled 1,400 tokens, accounting for over 4 per cent of the corpus. Other modal items which occurred with a frequency of over 20, but are not included in the quantitative analysis, include: *might*, *probably*, *maybe*.

Other lexico-grammatical features

The frequencies of all of the other lexico-grammatical markers investigated are much lower; the total number of occurrences for each category is:

hedges and intensifiers	497
idioms and metaphors	237
vague language	184

A number of other types of interpersonal marker could of course have been investigated, if it were not for limitations of time and space. Overall the focus is on more implicit stance markers and, except for idioms/metaphors and some types of vague language, the items investigated also tend to be more 'grammatical' than 'lexical'. One reason for this, as noted above, is that lexically encoded devices are fairly infrequent in the corpus. Evaluative adjectives and adverbs will receive some treatment, but will not be investigated in detail.

5.1.2 Summary

After describing the methods used for analysis, the remainder of this chapter will be devoted to an investigation of the four types of interpersonal marker (modal verbs, hedges and intensifiers, vague language and idioms) in the ABOT Corpus. As described in Section 3.2, this corpus is composed of the following genres:

I Transactional genres

A   unidirectional genres
      procedural and directive discourse
      briefing
      service encounters
      reporting
      requesting

B   Collaborative genres
      decision-making
      arrangements
      discussing and evaluating
      liminal talk

II Non-transactional genres

      small talk
      office gossip

In comparing the relative frequencies of the interpersonal markers across the corpus, one particular question to be addressed is whether any of them occur more frequently in non-transactional than in transactional genres. If interpersonal markers are seen as important linguistic resources for pursuing relational goals, it would be reasonable to predict a higher frequency of such items in discourse which is mainly relational rather than transactional.

5.2 Methods of corpus analysis

The frequency and use across the corpus of the selected interpersonal markers were investigated using mainly quantitative corpus linguistics methods. Wordsmith Tools' suite of analytical programs (Scott 1999) was used to compile frequency lists of all the words in the corpus, or in sub-corpora, as well as to create concordances for particular words or phrases. For each category of interpersonal marker, a list of items to be investigated was compiled and a concordance was created for each of the items. The concordance lines were then organized according to genre so that the use and frequency of the item could be compared across genres.

As it was not possible to collect equal amounts of data for each genre, two measures were used to allow cross-comparison between genres. First, the proportion of all uses of each item (or set of items) to occur in a particular genre is calculated as a percentage. This can be compared to the proportion of the corpus (again expressed as a percentage) which each genre represents. For example, 16.7 per cent of all uses of *could* occur in conversations involving requests, which is much higher than expected, as requesting discourse makes up only 3.7 per cent of the corpus (as shown in Table 5.1 below). Second, the density of the items in each genre was normalized to a frequency per thousand words. For example *could* has a density of 8 in requesting, which shows that it occurred on average eight times in 1,000 words of data. This measure allows easy comparison of relative frequencies across genres, as well as comparison with the average density of the item in the corpus as a whole. So the density of *could* in requesting is well above the average of 1.8 occurrences for every 1,000 words across the whole corpus, which can of course be explained by its politeness function in making requests.

Table 5.1 Could in non-transactional genres

	Corpus	Requesting
Total	60	10
Percentage of total		16.7%
Genre = percentage of corpus		3.7%
Density per 1,000 words	Average: 1.8	8

As the two transactional macro-genres – collaborative and unidirectional discourse – contain almost the same amount of data (they make up 42.6 per cent and 43.6 per cent of the corpus respectively) raw frequencies can also be compared for these two sub-corpora.

Reliability of results

A few issues need to be considered regarding the reliability of the results obtained through the methods described above. First of all there is the question of whether differences found in the relative frequencies of the items in the different genres are statistically significant or merely due to chance (see Bryman and Cramer 1990 and McEnery and Wilson 1996). Significance was calculated using the chi-square test for variations in the distribution of each item between the three macro-genres (collaborative, unidirectional and non-transactional discourse). This measure shows whether the observed frequency of each item in the three macro-genres deviates significantly from the expected frequency, based on the relative size of each sub-corpus.

One problem when using a small corpus is that of local densities (see Moon 1998: 68): certain items may be frequent in a particular genre simply because they are used a great deal in one particular encounter. This can skew the results for genres represented only by a few texts in the corpus (e.g., briefing and reporting in the ABOT Corpus), especially if there is a great discrepancy in the length of these texts. Clearly, the larger the text sample is for any genre, and the more texts are included in the sample, the more reliable the results will be. For this reason, comparisons are often made between the three macro-genres rather than between individual genres. Those individual genres which are analysed in greatest detail are decision-making and procedural/directive discourse. These are the two most frequently occurring genres (with 8,782 and 5,195 words respectively) represented by the largest number of texts (11 and 9 each). Where appropriate, comparisons are also made with larger corpora, e.g., the Cambridge and Nottingham Corpus of Discourse in English (CANCODE), The Cambridge and Nottingham Business English Corpus (CANBEC – see Chapter 2), the Longman Spoken and Written English Corpus (LSWE Corpus), containing 40 million words (described in Biber *et al.* 1999) and the British National Corpus (BNC). See Chapter 2 for a discussion of corpus-based methods and issues of reliability in small corpora.

5.3 Modality

Modality is not only the largest category examined, but modal items are also the most multifunctional and are used by speakers to express a multitude of different meanings: they can refer to possible, desirable or hypothetical states, and

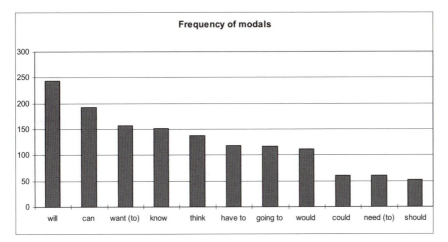

Table 5.1 Frequency of modals

some, e.g., *can/could*, to different time references (although 'true' modals are free of tense), and they can express different degrees and types of commitment (see Carter and McCarthy 2006: 638ff.). Modals thus represent a major resource for speakers in expressing interpersonal meanings, whether they are used for transactional or relational purposes. Modals perform a transactional function when they express the speaker's stance towards the content of what they are saying, and their function is relational when they convey stance towards the interlocutor; and, as Holmes (1983) points out, both functions may be performed simultaneously.

Figure 5.1 shows the relative frequency in the ABOT Corpus of the 11 most frequent modal items, which are all modal auxiliaries, semi-modals or verbs of cognition or desire.[1]

Similar relative frequencies of modal verbs are found in other larger spoken corpora. All these verbs occur in the same order of frequency in CANBEC (M. Handford, personal communication, 11 October 2005); and the relative frequency of the modal auxiliaries is the same in the spoken portion of the BNC (see Kennedy 2000).

5.3.1 *Modal meaning*

The semantics of modality are extremely complex, and it is beyond the scope of this chapter to go into the different, sometimes conflicting, descriptions and classifications found in the literature on modality (e.g., Ehrman 1966, Leech 1969 and 1971, Palmer 1979/1990 and Perkins 1982). The aim here is not to propose a comprehensive semantic classification of modal verbs, but to describe the functions of the modal items found in the corpus. Because of the polysemy or multi-functionality of the modal items examined, a further sub-classification of the uses of these items in terms of local meaning or function was carried out for most of the verbs. For example, all the occurrences of *will* in the corpus were categorized according to one of the following functions: futurity, habituality, probability or indirectness. Formal criteria were also taken into account if these were linked to differences in meaning, for example positive and negative polarity of *have to* (referring to necessity and absence of necessity respectively). It is important to point out, however, that the range of functions found in the data does not necessarily reflect the total range of possible meanings which these modal items can express. The analysis showed, for example, that even for modal items with recognizably discrete functions or meanings, one function tended to be much more frequent than the others

Many different types of meaning can be expressed through modality: possibility, obligation, necessity, ability, volition, intention, prediction, inclination, etc. However, in order to keep the classification as simple as possible, it makes sense to base the analysis very broadly on the two main types of modality generally recognized in the literature: epistemic modality, expressing degrees of commitment to the truth of a proposition; and deontic modality, expressing degrees of necessity to perform acts (see Lyons 1977). Most of the more specific modal meanings are linked in some way to one or both of these general modal categories. Although, as noted above, the modals examined here are polysemous and multifunctional, they can broadly be grouped into these two semantic categories, epistemic or deontic, according to their main or most frequent functions:

'Epistemic' modals

> can
> could
> would
> will
> be going to
> think
> know

'Deontic' modals:

> have (got) to
> need (to)
> should
> want (to)

5.3.2 Epistemic modality

According to Lyons, epistemic modality involves 'Any utterance in which the speaker explicitly qualifies his commitment to the truth of the proposition expressed by the sentence he utters' (1977: 797). However, in the ABOT Corpus, uses of the 'epistemic' verbs that strictly fit this definition, expressing degrees of commitment to the veracity or accuracy of statements, were not as common as other related uses, such as the expression of possibility for the verbs *can*, *could* and *would*. There are only six instances of *could* used to express tentative commitment to the factuality of the proposition, e.g.:

You say that. <u>could</u> mean anything,

The largest proportion of the 60 uses of *could* involved talking about the possibility of performing certain actions, e.g.:

Because you <u>could</u> write one cover memo explaining it

This is not surprising, as a great number of the conversations in the corpus involve the discussion of actions to be taken.

The modal *can* is of course also used to express ability, which is sometimes considered to represent a third type of modal meaning, next to epistemic and deontic modality (Halliday 1985/1994, Palmer 1979/1990). However, in the ABOT corpus *can* is used in 127 (out of a total of 192) instances to express possibility, which justifies its inclusion under the heading of epistemic modality. It is also used deontically to express negative imperatives (*can't/cannot*), e.g.:

I'm sorry I <u>cannot</u> discuss international sales (meant humorously)

and permission (*you can*), e.g.:

Mary <u>can</u> go because she's a director

In fact a number of the modals investigated (including *think* and *should*) have both epistemic and deontic uses, which illustrates their multifunctionality and the importance of distinguishing between the different uses when carrying out a corpus-based analysis.

Of all the verbs in the 'epistemic' category, the ones that are used most frequently to perform a 'true' epistemic function (to express commitment to or detachment from propositions) are *think* and *know*. But these verbs are multifunctional as well: both can function either as lexical or modal verbs, and *think* can also be used deontically to express an opinion.

5.3.3 Corpus findings for epistemic modals

Comparing first the frequency of the epistemic modals in the two transactional macro-genres, unidirectional and collaborative, we find that, with the exception of *can* (which is equally frequent in both), all occur more frequently in collaborative than in unidirectional genres. However, if we compare these modals in terms of some of their more specific functions, these results need to be qualified. First of all, 'purely' epistemic uses of *could*, *would*, *think* and *will*, expressing degrees of certainty (rather than other modal meanings such as possibility, opinions, intention) are fairly equally represented in both transactional macro-genres.

Subjective stance

It further emerges that while *going to*, *would* and *think* occur significantly more frequently in collaborative genres, *will*, *could* and *know* are slightly (but not significantly) more frequent in these genres. Take, for example the results for *would* and *could* in Table 5.2 below (raw frequencies are shown, as the two macro-genres, collaborative and unidirectional, contain about the same number of words).

Table 5.2 shows that while *would* occurs almost twice as frequently in collaborative genres, *could* is only marginally more frequent. Both modals are used primarily to talk about possibilities and hypothetical situations, so why should their use in the different genres vary to this extent? Examining the collocates of these two modal items is illuminating: the first person *I* occurs much more frequently in combination with *would*, than with *could*, which collocates more frequently with the second person *you*. Over half of these uses of *I'd* or *I would* occur in collaborative discourse – most in decision-making and discussing, and are often used to express opinions and evaluations, whether it be in discussing hypothetical situations, e.g.:

I <u>would</u> never say you will be doing this, that and the other

or showing a preference, e.g.:

I <u>would</u> go for the varnished one myself.

Table 5.2 *would* and *could*

	Collaborative	Unidirectional
would	60	33
could	27	23

Such uses of *would* involve quite a personal engagement on the part of the speaker in what they say, and thus reflect what could be called a 'subjective stance'.

Could, on the other hand seems to express more neutral possibilities, which may explain why it occurs practically as frequently in unidirectional as in collaborative genres. Unidirectional genres tend to occur in a more neutral mode as the focus is generally on information, rather than on expressing personal opinions or judgements. Thus *could* is used to refer to a possibility or option, without any particular preference being expressed, for example, in explaining a procedure:

> You <u>could</u> order them through the gratis order form,

or in briefing (referring to a printing process):

> We <u>could</u> do that, two up work in turn

A similar pattern can be found with the verb pairs *be going to* and *will*, and *think* and *know*, as shown in Table 5.3 below. Again, *be going to* and *think* are much more frequent in collaborative genres, and *will* and *know* only marginally so.

Will and *be going to* also have similar meanings, as both are used to refer to future events. However, in the corpus, *will* is often used for future actions and events which are seen as finalized and therefore referred to neutrally, whereas *be going to* is used more to talk about actions which are still negotiable, implying a more subjective and personal orientation., e.g.:

> I mean if you want something at the end of this week, <u>he's gonna struggle</u>

Be going to therefore plays an important role in conversations involving decision-making and discussing, where possible courses of action are negotiated, but final conclusions are often not reached.

Think and *know* can both be used either as lexical or modal verbs,[2] and when used modally, express mainly epistemic meanings (although they express different degrees of commitment/certainty). Besides expressing a relative degree of

Table 5.3

	Collaborative	Unidirectional
be going to	80	30
will	117	96
think	74	38
know	67	55

commitment (e.g., *I don't think she's there*), *think* can also be used to express opinions (e.g., *I think it's a good idea*), which can be considered part of deontic modality (see Section 5.3.4 below). Whereas epistemic uses of *think* are only slightly more frequent in collaborative genres, deontic uses are much more frequent in these genres, with 23 occurrences, compared to only six in unidirectional genres. Most of these deontic uses occur in conversations involving decision-making and discussing, where they express speakers' opinions and judgements in discussing and evaluating events, e.g.:

- I <u>think</u> it looks better without
- but I <u>don't think</u> it'd be good.

In summary, the three modal items which frequently convey a more subjective stance, *would*, *be going to* and *think*, are over-proportionally represented in decision-making and in discussing/evaluating discourse, which make up the bulk of collaborative discourse in the corpus. In unidirectional discourse, on the other hand, modal items with such a subjective orientation are used much less frequently, due to the focus in these genres on conveying information (giving information, explaining procedures, reporting, etc.), which implies, by definition, a more neutral stance.

Relational functions

Turning to non-transactional genres, the following modals have above-average frequencies in either office gossip or small talk or both: *will*, *could*, *would*, *think*, *know*. The high frequency of many of these items can be linked to the important role that narrative plays in these genres: most of the narrative past tense uses of *could*, *would* and *think* occur in office gossip or small talk. Many of the uses of *would* and the deontic uses of *think* (which are particularly high in these genres) reflect the relational orientation – the affective, interpersonal engagement – participants bring to these genres. For example, in small talk, speakers feel they can express their opinions more freely, for instance in discussing the likelihood of a mortgage application being accepted:

<u>they'd</u> be asinine to reject it,

or they may use *would* for hyperbole, as in the following example, to increase the involvement created by a narrative about a motorway accident:

I mean if <u>you'd</u> seen it, you <u>would</u> not believe that only two people were killed.

Another kind of function which *all* the modal items examined so far can perform is also a relational one: downtoning or hedging the force of the utterance (rather than hedging commitment to the proposition as such). It was only possible to distinguish such uses clearly from other epistemic uses – and count them as a separate category – for *can*, *could*, *will* and *would*. Most of these occur somewhat more frequently in unidirectional than collaborative discourse, but are infrequent in non-transactional genres. Looking at individual genres, *would* is used for indirectness most frequently in service encounters, for example in a conversation from a university office involving a student and a secretary:

Hello, <u>I'd</u> like to see you about my user name.

Can is used most frequently to make indirect requests in briefing, and *could* in requesting discourse. Thus the need to downtone the force of certain utterances seems to be somewhat greater in unidirectional genres. The unequal relationship in most unidirectional discourse, at least discursively and sometimes also institutionally (i.e. boss–employee, client–server, etc.) results in greater threats to face. Therefore the 'politeness' function of epistemic modality, which involves avoiding or mitigating threats to face, plays a more important role in these genres than in collaborative discourse, in spite of the overall higher frequency of all these modals in collaborative genres.

Comparing all three macro-genres, the overall pattern is that epistemic and possibility modals are used proportionally most frequently in transactional collaborative genres, followed by non-transactional genres, and finally least frequently in transactional unidirectional discourse. However, examining the results in more detail, as summarized in Figure 5.2 (overleaf), reveals a more complex picture.

The second most frequent modal item, *can*, is about equally frequent in collaborative and unidirectional genres. *Can* is used most frequently to express the feasibility of an action, and its relatively even distribution across the corpus can probably be explained by the fact that most transactional genres are action-oriented. Modals expressing strictly epistemic meanings (commitment to the truth value of an utterance) are also about equally frequent in collaborative and unidirectional genres.

Although modality indisputably plays an important role in non-transactional genres, the hypothesis put forward earlier in this chapter that interpersonal markers might be *more* important in these genres because of the relational function they often perform, is not confirmed so far. Even those uses of epistemic/possibility modality which clearly show one of the two types of relational orientation identified in Section 4.4 – politeness or solidarity – do not occur exclusively in non-transactional discourse. While modals showing a subjective orientation (i.e. *would* and *think*) are sometimes used relationally to express solidarity and affect

Figure 5.2 Epistemic modals

	← *least frequent* ——— *most frequent* →
can	← ——— non-transactional ——— collaborative / unidirectional →
other epistemic/ possibility modals	← unidirectional — non-transactional — collaborative →
subjective stance (*going to, would, think*)	← unidirectional — non-transactional — collaborative →
'true' epistemic modals	← ——— non-transactional ——— collaborative / unidirectional →
indirectness/politeness	← non-transactional — collaborative — unidirectional →

in non-transactional genres, such modals are overall more frequent in collaborative genres, where they are used for evaluations and to express opinions. And, as we have seen, there is evidence that using modals for indirectness and politeness is most important in unidirectional discourse, due to the unequal discourse roles of the participants. It will be interesting to keep this initial hypothesis in mind as we examine the other interpersonal markers in the corpus.

5.3.4 **Deontic modality**

Lyons says that deontic modality 'is concerned with the necessity or possibility of acts performed by morally responsible agents' (1977: 823), and there is general agreement in the modality literature that it involves the notions of obligation and necessity on the one hand (e.g., *must*), and permission (e.g., *may*) and absence of necessity (e.g., *needn't*) on the other.

Think, expressing opinions and judgements, can also be considered deontic, as such uses show speakers' views about what is necessary and desirable. A further area of meaning that will be included under the heading of deontic modality is that of desirability, inclination, volition, etc.; meanings expressed, for example, with such verbs as *hope*, *would like*, *prefer*. These notions can be linked to deontic modality in a number of ways. As Lyons (1977: 826) points out, in developmental terms, the instrumental function of getting things done can be seen as deriving from the 'desiderative' function (wanting things). This link is clearest with the verb *want (to)*, which can be used to express both desire and inclination (*I want to*) or obligation (*I want you to*). Halliday (1994: 356–8) in fact considers obligation and inclination to constitute two sub-types of deontic modality (or what he calls

Figure 5.3 Deontic modals in unidirectional genres

← *least frequent* ————————————————————————— *most frequent* →

have (got) to	need (to)	should	want (to)
(35%)	(36.5%)	(42%)	(55.5%)

← *most direct* ————————————————————————— *least direct* →

'modulation'), of which *want to* is just one of a number of realizations. Deontic modality will therefore be quite broadly defined as expressing degrees of commitment to the necessity *or* desirability of performing actions.

In the ABOT Corpus, *have (got) to*, *need (to)* and *should*, are most frequently used to express degrees of obligation and necessity, while *want (to)* is the only 'deontic' modal primarily expressing desire or inclination, rather than obligation and necessity. As with epistemic modality, classifying these verbs as 'deontic' merely reflects their main or most frequent function, and should not obscure the fact that they are all multifunctional.

5.3.5 Corpus findings for deontic modals

The only deontic modal in the ABOT Corpus to occur more frequently in unidirectional than collaborative genres is *want (to)*; the other deontic modals, *have (got) to*, *should* and *need (to)*,[3] all occur more frequently in collaborative discourse. This seems surprising, at first, as the 'proper place' for deontic modality would logically be in unidirectional genres, where one speaker has a dominant role. Furthermore, when we examine the relative frequency of all deontic modals, we find that their proportional frequency in unidirectional discourse varies inversely with the degree of forcefulness or directness with which they express obligation (percentages show which proportion of all uses occur in unidirectional genres) (Figure 5.3).

How can this apparent avoidance of deontic modals in unidirectional genres be explained?

As procedural discourse is the largest sub-corpus in unidirectional discourse (representing over 15 per cent of the corpus), comparing the use of the four deontic modals in this genre may be revealing. As the main aim of procedural and directive discourse is to get the addressee to perform certain actions, one would expect deontic modality to play a particularly important role here. And indeed, in contrast to the overall picture for unidirectional genres, all the deontic modals, except *need (to)*, occur with above-average frequency in procedural discourse (see also Chapter 3 for a more detailed description of procedural genre). However, the order of relative frequency is similar to the one seen in unidirectional genres in general (again, percentages show which proportion of *all* uses of each modal occur in procedural discourse):

want (to)	22.9%
should	21.2%
have (got) to	16.0%
need (to)	13.3%

Again, we can observe that the relative frequency in procedural discourse of the first three deontic modals varies inversely with the degree of directness they express.

There is, of course, one very direct way of expressing obligation with *want (to)*: *I want you to* ... , but this does not occur at all in procedural discourse (only *you want me* ...). *Want (to)*[4] can be used to express either obligation (e.g., *I want you to take a look at this*) or inclination (e.g., *She'll wanna be here*), but most uses in procedural discourse express inclination, not obligation. When used in giving directives, they often involve giving the addressee choices, e.g.:

Example 5.1

Mm, if you want to, you can ... separate them. But it's usually probably not worth the ti:me

Even directives expressing obligation sometimes *seem* to express the addressee's inclination (i.e. using *you want to*) and therefore come across as quite indirect, e.g.:

Example 5.2

So basically you wanna see if you have those invoices already

Deontic uses of *can* expressing permission, of which a large proportion (8 of 19) occur in procedural discourse, are very similar. Directives are sometimes expressed *as if* they were optional:[5]

Example 5.3

Just – assuming that our packing slip's gonna come from upstairs, you can go ahead an' put it back in here

But *can* is used most frequently to refer to real options, sometimes in conjunction with *want to*, as in Example 5.1 above.

Should occurs proportionally only slightly less frequently than *want (to)* in procedural discourse, but it is only used twice in directives with the second person pronoun (e.g., *either you or Julie should call*), whereas *want (to)* is used 12 times with *you*. Over half of the uses of *should* are in fact with the first person singular, involving speakers asking what actions they should take, e.g.:

Example 5.4

What should I do. Just– get the estimate ...

Have (got) to occurs only marginally more frequently in procedural discourse (with 16 per cent of all occurrences) than one would expect from the size of the sub-corpus (15.4 per cent of the corpus), and it only occurs once with the second person pronoun.

The relative frequencies of these three deontic modal items in procedural/directive discourse, as well as the frequency with which they combine with the second person pronoun *you* for giving directives, indicate that speakers use deontic modality with circumspection in this genre. The modal expressing necessity and obligation most directly and with the most force, *have (got) to*, is used proportionally least frequently. *Should*, expressing a lesser degree of obligation and necessity, is used more (relatively speaking), but even here, direct second person address is avoided. Finally *want (to)*, which most commonly expresses inclination (rather than externally imposed obligation or imperative), is used most frequently in procedural discourse (in proportional as well as absolute terms). It is also worth pointing out that many of the uses of these modals are not in actual directives, for example *want (to)* is often used to talk about wishes of third parties, such as customers. Instruction-givers in fact tend to use more subtle and indirect means to impart instructions, as we shall see in the next chapter.

This avoidance of direct expressions of deontic modality in procedural discourse, and preference for using more indirect means, can be linked to the unequal relationship between the speakers in this genre, and the increased danger of threat to face this entails. Chapter 6 explores these issues in more detail by examining the ways in which discursively unequal encounters are managed in procedural/directive discourse.

While modality *does* play an important role in procedural discourse (although used with circumspection), it is less frequent in the other unidirectional genres, except to some extent in briefing (where it is also fairly well represented). The reason for this is probably two-fold:

1 except for procedural/directive discourse and requesting, unidirectional genres focus more on information than action, and deontic modality is of course directly linked to action, and
2 as with procedural discourse, the use of deontic modality is associated with

the risk of performing a face-threatening act in these genres, as a result of the unequal discursive relationship.

Want (to) on the other hand, is quite multifunctional: although it can express obligation, the main function of *want (to)* is expressing inclination, and it is fairly well represented in all unidirectional genres.

There may be a further explanation for the frequency of *want (to)* in unidirectional genres. The analysis of epistemic/possibility modals showed that the focus on facts and information in these genres results in a more factual, neutral type of discourse with fewer modals showing subjective stance. The frequent references, through the use of *want (to)*, to one's own and others' wishes and preferences may serve to personalize this whole process of information transfer. *Want (to)* has an interpersonal and interactive function, especially when used with *you*, which, as we have seen, is the pronoun with which it is used most. A large number of these uses occur in the interactive structures:

> *(do)/did you want* … ? (19 instances in the whole corpus)
> *if you want* (12 occurrences),

both of which show speakers attending to the interpersonal nature of the encounter they are engaged in with the addressee, and not merely to the information they are trying to convey, as illustrated in Example 5.5 from a briefing conversation:

Example 5.5

Dave	↓ S– it's a bit confusing. ↑ I'll come an' show you.
Val	⌊Yeah Okay
Dave	<u>Did you want</u> this copy anyway, for this one

Turning to non-transactional genres, it is not surprising that deontic modality does not play an important role in office gossip and small talk, as relational discourse does not usually involve talking about obligation and necessity. Although *have (got) to* and *need (to)* occur proportionally more frequently than *want (to)* and *should*, they all occur with below-average frequencies in these genres. The only exception is the use of *got to/gotta* (but not *have to*), which may be related to the greater informality of this structure.

5.4 Vague language

Three types of vague item were analysed in this category:

1 **Vague nouns**, that is, vague words used to refer to entities: *things, thing, stuff, bit* (e.g., *the extra bit*).

2 **Vague categories**, consisting of an 'exemplar' (e.g., *the servers*) and a vague tag (e.g., *and things like that*), where the exemplar is meant to allow the listener to identify the category referred to (see Channell 1994), as in:

Because she's missing <u>the servers and things like that,</u>

3 **Vague approximators**, used to refer vaguely to amounts, times and dates: *about, around, or so*

The notion of vagueness is restricted here to 'purposely and unabashedly vague' uses of language (Sadock 1977, cited in Channell 1994: 19).[6]

Unlike modals and idioms, which always express interpersonal rather than ideational meanings (see Chapter 4) whether used transactionally or relationally, vague language and some hedges and intensifiers can express ideational meanings when used for transactional purposes. Although vague language is imprecise, it can still convey information in terms of approximate amounts (*around*) or vague entities/categories (*things, stuff like that*); the same is true of hedges and intensifiers like *a bit* and *very*. The following example from the corpus was no doubt meant by the speaker to be informative, although he uses the vague item *stuff*:

Example 5.6

We supply lots of stuff for them on a gloss acetate

There may of course also be a relational dimension to the use of the vague item in this example: the speaker may be using such vague language only because the relationship with his co-worker is very informal and relaxed, or even in order to create an informal atmosphere, or to project a very high degree of shared knowledge. Example 5.6 illustrates how difficult it often is to distinguish between transactional and relational uses of the markers investigated, especially as transactional and relational functions may be performed simultaneously by the same item.

In the ABOT Corpus a total of 184 vague items in the above three categories were found. All three types of vague language are most frequent in unidirectional genres. Table 5.4 shows the absolute frequencies and the density per thousand words of vague language in each of the macro-genres, as well as the average density across the corpus. If we compare the two transactional macro-genres, we see that vague language is much more frequent in unidirectional than collaborative discourse, and this difference is statistically highly significant. This finding

Table 5.4 Vague language

Macro-genre	Frequency	Density
Unidirectional	102	6.9
Collaborative	66	4.6
Non-transactional	16	3.5
Total frequency	**184**	
Average density across corpus		5.5

is initially surprising, as unidirectional genres deal mainly with the transfer of information, with frequent references to facts and figures. Such a focus on factual information would seem to require precision and specific details from speakers. A look at how vague language is used in these genres, however, shows that facts and information are often talked about in vague terms, as illustrated in the discussion below of their transactional and relational functions.

5.4.1   Transactional functions

Vague nouns

A substantial portion (108 of a total of 184) of the vague markers found in the corpus are vague nouns, and we can identify a number of reasons why speakers use such items instead of more specific ones. First, vague and general words are often used cohesively to refer anaphorically to a more specific term mentioned earlier, e.g., *these things* in the example below:

Example 5.7

But yesterday I gave her a list, of <u>everything that I have on my desktop</u>, .hh and I said this is what you nee:d, and tell Ed that you have– ↓ he has to get <u>these things</u>.

Other vague nouns refer deictically to items in the physical environment (e.g., *this/that stuff*), but most frequently they are used to refer implicitly to items or concepts in the participants' world of work which the hearer can easily identify without needing a more specific referent, e.g.:

Example 5.8

There's a fair amount of sort of … standard <u>stuff</u> at Belvedere […]

Both speaker and hearer (a supplier and a customer) know what *stuff* refers to (paper, as this is the business they are in), because of the knowledge they share as members of the same professional discourse community. Such uses of vague nouns can also have an interpersonal function, as referring to shared knowledge can be a way of creating a sense of familiarity and common ground (see below).

Vague categories

Although vague tags are much less frequent in the corpus than vague nouns, with only 49 instances in total, 14 different types were found, including *or something (like that), and stuff (like that), and everything, and things (like that), this sort of thing.* By using a vague tag (or 'vague category identifier'), the speaker refers to non-specified items similar to the specific item(s) mentioned, for example in briefing a co-worker about a printing job:

> So you'll get <u>photos</u> coming down <u>and everything</u>

One of the more obvious reasons for using a vague tag is to show uncertainty about specific information, e.g:

Example 5.9

> Chris Oh the NC– the NCOA stuff won't be back until next week (<u>or
> something</u>)?
> Mike Right. Until ... Wednesday or Thursday earliest,

But vague categories can also perform a number of more specific functions. As with vague nouns, speakers often use vague tags to refer implicitly to shared knowledge. This occurs most noticeably in procedural discourse, where instruction-givers sometimes use vague category identifiers to exemplify their explanations:

Example 5.10

- you can give a reason for the free, you know, like <u>gratis copy or something</u>
- So instead of like the old way you know, we used to <u>fax and stuff</u>

Appealing to shared knowledge is a useful strategy in this genre, as it allows the addressee to link the new information with pre-existing knowledge, as reinforced by the use of *you know* in both examples.

Vague approximators

With a total of only 27 occurrences in the whole corpus, vague approximators (*about*, *around*, *or so*) are the least frequent of the three categories of vague language examined. The overwhelming majority of occurrences are in unidirectional genres, and they are nearly three times as frequent here as in collaborative discourse. They are used to be vague about facts and figures, mainly quantities, dates and times, e.g.:

- <u>about</u> twelve thousand <u>or so</u>
- we should have 'em ... within <u>about</u> a week
- I'll have to leave <u>about</u> ... two thirty

Speakers use vague approximators because they do not have the exact information or because it is not relevant, e.g.:

Example 5.11

I don't know if I explained this already or not. but ... the stuff that's already been pai:d: COD, ↓ which is indicated by that little green stub attached, ... ↑ is no:t ... that high of a priority, ... to code an' enter, ... until: <u>around</u> the end the of the month.

In this example from procedural discourse, the approximate not the exact time period is important.

5.4.2 Relational functions

Many of the uses of vague language discussed above can simultaneously perform relational functions. Referring to shared knowledge (Examples 5.8 and 5.10) can be a way of creating a sense of familiarity and common ground; and being vague (e.g., about dates and times) makes the discourse more informal, which can also be a solidarity strategy.

But vagueness can also be used interpersonally as a kind of shield, whereby speakers avoid committing themselves to concrete views, e.g.:

I'm just saying that this <u>thing</u> uh it's complicated

This kind of relational function comes across particularly clearly in examples where the vague item does not seem to convey a great deal of information, for example:

> You're not winding me up here <u>or something</u>

The function of *or something* does not seem to be to refer to some more general category, but to tone down and weaken the assertion *you're not trying to wind me up here* (which could be heard as an accusation). Vague language can therefore also be used to mitigate a face-threatening act.

5.4.3 Summary: vague language

Although there are some differences in frequency between the individual genres, overall vague language occurs most frequently in unidirectional genres, with the highest density in procedural discourse. The results for vague language are therefore different from those for modality, which was found to be most frequent in collaborative genres; however, a link can be established between these differing results.

The analysis of modal verbs in Section 5.3 showed that the lower incidence particularly of deontic modality in unidirectional genres reflects a more neutral stance on the part of the speakers, due to their focus on information in these genres, as opposed to a more subjective orientation in collaborative genres. The more frequent occurrence of vague language in unidirectional discourse can also be linked to the speakers' concern with the transfer of information. It seems that facts and information are often talked about in vague terms for a number of reasons: the exact information may not be known, speakers may be referring implicitly to shared information, or they may use vague language (i.e. vague nouns) for deixis or to refer back to items talked about previously. Thus a focus on facts and information actually seems to result in an increased use of vague language compared with genres such as decision-making or small talk, which are less concerned with the transfer of information.

However, the higher incidence of vague language in unidirectional discourse can also be linked to relational factors. Because of the discursive imbalance in these genres (one speaker has a dominant role), and in many cases a power imbalance (e.g., boss–employee, server–customer), the risk of performing face-threatening acts is higher than in collaborative discourse, where participants are on a more equal footing. As we have seen, vague language, particularly vague tags, can be used to mitigate potentially face-threatening acts.

But vague language can also have a different sort of relational function. The analysis of modality showed that there also seems to be an effort on the part of dominant speakers engaged in unidirectional discourse to reduce the asymmetry in their discursive roles and make the discourse more 'personal', for example by using the modal verb *want to* in giving instructions. The use of vague language can also be a way of personalizing the discourse: by referring vaguely to items or categories, speakers can draw attention to the common ground and shared worlds that exist between themselves and their interlocutor. This can lend an atmosphere of informality or even intimacy to the discourse.

All three types of vague language were least frequent in non-transactional discourse, vague categories and vague approximators being particularly infrequent. Only vague nouns are fairly well represented here (but still below average), probably due to the relatively frequent occurrence of the informal vague referent *stuff*. It may seem surprising that vague language is less frequent during small talk than work-oriented talk, as such language is usually associated with a very informal, colloquial type of discourse. Overstreet and Yule (1997b) for example report that vague tags occurred more frequently in a corpus of informal compared to more formal spoken interaction. But distinguishing between interactions simply in terms of formality, and not taking genre into account, may mean disregarding fundamental differences which can cut across these distinctions. The analysis shows that using vague language is not just a question of formality or informality (although none of the language in the corpus is very formal). As results for unidirectional genres demonstrate, discourse which is information-focused and 'unequal' tends to contain more vague language. The non-transactional discourse in the corpus is neither of these things: it is not usually concerned with the transfer of information, and the discursive roles tend to be equal.

5.5 Hedges and intensifiers

Hedges have been investigated primarily as negative politeness devices, and a range of linguistic devices, including adverbs, modals and if-clauses, are usually included in this category (Brown and Levinson 1978/1987, Hyland 1996). Here the term 'hedges' is much more restricted: hedges are defined as lexical items which downtone or mitigate the force of the word, phrase or clause they modify. As we shall see, expressing negative politeness is an important function of hedges, however the notion of politeness is not an a priori part of its definition, which is based on a lexico-pragmatic classification.

The hedges examined in the ABOT Corpus are mostly adverbs, the most frequent being: *just, like, actually, quite, really, little, sort of, basically, a (little) bit (of), kind of*. A number of these items (*just, actually, quite, really*) can also function as intensifiers, which were counted separately in the corpus, along with other intensifiers, such as *very, so, completely, absolutely*.

Many of these items have a very high frequency in the corpus – *just* for example is the 33rd most frequent word in the whole corpus. Studies using large corpora have found that some of these words, including *really, actually, quite, sort of*, are among the most frequent lexical items in the spoken language (Stenström 1990, Conrad and Biber 2000). What they all have in common, according to Stenström,

Table 5.5 Hedges

	Density
Unidirectional	13.0
Collaborative	9.5
Non-transactional	6.3

Table 5.6 Intensifiers

	Density
Unidirectional	3.8
Collaborative	3.7
Non-transactional	6.9

is that their primary function is interactive and pragmatic, and that it is often diffi-cult, or even impossible, to analyse them syntactically.

In total, 356 hedges and 141 intensifiers were examined, which, as far as possible, is an exhaustive coverage of these items in the corpus. The quantita-tive analysis of hedges and intensifiers shows that hedges are considerably more frequent in unidirectional than in collaborative genres, and least frequent in non-transactional discourse, as shown in Table 5.5, comparing densities per thousand words.

Intensifiers, on the other hand, occur most frequently in non-transactional dis-course, and are about equally frequent in the two macro-genres which make up transactional discourse, as shown in Table 5.6.

The density of intensifiers per thousand words is almost twice as high in non-transactional compared to transactional discourse. If we add to this intensifiers which occur in relational sequences within transactional genres, we see that a total of 34 per cent of all intensifiers occur during relational talk.

5.5.1 Hedges

The distribution of hedges in the corpus is very similar to vague language, and the prevalence of hedges in unidirectional discourse can also be related to the unequal discursive relationship between the participants. The use of hedges reflects an attempt on the part of the speakers to reduce or mitigate this imbalance. Looking at specific genres, hedges occur most frequently in the three unidirectional genres which make up the bulk of this macro-genre, with densities per thousand words well above the corpus average of 10.6 (Table 5.7).

However, there are some differences between these genres in the frequency

Table 5.7 Hedges in unidirectional genres

	Density
Service encounters	17.7
Procedural discourse	15.6
Briefing	13.3

of certain hedges. *Really* and *quite*, for example, occur more frequently in service encounters, whereas *just* and *like* are particularly frequent in procedural discourse. Very generally, one can distinguish between hedges which downtone or minimize the modified proposition (*just, little, a bit, quick*) and those that merely make it fuzzier and more vague (*really, actually, quite, like, sort of, kind of*).

On the whole the downtoning/minimizing hedges (*just, little*) are most frequent in procedural discourse and briefing, and this can be linked to the nature of these genres: speakers giving instructions, explaining procedures or briefing a co-worker attempt to make what they are talking about seem as simple and uncomplicated as possible.

In procedural discourse, *just* is used in particular to hedge instructions, and frequently collocates with verbs such as *put, take, say*, e.g.:

- over here just put in [...]
- and you just say well that took me about four hours to deliver it

Aijmer (1985) remarks that *just* used with an imperative conveys to the listener that what they are asked to do is very little and not difficult. Minimizing and downtoning are very useful strategies here: on the transactional level, they facilitate the task for both parties, and on the relational level, they convey the message that what the addressee is being asked to do or understand is not too much of an infringement on his or her freedom of action.

Many of the 'fuzzy' hedges (*really, quite, sort of*) are used particularly frequently in service encounters, where their main function is mitigating or softening actions performed through talk. Many of the hedges in this genre occur in a fairly lengthy supplier–customer encounter, and serve (mainly negative) politeness functions; for example the use of *really* by the supplier to mitigate the imposition on the customer of trying to sell him his goods and services:

Example 5.12

Um so <u>really</u>, ... what I'm trying to do is to: get your– troops to: give us a ... shot[7]

This is a situation where both discourse participants frequently need to make use of politeness strategies: the supplier must avoid appearing to impose too much on the customer's time and freedom; the customer, on the other hand, must not appear rude, even if he is not interested in all the supplier's offers.

The somewhat different functions of these two types of hedges (mitigating versus minimizing) seem to correspond more or less to Robin Lakoff's (1973) first two rules of politeness:

> Rule 1: Don't impose
> Rule 2: Give options.

According to Lakoff, the first rule involves the use of linguistic devices which are distancing and formal, whereas Rule 2 leads to more informal linguistic choices (here Lakoff mentions hedges and euphemisms). By distinguishing between these two rules, Lakoff identified two slightly different relational goals, which in Brown and Levinson's (1987) model are both subsumed under negative politeness (and which Lakoff says are easily confused).

Hedging is usually associated with politeness (see Brown and Levinson 1987), but Chafe (1982) and Tannen (1989) mention that indirectness and fuzziness can also contribute to involvement. As we have already seen with the use of modals and vague language in unidirectional discourse, speakers in these genres seem constantly to be attempting to reduce the inequality between their discursive roles. Many of the hedges used by co-workers in procedural discourse and briefing reflect such an attempt to reduce distance and project more equality, or even intimacy, and their function is perhaps more accurately described as showing solidarity rather than politeness. Chapter 6 will examine in more detail the devices used by speakers in procedural/directive discourse to pursue these relational goals.

5.5.2 Intensifiers

The proportionally very high frequency of intensifiers in non-transactional genres (especially small talk, where the density is 9.7 compared to an average of 4.2) can be explained in terms of the speakers' relational orientation in these genres in creating a sense of involvement with their interlocutors. In small talk, narratives are very common, and here intensifiers are frequently used to heighten the drama of a story:

Example 5.13 (a)

Vicky   You could actually smell– all the smoke coming up, /??/ was <u>just</u>
         being blown, it was horrible =
Liz   = ↑ O:h glo:ry!

Example 5.13 (b)

Kate   So there was a mad dash up to [name of hospital], and … um …
Mary   Oh my God!
Kate   And … I mean this child's, hand, it was … <u>just</u> bleeding […]

They are also used in small talk to intensify evaluative comments, and frequently collocate with evaluative adjectives, for example:

Example 5.14

I mean <u>just</u> all these … <u>stu</u>pid little things heheheh it's <u>just</u> <u>*dreadful*</u>,

5.6 Idioms

While there is a large body of research in the field of idiomatology, only a few studies have looked at the use of idioms in naturally occurring spoken discourse (see Strässler 1982, Moon 1992, 1997, 1998, Drew and Holt 1998 and McCarthy 1998), and none at all, to my knowledge, at workplace discourse.[8]

5.6.1 Defining idioms

A fairly broad definition of idioms was taken here, based on Moon's (1998) corpus-based classification of a large number of fixed expressions and idioms, which considers three factors:

1   opacity/ non-compositionality: the degree to which an expression is figura-
     tive and non-literal
2   institutionalization: the degree to which a string of words has become
     conventionalized
3   lexico-grammatical fixedness, e.g., restrictions on inflections or word order.

The definition and classification of idioms used here is based on these three criteria, which yielded the following broad categories of idiomatic expressions
(examples from the ABOT Corpus are given for each type).

1   Metaphors (non-compositionality)
*   Extended opaque frozen metaphors ('classic' idioms): *get in under the wire,
    clear the deck*
*   Extended spatial/motion metaphors: *You know where you stand, get it moving*
*   Other metaphors and metaphorical collocations: *to have a word (with someone),
    a safe bet*

2   Formulae (institutionalization)

- Cultural allusions: proverbs, maxims, catch phrases: *That's life (isn't it)*, *Murphy's Law*
- frozen similes: *It's like pulling teeth*
- Idiomatic prefabricated phrases or clauses: *What's the story? The good news is …*

3   Anomalous collocations (lexico-grammatically anomalous strings)

- ill-formed and defective collocations: *every once in a while, on the off-chance*
- irreversible binomials and trinomials: *doom and gloom, neither here nor there*

4   Idiomatic phrasal verbs: *foul up, trickle down*

Single-word metaphors were also included, as these have non-literal meanings and (at least in speech) are usually conventionalized and not original. In addition, the same item often occurred either on its own or in a fairly fixed collocation (e.g., *a pain* or *a bit of a pain*), and it made sense to include both types of item. Phrasal verbs were counted as a separate category, as there were a large number of them.

5.6.2 Corpus analysis of idioms

Because of the small size of the corpus, individual idioms are relatively infrequent, and most occurred only once. As a result, it was not possible to quantify and compare idioms in the corpus by creating computer-generated concordances, as was done for the analysis of the other interpersonal markers. This meant the list of items was established by going through the corpus 'by hand'; a method which is obviously prone to human error. A total of 237 tokens were identified (although a number of items may have been missed) with the following totals for each category:

metaphors	116
formulae	37
anomalous collocations	29
phrasal verbs	55

As shown in Table 5.8 below, idioms occur most frequently in collaborative genres (this was statistically significant, but not highly significant) and least frequently in non-transactional discourse. An idiom (or metaphor) occurred on average seven times every 1,000 words in the corpus, which represents a much higher density than found for idioms by Strässler (1982) in a study of idioms in conversation. This is probably due to the fairly broad definition of idioms taken here. However, as shown in the subsequent analysis, idioms are not distributed evenly throughout the corpus, but tend to cluster in certain parts of the discourse. In addition, we find a high concentration of idioms in certain genres.

Table 5.8 Idioms

	collaborative	unidirectional	non-transactional
frequency	123	89	25
density	8.5	6	5.4

As the corpus findings indicate, the frequency of idioms varies considerably from genre to genre, and this variation can be linked to a number of different discourse functions that idioms were found to perform.

5.6.3 Summarizing/closing function of idioms

In some conversations in the corpus, speakers used no idioms at all, frequently only one or two; however, when they did occur, it was noticeable that they were particularly frequent at certain points in the conversation. This is illustrated in the following extract from the end of a longer meeting between an executive, Carol, who has just returned from a business trip, and her assistant, Beth. Beth has just finished updating Carol on important developments in her absence:

Example 5.15

1 Beth   I just wanted to like <u>clear the deck</u>,
2 Carol Mhm,
3 Beth   and so at least I know what I'm … <u>hittin' the ground with</u> next week,
4 Carol Mhm,
5 Beth   ⌊when I come in. you know,
6 Carol Okay, Okay, Well it sounds like uh …
7 Beth   ⌊Get moving.
8 Carol everything's gone *very* well.
9 Beth   Yes. <u>The fort has been held down</u>. Hehehehehe
           (from the Cambridge International Corpus © Cambridge University Press)

A whole cluster of idioms (underlined) is produced here, mainly by Beth, and the meeting ends soon after the extract shown. The function of these idioms seem to be to sum up the meeting, e.g., *I just wanted to <u>clear the deck</u>*. There are a number of other, similar examples from across the corpus, where one or more idioms are used to summarize previous discourse, and either move towards closure of the encounter or move on to another topic or task. In these examples, idioms seem to be performing an important discourse function. Drew and Holt (1998) observed a similar phenomenon in informal telephone conversations, with idioms occurring at topic transitions to summarize the current topic, before opening a new topic.

But in addition to performing the transactional job of summarizing and closing the encounter, the idioms used in these conversations simultaneously have a relational function. The idiomatic expressions used in Example 5.15 (e.g., *clear the deck* and *the fort has been held down*) also express a positive evaluation of the meeting, i.e. that a great deal has been accomplished and that things have gone well in Carol's absence. This allows the participants to feel good about themselves and what they have accomplished, and thereby reinforces solidarity and common ground between them.

This discourse-summarizing function of idioms does not seem to be genre-specific, as it occurred in conversations in all three macro-genres: collaborative, unidirectional and non-transactional. Nevertheless, the frequency of idioms is well below the average (of seven per thousand words) in three of the five uni-directional genres; for example only about three idioms occur in a thousand words of speech in procedural discourse. The few that do occur here (only 15 in total) almost exclusively perform such a summarizing function. In other genres, where idioms occur more frequently, they also occur in other parts of the discourse and perform a greater range of functions, which are all evaluative in some way.

5.6.4 Evaluating with idioms

Problem-solution patterns

Idioms occur with above-average frequency in decision-making and discussing, genres in which evaluation clearly plays an important role. As discussed in Chapter 3, decision-making always focuses on a problem which needs to be resolved, and usually follows a problem-solution pattern (Hoey 1983, 1994).

Hoey found that this pattern was often signalled lexically through the use of certain key words (e.g., *problem, difficult, response*). In decision-making con-versations in the ABOT Corpus, such lexical signals are often idiomatic or metaphorical, for example:

- problem phase: *a (bit of a) pain, a real headache, kinks (to work out), foul up, screw up, goin' crazy, hangin' over our heads, (be) an arm and a leg, rough day(s)*
- response/solution phase: *come up with, sit down (together) (and talk/think about), figure out, have a word, wrack our brains, get it moving, get it sorted, have a word*
- evaluating phase: *dead easy, it's not that big a deal, it never hurts, makes sense, works for me, that's where we stand, par for the course*

In the CANBEC Corpus, idioms and metaphors (e.g., *it's a nightmare, can of worms*) also frequently occur in discussing problems (see McCarthy and Handford 2004).[9]

Among these items were some of the few idioms in the corpus that occurred more than once, and in a number of different conversations; for example idioms used as response/solution signals:

- *sit down (together)(and talk/think about)* (5 times, 2 conversations)
- *figure out* (7 times, 4 conversations)
- *have a word* (4 times, 2 conversations)

The fact that these idioms recurred in different conversations to discuss solutions to problems is an indication that they have become pragmatically specialized as signalling devices. Such a signalling function is quite clear in an example where the speaker first reluctantly agrees to *have a word*, but then evaluates this negatively as not likely to lead to a solution:

Example 5.16

I uh— I can <u>have a word!</u> ↓ But I don't know if it'll do any good,

This was confirmed by examining *have a word* in CANCODE, where it occurs 22 times, with most uses involving possible solutions to problems. A search for *sit down (together) (and talk/think about)* in CANCODE yielded similar results: *sit/sat down* occurs 29 times with a similar pragmatic function, frequently in combination with *and think* or *and talk*.

Why should idioms and metaphors be used so frequently as signal words in a problem-solution pattern? On the discourse level, these items are useful signalling devices, because they draw attention to themselves and thus foreground key elements and phases of the discourse; but they also function interpersonally. Talking about problems is a highly evaluative business and, like the idioms used for summarizing, the idioms in problem-solution patterns also perform an evaluative function. Like certain modal verbs (*going to*, *would*, *think*), idioms are markers of subjective stance and are used by participants in these genres to make evaluations and express judgements and opinions. Other studies looking at the use of idioms in naturally occurring spoken discourse (Strässler 1982, Moon 1992, 1998, Powell 1992) have also shown that idioms often have an evaluative function.

Negative evaluation

Idioms are used particularly frequently to talk about problems, as many of the above examples show, and therefore often have a function of *negative* evaluation. This can be seen in many conversations from across the corpus, for example in a university office conversation, where colleagues discuss the bad news that one of the secretaries has resigned, and evaluate this situation using a number of idioms or metaphors:

Example 5.17

```
1  Jean    It is– It is a blow, but … you know,
2  Susan                            ⌊Yeah.
3  Jean    i– i– She needs more money.
4  Liz          ⌊That's life isn't it
```

In investigating a much larger corpus, Moon (1998) found that idioms were used for negative evaluations twice as frequently as for positive ones. She suggests that this is because idioms allow speakers to express themselves more indirectly than with literal expressions, and that they are therefore useful politeness and mitigating devices in performing negative evaluations.

5.6.5 Summary: idioms

Overall, idioms occur most frequently in collaborative genres, due to their evaluative function as interpersonal markers of subjective stance in conversations involving decision-making and discussing. In unidirectional genres, idioms are not as frequent, as here the focus is on facts and information, rather than on evaluating and making judgements. In these genres, idioms often occurred only as summarizing devices at the end of the encounter or to close off phases within the encounter.

The analysis shows that, although they may be infrequent (as individual items), idioms are important interpersonal devices for the accomplishment of both transactional and relational goals. In terms of relational goals, a distinction can be made between uses of idioms which reinforce solidarity between the participants and those that mitigate threats to common ground or face. Idioms which perform a discourse-summarizing function also usually evaluate the encounter positively, thus creating a bond of solidarity between the speakers. In non-transactional genres, idioms are used mainly for solidarity, for example in the following small talk episode, where the second speaker, Beth, shows she sympathizes with Carol by relexicalizing her words:

Example 5.18

```
Carol   That's … that's not my style.
Beth    That's not your thing. No, seems it's kind of wild. Hehehe
```

The density of idioms in relational genres is below average (about 5.5), but still higher than in briefing, procedural discourse and requesting. Furthermore if one takes into account all idioms occurring in closing sequences (which can be considered relational – see Chapter 4 on 'phatic communion'), nearly 20 per cent are used in relational talk. Clearly then, idioms *do* play an important role as relational solidarity devices. The relational function of idioms as mitigating devices will be discussed in Chapter 6.

What sets idioms apart from the other items investigated, besides the fact that they tend to be much more lexicalized, is the fact that they are ready-made, recognizable phrases, and are therefore always 'acts of quoting' (as Norrick 1985 says of proverbs). This means that to some extent speakers always invoke cultural values and norms when they use idioms, in particular cultural allusions and 'classic' idioms.

5.7 Summary: analysis of interpersonal markers

The corpus analysis of interpersonal markers in this chapter has shown that interpersonal markers *do* play an important role in workplace discourse, and that there are significant differences in the frequency of such markers from genre to genre. Figure 5.4 summarizes the results for the five types of interpersonal marker analysed in the ABOT Corpus: modals, vague language, hedges, intensifiers and idioms.

Figure 5.4 shows that modals and idioms were most frequent in collaborative genres. Evaluative interpersonal markers expressing judgements and opinions, such as modal verbs (e.g., *have to*, *need to*, *would*) and idioms (e.g., *sit down and talk about*) are particularly frequent in decision-making encounters, as illustrated in Example 5.19. Notice also the use of other markers of subjective stance here: *It's complex*, an evaluative comment, and I'm *wondering*, expressing an opinion.

Figure 5.4 Frequency of interpersonal markers in the three macro-genres

	← *least frequent* ——————————————— *most frequent* →
modal verbs	← non-transactional ——— unidirectional ——— collaborative →
vague language	← non-transactional ——— collaborative ——— unidirectional →
hedges	← non-transactional ——— collaborative ——— unidirectional →
intensifiers	collaborative ←——————————————— non-transactional → unidirectional
idioms	← non-transactional ——— unidirectional ——— collaborative →

Example 5.19

1 Beth   I'll update *this*. <u>I don't need</u> to keep this as it is now
2 Carol   └<u>You need to</u> update *this too.*
3 Beth   Right.
4 Carol   However, … it's– <u>it's complex.</u>
5 Beth   └You know <u>I'm wondering</u> whether we <u>should</u> have new
            columns
6 Carol   We <u>have to</u>– we <u>have to sit down and think about</u> how we can
7 Beth   └Yeah. <u>I'd like to sit down and</u> …
8 Carol   turn it into a something that could be updated every–
         (from the Cambridge International Corpus, © Cambridge University Press)

The use of such evaluative interpersonal markers in collaborative genres can be linked directly to participants' transactional goals in these genres: particularly in decision-making and discussing, making evaluations and expressing judgements and opinions form an essential part of the performance of these genres. In terms of relational goals, the discursively equal roles of the participants in these genres license the often more direct expression of necessity, obligation and opinion through linguistic devices such as deontic modals (*need to*, *have to*, *should* in the above example).

Vague language and hedges were most frequent in unidirectional genres. These interpersonal markers are useful in referring vaguely or implicitly to facts and information (e.g., *things*, *stuff*), which are the focus of these genres, and in exemplifying or elaborating on explanations (e.g., *like*, *sort of*, *or something*), for example:

- I don't know if I already explained this or not, but … the <u>stuff</u> that's already been paid …
- You can give a reason for the free, you know, <u>like</u> gratis copy <u>or something</u>

But these interpersonal markers also play an important role in terms of speakers' relational goals: being vague and using hedges allow speakers to mitigate or minimize the unequal discursive relationship in these genres. These devices therefore often perform a face-saving politeness function, as in the extract below from a procedural conversation, where a manager instructs a subordinate on how to keep a record of his response-time in dealing with requests:

Example 5.20

An' it's an' it's <u>kind of</u> a– you know you don't have to <u>like</u> write down the minute that you– got the request and the minute that you got– it done, an' you <u>just</u> say well that took me about four hours to deliver it.

Finally, intensifiers, while occurring with about equal frequency in collaborative and unidirectional genres, are used most frequently in non-transactional genres – office gossip and small talk – reflecting a relational orientation towards solidarity and heightened involvement. Intensifiers often modify evaluative adjectives (e.g., <u>*just*</u> *dreadful*, <u>*really*</u> *great*), which according to a preliminary analysis of such items in the corpus, are also most frequent in these genres. The small talk extract below illustrates such relational uses of intensifiers and evaluative adjectives (here Andy describes how he discovered that he had been given two jars of French chestnut butter; see also Example 7.1):

Example 5.21

```
 1  Andy   And ... looked on my shelf and there was a— a— jar of it.
 2  Don    You're joking!
 3  Andy              ⌊Someone obviously gave it to us for Christmas
 4  Don                         ⌊That's hilarious!
 5  Don    That's so funny
 6  Andy                   ⌊So funny, I never heard it, an' now I got – /inaudible/
 7  Don                                     ⌊Now you have
        two of them
 8  Andy   And we had brunch, and Shelly put it in a bowl, with all this cut fruit.
        and just dipped the cut fruit, and it was great!
 9  Don    It was delicious?
10  Andy   It was really great!
```

5.8 Conclusion

The corpus-based study discussed in this chapter shows that the frequency and use of the interpersonal markers investigated varied considerably according to genre. This finding indicates that genre has a significant impact on linguistic choice and is thus a central factor accounting for language variation within workplace talk. Furthermore, the study demonstrates the important role played by interpersonal or evaluative elements in workplace discourse.

One interesting and somewhat unexpected result of the analysis is that most of the interpersonal markers investigated actually occurred less frequently in genres in which participants focused more on relational goals (office gossip and small talk). This is particularly surprising for idioms and vague language, which are generally considered to be typical features of informal, casual talk. One reason for these results is the fact that all the markers investigated can perform transactional as well as relational functions, and can therefore play an important role in terms of the transactional goals of a particular genre. So, for example, interpersonal markers which are evaluative and express necessity or obligation are central to a genre like decision-making, but play a negligible role in relational talk. In addition, while a relational orientation towards solidarity seems to find most frequent (but not exclusive) expression in non-transactional genres, markers which show an orientation towards politeness (avoiding or mitigating face threats) occur most frequently in transactional discourse which is unidirectional.

This chapter has also illustrated some ways in which corpus-based methods can be used to analyse even a modest-sized corpus of workplace discourse. As we have seen, such methods are particularly useful in identifying some of the specific linguistic features of different workplace genres, and highlighting differences between them. Such features cannot necessarily be identified by analysing only individual encounters. Based only on the analysis of a number of examples of decision-making and procedural encounters in Chapter 3, we might have concluded that deontic modals are more frequent in procedural discourse; however the corpus-based analysis shows that almost *all* modals (including deontic ones) are more frequent in decision-making.

While many insights can be gained that cannot easily be obtained by other methods, focusing on a limited number of individual lexico-grammatical items, as we have done in this chapter, still does not provide us with a complete picture of the discourse investigated. Speakers' transactional and relational goals do not reveal themselves exclusively in such 'snapshots' of isolated features, but are jointly negotiated in discourse as it unfolds and develops over time. The next chapter picks up on many of the observations made here about interpersonal markers, but shows how these and other devices are embedded within longer stretches of discourse in workplace conversations. The focus will be on the linguistic and discursive strategies used by co-workers in the sometimes tricky business of building consensus, managing conflict and negotiating unequal encounters.

6   Negotiating consensus and conflict in workplace talk

6.1 Introduction

As discussed in Chapter 1, one of the key characteristics which distinguishes workplace discourse from ordinary conversation is the fact that the discourse participants have specific institutional roles and identities. Many interactions are therefore asymmetrical or unequal in terms of the power relationship which these institutional identities entail. However, the analyses of different workplace genres in Chapters 3 and 5 have shown that the discursive roles participants take on in relation to the goals of the genre can also entail a type of power or 'dominance' which is a key factor influencing the discourse. Furthermore, we have seen that talk at work is not simply a reflection of speakers' transactional goals in performing a given genre, but that participants' relational goals are also central in shaping the interaction and influencing linguistic choice and discourse strategies.

This chapter explores the complex interplay between institutional and discursive roles, and speakers' transactional and relational goals. It draws on the corpus-based findings from Chapter 5, but takes a more qualitative approach by examining in some detail a number of different encounters from a variety of genres in the ABOT Corpus. In the first part of the chapter we examine the ways in which speakers negotiate institutional or discursive dominance through the use of relational politeness and solidarity strategies. After that, we turn to encounters in which conflicts arise, and explore the features of conflictual talk, the discursive roles taken up in the course of such arguments, and the ways in which a resolution is negotiated.

6.2 Negotiating politeness and solidarity in unequal encounters

All the interpersonal markers analysed in the last chapter can be used in workplace talk for transactional *or* relational purposes, and two types of relational orientation were identified: politeness and solidarity (see Chapter 4). The chapter will begin by continuing the discussion from the last chapter regarding the relational function of idioms in workplace talk: here the focus will be on their role as politeness devices in mitigating face-threatening acts. We will look at the particularly useful role idioms can play in negotiating delicate situations involving issues of power related to the institutional roles of the discourse participants. After that we turn to one particular genre – procedural and directive discourse – and, again building on the discussion in Chapter 5 of interpersonal markers in this genre, try to identify the strategies used by co-workers to build and maintain solidarity in situations where one of the participants is discursively and often also institutionally dominant.

6.2.1 Idioms and politeness in the negotiation of unequal encounters

Idioms as politeness devices in negative evaluation

The study of interpersonal markers in the ABOT Corpus discussed in the last chapter showed that idioms have an evaluative function, and that they are used particularly frequently for negative evaluation. In view of their evaluative function, it is not surprising that idioms had an above-average density (about nine every thousand words) in the corpus in conversations involving discussing and evaluating, a genre obviously centrally concerned with evaluations.

The items which are most clearly evaluative in the corpus are those classified as 'cultural allusions': proverbs, maxims and catchphrases, e.g.:

> *(You) can't win 'em all*
> *Win some lose some*
> *That's life, isn't it.*

Norrick (1985) notes that proverbs signal group membership, and Moon (1992 and 1998) suggests that idioms, and proverbs in particular, reduce the interpersonal risk of evaluation, because they are generalizing statements referring to culturally accepted truths and values, and therefore allow speakers to 'shelter behind shared values' (1992: 24).

Four such cultural allusions (there are only 10 in the whole corpus), as well as two other idioms/metaphors, occur in an encounter that took place in the sales office of a British paper supplier, in which a sales rep, Mark, and his boss, Paul, discuss and evaluate a situation in which they have lost an order to a competitor:

Example 6.1 'Lost order'

Paul: Office manager
Mark: Sales rep

1   Mark   We lost that one ... that /??/ one,

2   Paul   ↑Did we?

3   Mark   Yeah. Someone quoted seven hundred pound a ton,

4   Paul   On what.

5   Mark   ⌊/Didn't say,/ Well ... say equivalent sheet. but ... as far as
            I was aware, we was the only ones who could get hold of [name of
            paper].

6   Paul   No. various mills ... various merchants can get hold of it,

7   Mark   Just ... they call it something else. yeah.

8   Paul   Yeah. [name of paper] or whatever

9   Mark   (Yeah)

10 Paul   That's a bit of a *pain*, isn't it.

11 Mark   Yeah. So ... so–

12 Paul   ⌊Remember that next time

13 Mark   I said to him uh ... let us know next time you know ... what ... prices
            you're getting in and we'll always see if we can better ... that /?/.

14 Paul   Well you'll know it for next time,

15 Mark   Mm

16 Paul   [funny voice] Trying to be too greedy,
            [2]

17 Mark   Mm

18 Paul   ⌊Well I m– we won't– y' know don't know do yous

19 Mark   You don't know
            [3]

20 Mark   Well it's annoying that he's got an order in if you think about it at forty
            pound a ton or whatever,

21 Paul   Mm

22 Mark   It's not exactly like not getting an order at all though

23 Paul   ⌊Annoying, isn't it
            [3]

24 Mark   (That would have been quite nice)

25 Paul   Oh well,
            [11]

26 Paul   It's a pain, isn't it.

27 Mark   Mm
            [1.5]

28 Paul   Can't win 'em all,
            [9]

29 Paul   About a *grand* that, isn't it.

30 Mark   Yeah

31 Paul   Oh well,

[4]
32 Paul   <u>Win some you lose some</u>. /so/ [1.5] We coulda made seven hundred
             quid out of it, couldn't we.
             [1]
33 Mark   (Mm)
34 Paul   Oh well
             [2.5]
35 Paul   It's an*noyi*n' though, isn't. hhh

From about turn 16 onwards, Mark and Paul's talk consists entirely of negative
evaluations of what has happened. It is as if they cannot stop expressing their
annoyance: instead of moving towards closure after producing an idiom, as tends
to happen in other conversations (see Section 5.6), they keep reopening the topic
with further comments (after fairly lengthy pauses). This frustration about the
lost order is sometimes expressed with direct evaluative statements (*annoying*
– turns 20, 23 and 35 and *that would've been quite nice* – turn 24), but more frequently with 'cultural allusions':

18 Paul   don't know do yous
19 Mark   You don't know
28 Paul   Can't win 'em all
32 Paul   Win some you lose some

or metaphorical expressions:

10 Paul   That's a bit of a pain, isn't it
26 Paul   It's a pain, isn't it

The function of all these idioms is clearly to evaluate this negative turn of events.
The question is why the speakers, in particular Paul, should so frequently choose
to use idioms for this purpose instead of more direct evaluative language.

    Low (1988: 128) found that metaphors can function as distancing devices,
allowing speakers to discuss emotionally charged subjects or avoid committing
themselves, and this is clearly their function here. This encounter involves a particularly delicate situation, where a subordinate (Mark) has admitted to a mistake.
The use of idioms and metaphors allows his boss (Paul) to express his displeas-
ure without directly blaming Mark, thereby allowing Mark to save face. The
only direct reference to what the sales rep may have done wrong is spoken with
a 'funny' voice, thus distancing the speaker from what he is saying: *trying to be
too greedy* (turn 16). But for the most part, Paul's evaluations are expressed indirectly through idioms, especially 'cultural allusions' (e.g., maxims like *can't win*

'em all, win some lose some). While all idioms are evaluative to some extent, cultural allusions seem to be the most strongly evaluative. McCarthy (1998: 145) notes that proverbs 'express cultural and social solidarity' even more than other idioms. These maxims are not only devices for indirect evaluation, but as they appeal to culturally shared values, they also allow Paul to establish solidarity with Mark. This encounter illustrates how, in delicate situations like this where a mistake has been made, idioms can play an important role in delivering negative evaluation, while at the same time preserving the working relationship.

Idioms and the negotiation of discursive roles

The above analysis shows that the use of idioms can be related to the speakers' relative institutional roles and the power relationship linked to these. In a number of encounters, speakers seem to use idioms or metaphors for self-abasement as a kind of defensive strategy to ward off possible threats to positive face, e.g.:

- sorry I– <u>spaced</u>,
- I mean *I* <u>screwed up</u>.

Strässler (1982) found that idioms were sometimes used for self-abasement (using the first person) by speakers of lower status. Such a use of idioms is particularly noticeable in a service encounter, in which a supplier, Angus, visits the office of the British paper company (the same as in Example 6.1 above) in order to try to drum up some business:

Example 6.2

> [...] I: had a meeting with Stan White, abou:t oh: eight weeks ago. S– An' I was saying well how can I: you know, get more business out of um: [name of company], 'cause it's been growing, it's been doing very well ⌊<Paul>: Mm.⌋ So he said well first thing is to <u>get off your back side</u> an' go round an' see the– see the branches, so I'm doing a <u>grand tour</u> of the: [name of company] branches.

and later:

> I'm sort of tottin' around

In the above example, Angus uses a number of idioms in a self-deprecating manner to downplay the importance of his visit. He thus seems to position himself asymmetrically as less powerful in relation to his customer, Paul.

This difference in the positioning of the two speakers can also be seen in the way they use idioms to relexicalize each other's words. McCarthy (1998) and Moon (1998) found that idioms used for relexicalization are loci for the negotiation of meaning and evaluation. By using idioms which refer to general, culturally accepted values, speakers are able to avoid precise meanings which might pose a threat to common ground and convergence, e.g.:

Example 6.3

Angus	Aha. An' that was a lot of <u>odd sizes</u> in that
Paul	Yeah. There's a lot of weird st– <u>weird an' wonderful</u>–

Here Paul uses an idiom (*weird an' wonderful*) to relexicalize Angus's description of certain paper being in *odd sizes*.

However in other parts of the same encounter, the opposite happens: Paul relexicalizes Angus's idioms with a more literal expression:

Example 6.4 (a)

Angus	Um so really, … what I'm trying to do is to: <u>get your– troops to: give us a … shot</u>
Paul	⌊<u>Phone you a bit more</u>.

Example 6.4 (b)

Angus	You know, we'll ⌊Paul: Mm⌋ give you first refusal on it, you know, we'll tell you we've got it, ⌊Paul: Mm⌋ an' we'll hold it for you, on the basis that if somebody else comes along, we'll give you a ring, an' say well look, <u>make up your mind</u>–
Paul	⌊<u>Do you want it or not</u> yeah

In Example 6.4a Angus uses a 'classic' idiom to express indirectly what the purpose of the visit is (i.e. to get more business): *get your– troops to: give us a … shot*, as saying this too directly might seem too pushy on his part. Paul, however, relexicalizes this directly, even bluntly, as *phone you a bit more*. In his position of power as a customer, he seems to have the liberty to be more direct, which Angus does not. The same sort of thing can be seen in 6.4b, although the idiom (*make up your mind*) is less opaque and the more literal relexicalization (*do you want it or not*) therefore seems less blunt.

At one point during the meeting, Paul in fact momentarily threatens convergence by being 'cheeky':

Example 6.5

1   Angus […] Uhm … because– one of the things which we've changed. U:
        hm since u:hm … I spoke to you last, is that we've gone very heavy on
        this um ⌊Paul Yes. Yeah.⌋ bespoke sizes … hh Uh:
2   Paul   ⌊Well they didn't have
        any when I phoned you yesterday you buggers
3   Angus Oh. Wait. Well it's not– not /perfect/
4   Paul   ⌊You can't win 'em all.

In turn 2, Paul uses a mock insult (*you buggers*) to point out that Angus's company
was in fact not able to deliver one of the services which Angus says they offer.
When Angus then gets somewhat defensive, Paul seems to try to redress the
balance by relexicalizing *it's not perfect* with the placating maxim *you can't win 'em
all*.

     Angus is on delicate ground in this encounter. He is the one who wants some-
thing from Paul (he is trying to get more business), and Paul seems to take
advantage of this situation by taking some liberties in the interaction (i.e. by
being a little cheeky). In an interview conducted afterwards with Paul, he showed
awareness of this situation by remarking that he was 'ribbing' Angus. Angus also
seemed to be aware that Paul was playing with him a little, as at one point in the
conversation he says:

     you're not winding me up here or something

In this encounter, idioms clearly perform the function of reducing threats to face
and common ground. However, differences in the roles and positioning of speakers, as we have here, can mean that the onus is more on one of the speakers to
work towards convergence and mitigate potential face-threatening acts.

     In the above two conversations we have seen how idioms can be used in unequal
encounters by both more and less powerful speakers to mitigate face-threatening
acts which arise in the course of transactional talk: in the first instance to evaluate a subordinate's performance, and in the second conversation, to try to get
more business from a customer. By using metaphors and maxims that appeal to
culturally shared values, speakers avoid committing themselves to the evaluations
expressed, thus negotiating relationally delicate transactional tasks.

6.2.2 *Building and maintaining solidarity in procedural discourse*

Procedural workplace discourse

One of the findings of the corpus-based analysis of interpersonal markers in Chapter 5 was that, in workplace conversations involving directives and instructions, direct forms occurred less frequently than more indirect or mitigated alternatives. While, as one would expect, deontic modality occurred with above-average frequency in procedural and directive discourse in the ABOT Corpus, the frequency of the modals analysed varied inversely with the degree of directness with which they express obligation. Furthermore, both hedges (in particular *just*) and vague language (e.g., *things, stuff, or something*), were used very frequently in such conversations.

It is also striking that besides the four deontic modals analysed in Chapter 5 (*have to, should, need* and *want to*) only three others occur in procedural discourse in the ABOT Corpus (*mustn't, ought to* and *be supposed to*) and each is used only once. Imperatives are also used less frequently for giving directives or instructions than one might expect: only 17 times in a sub-corpus of over 5,000 words, and only six of these are bald imperatives (i.e. *do X*). The rest are *you*-imperatives (e.g., *you open this up*) or imperatives hedged with *just* (e.g., *just call it in off the copy*). Other studies of white-collar contexts like the ones recorded for the ABOT Corpus have found similar results for the language of directives. Modalized forms, such as *you can* ... were more frequent than bald imperatives in a study of directives in an American university office (Pufahl-Bax 1986); and in procedural office conversations from the Language in the Workplace (LWP) database (Holmes and Stubbe 2003), mitigation and hedging were very frequent (in contrast to instructional data from factories, where imperatives were the most frequently used form[1]).

Comparing procedural and directive discourse to other workplace genres, the findings from the ABOT Corpus show that, overall, direct forms are less frequent (and indirect forms more frequent) than in other genres like decision-making (see also Chapter 3 for the characteristics of procedural discourse compared to other genres). The generic goal itself – getting someone to perform an action – creates a discursive imbalance which the discursively dominant speaker often seems to try to offset by using relational strategies, compared to more collaborative genres. But beyond these generally shared features that a corpus-based analysis reveals, speakers clearly use a multitude of different strategies in instructing or directing co-workers, as confirmed by the different procedural conversations in the ABOT Corpus and Holmes's and Stubbe's (2003) LWP database.

Many different factors can influence the chosen strategies, including the nature of the task (routine or new), whether the instructions are solicited or not, the degree of imposition of what is asked, the institutional (hierarchical) relationship, how well the participants know each other, and so forth. Holmes and Stubbe

(2003) found that imperatives and other direct forms were used more frequently when talking to a subordinate and when routine procedures were involved. There is also some evidence in the ABOT Corpus that routine procedures required less hedging, and that the institutional relationship can influence the way in which directives are delivered. According to Holmes and Stubbe, power (the institutional relationship) and politeness (concern for relational goals) are two major factors which influence speakers' choice of strategy in all types of workplace interaction. Corpus-based analyses indicate that genre, or the nature of the activity in which speakers are engaged, is a further crucial factor. What is also clear from the conversations in the ABOT Corpus, as well as the LWP database, is that dominant speakers orient not only to the task goal of procedural genres (getting the addressee to perform an action, or showing them how to perform it), but also to relational goals involving both attention to face wants (politeness) and the creation of rapport (solidarity).

In order to explore in more detail the complex interplay between speakers' discursive and institutional roles on the one hand, and their relational goals on the other, we will examine a number of procedural encounters from the ABOT Corpus.

Solidarity strategies in procedural discourse

Examples of both types of relational orientation, politeness and solidarity, can be found in procedural discourse. Vague language and hedges occur as negative politeness devices to mitigate potential threats to face which directives can sometimes entail (see Example 5.20). The same kinds of device can also be used to express solidarity, for example the use of hedges can make the task sound easy, and a clustering of interpersonal markers can lend a friendly, informal tone to the discourse (see Example 4.7). Many examples from the ABOT corpus show politeness and solidarity strategies being used by instruction-givers *both* to 'talk down' to a subordinate *and* to 'talk up' to someone who is senior in the organization. Here we will focus on the use of solidarity strategies, as one might not initially expect to find such strategies in procedural and directive discourse, with its focus on information and its unidirectional nature.

The two examples below (6.6 and 6.7) illustrate the use of the same kinds of relational strategy by discursively dominant speakers in procedural talk, regardless of their hierarchical position in relation to their co-worker.

In the first example Beth, an assistant editor in an American publishing company, tells a more senior editor what the procedure is for ordering free books:

Example 6.6 (a)

Beth	a:nd <u>I'll show you</u> it now because I'm not sure if you have it on *your* computer?
Judy	I may not.
Beth	You might not have it yet.
Judy	⌊Yeah.
Beth	But <u>I'll show you</u>, and you can just put it in and you can sa:y um … you can give a reason for the free, you know, like gratis copy or something.

Example 6.6 (b)

Beth	Yeah. <u>If</u> you wanna do it where you're … where you're paying *part* of it, then <u>I would</u> call someone in Porchester. You know, ⌊Judy: Yeah.⌋ like someone in customer service.

Example 6.6 (c)

Beth	Um … but if you don't have it up on your desktop, <u>we</u> can get it.
	(from the Cambridge International Corpus © Cambridge University Press)

The above extracts from different parts of the conversation show Beth using a number of devices which project solidarity with Judy. In a number of instances, she uses first person pronouns (*I*/*we*), instead of the second person (*you*), which is more usual for instruction-giving. She says *I'll show you* twice (extract a), and thereby shows her willingness to be helpful; and she also uses *we* (*we can get it*– extract c), which makes the proposed action sound like a joint endeavour.[2] There is also an 'if'-clause, which projects the proposed action as Beth's *own* action in a hypothetical situation: *If you wanna do it where you're … then I would call someone in Porchester* (extract b).

In this encounter the addressee, Judy, has just returned to the office after spending two years abroad, and has asked Beth how to order some books. Throughout this encounter, which comprises a number of generic episodes, Beth seems to make a particular effort to make Judy's transition back to the office as easy as possible, and this relational orientation is reflected in her use of inter-personal markers (see also Chapter 7, where a requesting episode from this encounter is analysed).

The same solidarity strategies are used by Ann, a bookkeeper in the back office of an American food retailer, in training a new assistant, as shown in extracts from Ann's explanations:

Example 6.7 (a)

I'll show you what to do with it

Example 6.7 (b)

↑ There *should* also be a ↓ packing slip for this one here. So ... I would do this ... staple that bill of lading onto that *invoice*, 'cause we know *those* two go together

Example 6.7 (c)

Then: ... we wanna keep the two cover sheets, ... for that day's invoices,

Ann also uses *I'll show you* twice in this conversation (extract a shows one example); she frames an instruction as something she herself would do in this situation (*I would do this* – extract b); and she uses *we* twice, thereby projecting the action as joint, rather than as something the addressee will actually do on her own. As in Example 6.6, the high concentration of such solidarity strategies can be linked to the specific circumstances of this encounter: Ann is training a new employee, so she seems to be making a particular effort to make her new assistant feel at ease and to establish a good relationship with her.

These examples, and other examples from the corpus, demonstrate that, regardless of their institutional roles, discursively dominant speakers often seem to make an effort to 'personalize' the one-sided transfer of information which procedural discourse involves. Both types of first person reference by the dominant speaker, referring either to own (*I'll show you*) or joint action (*we can get it*), make the process of giving instructions and explaining procedures less 'unidirectional' and more interactive. By referring to their own role in the procedural process, dominant speakers temporarily take the focus away from actions to be performed by the addressee. References to actions as joint (even if they in fact are not) add an interpersonal dimension to the discourse, and bring it closer to collaborative types of discourse, where the focus is on joint action.

Institutional relationship and discursive strategies

However, there are occasions where the institutional role does seem to influence linguistic choice. For example, it is noteworthy that in the encounters in which the discursively dominant speakers are institutionally subordinate, they do not use any of the stronger modal forms: *have to* (with positive polarity), *should*, *ought to*, *must* or *supposed to*.

Turning to encounters where the discursively dominant speaker is the institutional superior, there is also evidence that those with power do have the option of using more direct and forceful forms, if necessary. One encounter in particular stands out, as the avoidance of direct forms generally observed in procedural discourse does not seem to apply. In this encounter ('Mistake with order'), both speakers, Paul and Sam, use direct modes of expression and the tone of the interaction is quite argumentative.

Example 6.8 'Mistake with order'

Paul: Office manager
Sam: Rep

1	Paul	Yeah. Your ten and a half thousand sheet order for um ... /Phoenix./ It was two and a half thousand sheet.
2	Sam	↑*What!*
3	Paul	He reckons it was *two* and a half.
4	Sam	↑When was this!
5	Paul	↑This *morning*. You put *ten* and a half thousand. [4]
6	Paul	You /?/
7	Sam	No? He said ten– *ten an' half.* That's what he said to me.
8	Paul	An'– I– I'll find you some cotton buds soon, all right,
9	Sam	↑No, He said– I wa– I wa– ... I hate people that lie,
10	Sam	'Cause he said– if it's like ten and a half thousand, /?/
11	Paul	⌊Yeah but–
12	Sam	I go is that ten– he goes ten an' a half. I go is that ten an' a half thousand. he says yeah.
13	Paul	⌊Yeah but Sam, they're packed in *two* an' a halfs.
14	Sam	Huh?
15	Paul	So didn't you tell him he couldn't have ten an' a half. [8]
16	Paul	You should have basically mentioned to him that uh:m ... he couldn't have ten an' a half in any case.

This encounter is from the sales office of the British paper supplier (see also Examples 6.1–6.5), and involves the office manager, Paul, reprimanding a junior sales representative, Sam, for a mistake he made with an order: he ordered ten and a half thousand sheets of paper for a customer instead of two and a half thousand. The direct tone of the discourse seems to be due, on the one hand, to the nature of the relationship between the two speakers – Sam is a relatively new junior (and very young) member of the sales force – and on the other to the general tone of interaction in this office: it is an all-male office, the atmosphere is very informal, and a great deal of bantering goes on between the sales reps. As Holmes (2001) notes, workplace culture can influence interactional style, particularly in the way conflicts are handled.

It is interesting to look not only at the language of the dominant speaker, Paul, but also at how Sam reacts to the reprimands. He does not accept that he has made a mistake, but defends his actions quite adamantly. Rather than acknowledging his mistake, Sam repeatedly challenges Paul:

3   Paul   He reckons it was *two* and a half.
4   Sam   ↑When was this!
5   Paul   ↑This *morning*! You put *ten* and a half thousand.

Instead of responding to Paul's 'accusation' with an acknowledgement of his error (which would be the expected 'second pair part' in conversation analytical terms), Sam counters with a question of his own, which initiates a side sequence[3] regarding the time when the action he is accused of took place. This results in a very unco-operative type of interaction, as the speakers' frequent emphatic stress (italics) and high key pitch (arrow up: ↑) serve to reinforce.

Sam's persistent refusal to acknowledge he has made a mistake seems to push Paul into expressing himself more and more directly. Although Paul's language is quite direct and abrupt from the beginning, he does not initially attribute blame to Sam in such a direct manner. He begins by pointing out Sam's error using an impersonal form – *it was*

1   Your ten and a half thousand sheet order for um … /Phoenix./ It
           was two and a half thousand sheet.

In his next attempt he again avoids directly attributing blame to Sam, by couching the recrimination as a third person report:

3   He reckons it was *two* and a half,

until finally, in his third attempt, he makes a direct reference to what Sam did wrong, using the second person pronoun *you*:

5   […] You put *ten* and a half thousand.

But it is still not until turn 15 of the encounter that Paul actually indicates what action Sam should have taken, phrasing this as a negative past tense question:

15   So _didn't you tell him_ he couldn't have ten an' a half.

When this still does not elicit a recognition of the error by Sam, Paul finally produces a direct reprimand using *you should have* in turn 16:

16   You _should have_ basically mentioned to him that uh:m … he couldn't
          have ten an' a half in any case.

This is one of the only two uses of *you should* in procedural discourse in the ABOT Corpus, and it is interesting that Paul only uses this fairly forceful deontic modal with second person at the very end of the encounter, after various other attempts to get Sam to acknowledge his mistake have failed.

Thus in trying to convey that a mistake was made by the rep, and that a different course of action should have been taken, the office manager moves from less direct to more and more direct methods of trying to communicate this message. It is only in the face of repeated challenges from the subordinate that more direct forms are finally resorted to. It seems, therefore, that even when the speaker is in a position of power, and the office culture encourages a fairly direct mode of expression, very bald and forceful forms of expressing obligation are nevertheless marked, and tend to be avoided. Not only that, but even in this argumentative mode, Paul still attempts to build solidarity through humour:

8   An'– I– I'll find you some cotton buds soon, all right,

Solidarity strategies in procedural discourse – conclusion

The above examples have illustrated some of the complex ways in which speakers' transactional goals (in these examples, getting the addressee to perform an action, or enabling them to do so) interact with their relational goals of building and maintaining the relationship, as well as with the power relationship between the speakers. One finding was that whether instruction-givers are talking 'up' or 'down', solidarity strategies seem to play an important role in procedural discourse. The only procedural encounter in the corpus (not shown here) in which the dominant speaker does not use any such strategies is the only one which does not take place between close colleagues, but between people who work in different departments. The reason there is no evidence of any 'relationship work' in this encounter may be because there is no relationship to maintain (of course there may be other reasons as well, such as individual style). So whether or not discourse participants are in a long-term working relationship is also an important factor affecting speakers' choice of discourse strategies. But, as we have seen, the power relationship between the speakers can also influence linguistic choice:

there is evidence in the corpus that direct forms may be avoided more when speaking to a superior than when speaking to a subordinate, and that ultimately superiors do have the authority to use more direct forms. In the 'problematic' encounter examined ('Mistake with order', Example 6.8), the manager eventually uses 'bald on-record' strategies to assert his authority in the face of continued resistance. Nevertheless, he also uses humour as a solidarity strategy, showing that even in such a confrontational situation, he is concerned with maintaining the relationship.

There can of course be many different reasons for using solidarity strategies in procedural discourse. On the one hand, the nature of the task itself seems to play a role: the speaker playing a dominant role as instruction-giver or issuer of directives seems to try to compensate for the discursive imbalance by avoiding direct forms (which might indicate a presumption of dominance) as well as by using various solidarity devices to make the encounter less one-sided and more interactive and interpersonal. But various other factors may also come into play, including the exact nature of the relationship, the difficulty or novelty of the task, and so forth. One of the encounters examined above involves training a new employee (Example 6.7). As the relationship between the speakers is new, solidarity strategies play a particularly important role here in establishing a good working relationship with the new member of staff.[4] In another encounter (Example 6.6), the speakers, Beth and Judy, re-establish their relationship after Judy's two-year stint abroad, and Beth (although she is in a junior position to Judy) seems to make a particular effort to ease her transition back into the office.

6.3 Dealing with conflict in collaborative talk

So far we have looked mainly at how discourse participants at work use strategies of politeness and solidarity in building common ground and consensus. However, in a few of the examples, problems or conflicts of some kind arise, and we have seen some of the ways in which speakers negotiate such tricky situations using politeness and solidarity strategies, occasionally also asserting their institutional power. As maintaining good working relationships is important, co-workers tend to avoid outright conflict, as shown for example by Holmes's and Stubbe's analysis of many different workplace interactions involving problematic talk (2003: 137–63).

However, overt disagreement does sometimes arise between co-workers, although it is perhaps not so easy to capture such conversations on tape! This section examines two decision-making encounters from the ABOT Corpus involving conflict, and analyses how interpersonal markers and other discursive devices are used to express disagreement and conflict, structure arguments and negotiate consensus. It should not come as a surprise that conflict and disagreement can occur in the process of decision-making. Participants may have differing opinions about which course of action should be taken or how a particular problem should be resolved. In addition, the discursively equal roles played by participants in collaborative discourse makes the voicing of differences of opinions more likely than in more unidirectional genres such as procedural discourse.

Although most discourse analysis focuses on co-operative talk, a number of studies have looked at the nature of arguments or disputes from both linguistic and sociological perspectives. Coulter (1990), who examines the structure of arguments using a CA approach, characterizes arguments as follows:

> An argument, as it arises in conversational interaction, characteristically comprises two or more disputants articulating adversary positions (or 'theses') with respect to some topic, including at least an exchange of assertion and counter-assertion with some attendant expansion.
>
> (Coulter 1990: 185)

There is general agreement in the literature that arguments have specific recognizable structures: they involve discourse participants displaying 'opposition' or 'disagreement' and are terminated either by some kind of settlement, or by disengagement of the participants or shift to another topic/ activity (see also Corsaro and Rizzo 1990, Vuchinich 1990, Muntigl and Turnbull 1998).

6.3.1 Negotiating conflict and consensus

Expressing disagreement

The first encounter, 'Discussing applications', was recorded in the registrar's office of a small graduate school in a North American university. The two speakers are Don, the staff assistant, who works at the reception desk, and Andy, the assistant registrar, who is Don's boss. They are discussing how often they should check the incoming student applications. The encounter begins with a simple exchange of information (turns 1–5), but a disagreement arises in turn 7, after Don makes a suggestion in turn 6 regarding how often applications need to be checked:

Example 6.9 'Discussing applications'

1 Andy Did you check all these people out next door?
2 Don   Ah yes.
3 Andy Okay?
4 Don   As of … this day.
5 Andy ↑Oh. ↓(Aha)
6 Don   So I can do 'em … Let's say weekly. ↓or something like that from here on out. ↓I don't think it pays to do it any more often than that.

7   Andy   ↑Well weekly, I mean you have to do it … [1.5] ah … more often
            than that right now, for this week an' next week, 'cause we gotta– .hh
            … have 'em all /entered into the system/ by a week on Friday. [1] so–
            any ones that are complete /a-/

Turn 7 marks a change in the nature of the discourse from information exchange
to a decision-making sequence, in which the participants disagree about the
course of action to take. Conversation analysts have observed that agreement
is the expected or 'preferred' response to a large number of first parts of adjacency pairs (e.g., invitations, suggestions, assessments), whereas disagreement is
'dispreferred' (Levinson 1983, Pomerantz 1984, Sacks 1987), and is characterized by a more complex turn shape. Andy's response to Don's suggestion has the
typical structure of a dispreferred second pair part: the disagreement is delayed
by a preface (*Well weekly, I mean*[5]), hesitations in the form of pauses and fillers
(*ah, .hh*) and Andy produces an account (introduced with the discourse marker
'cause) – an explanation of why the dispreferred action is being done (see Levinson 1983: 334).

   In the ensuing discussion, although initially some elements of dispreferred
responses still occur, e.g., token agreements (turn 8: *yeah, but*) or hesitations
(turn 9: *ah* …), there are fewer such markers and disagreement becomes more
direct:

Example 6.10

 7   Andy   […] we gotta– .hh … have 'em all /entered into the system/ by a
             week on Friday. [1] so– any ones that are complete /a-/
 8   Don   ⌊↑Yeah. ↓but we're <u>only</u> talking about …
             a comparatively small number of *stray* … ⌊<Andy>: Yeah⌋ individual
             stray fo– ↑you know you know you don't <u>even</u> *enter* ↓the individual
             letters an'– and transcripts <u>do you</u>?
 9   Andy   Ah … *no.* but we wan'– but–
10   Don   <u>So</u>?
11   Andy   I'm holding off entering these– *this* week ↓until they're complete.
             [3]
12   Don   Well then we'll check 'em at the end of this week or at the beginning
             of *next* week. that's what I'm *saying.*
13   Andy   I might check 'em tomorrow or something just to–
14   Don   Okay,
15   Andy   just to have more–
16   Don   ⌊Whatever you *want*. but I– I honestly don't even
             think it's worth it.

17 Andy Yeah
18 Don   I don't think you're gonna ... come up with enough to make it worth–
             the ti–
19 Andy $\lfloor$(/Yeah, ??/)
       [1]

Don's discourse in particular becomes quite direct and forceful: in turn 8 he uses intensifiers (*only* and *even*), tries to elicit consent from Andy by using a question tag (*do you?*) and then in turn 10 he openly challenges Andy's point of view with a blunt *So?*[6] (these feature are underlined in the above example). This corresponds to what Kotthoff (1993) observed for the structure of disputes: she found that initially disagreements with dispreferred turn shapes occur, but that as arguments develop, disagreement is expressed in a more unmodulated way, and eventually the preference structure is reversed; that is disagreements become the preferred response. The above disagreement sequence also has a number of interruptions or intrusive overlaps and pauses between and within turns (e.g., after turns 11 and 19), which are all features identified by Boden (1995), in examining workplace meetings, as markers of conflictual discourse.

   Turn 12 is a particularly interesting example of a conflictual mode of discourse, as it is a reformulation of Don's original suggestion in turn 6, but contrasts with this first suggestion in a number of ways:

6   So I can do 'em ... <u>Let's say weekly.</u> $\downarrow$<u>or something like that from here</u>
          <u>on out</u>.
12   Well then we'll check 'em <u>at the end of this week or at the beginning</u>
          <u>of *next* week. That's what I'm *say*ing</u>.

The first time he hedges his suggestion modally with *let's say* and refers to a vague category (*weekly or something like that*) to say how frequently they should do the task. In the reformulation he is much more specific and explicit – *at the end of this week or at the beginning of next week* – and not only is his suggestion now unhedged, but he fully commits himself to the illocutionary force of his utterance with a metalinguistic comment: *That's what I'm saying*. Thomas (1984: 227) refers to such items as 'metapragmatic acts', where the speaker 'effectively denies his or her interlocutor the possibility of escaping into "pragmatic ambivalence" – of leaving the precise illocutionary intent of his or her utterance diplomatically unclear'. Lakoff (1973: 304) describes such 'outright insistence on the force of the speech act' as 'incontrovertibly rude', as it destroys the addressee's options: 'he must recognize the speech act for what it is, and must respond appropriately'.

   So the reason for Don's more specific and unhedged reiteration is not that he thinks he did not express himself clearly enough the first time, but can be found in its function at this stage of the discourse. The first proposal is made in the context of a simple exchange of information, whereas the reformulation later occurs after Don and Andy have started arguing. The first hedged and vague formulation is thus made in a neutral mode, where consensus is assumed, whereas the reformulation is made within an argumentative, conflictual frame. It seems, therefore, that vague language and modality are associated here with a consensual type of discourse, whereas explicit on-record language is associated with a conflictual mode. Channell (1994) argues that vague language forms a considerable part of language use and cannot therefore be treated as a marginal phenomenon. The above analysis indicates that one can go even further and suggest that in certain situations vague language may be the unmarked neutral form, whereas more explicit/direct language may be marked and signal a special interactive frame, e.g., a conflictual type of interaction, as in this example. It is of course not possible to generalize from one example, but as we shall see in Section 6.3.2 below, there is further evidence for this elsewhere in the ABOT Corpus.

Reaching an agreement

Despite the features of conflictual discourse identified above, both participants are interested in finding the best procedure for accomplishing the task (i.e. checking the applications), and the argument is settled fairly rapidly, after only about 20 turns. The first move towards consensus comes in turn 21, when Don agrees to do the task Andy's way. This is marked by a change in Don's tone of voice to a lower pitch and a more 'confidential' timbre, which signals a change in footing and alignment (see Goffman 1981).

Example 6.11

[1]
20 Andy   (/Right/)
21 Don   [voice changes] On the other hand it doesn't really take *that long*. It takes about fifteen minutes to go through the whole box.
22 Andy   ⌊Yeah it's–   ⌊(/Alright yeah/)
23 Don   It's not that big a deal. <u>You want me to do it? I'll be happy to do it.</u>
24 Andy   No don't. [1] ↑ You know– lemme– *I'm* gonna do it. ↓I'm looking for something to *do*: honestly so–
25 Andy   [takes the box with the applications] (I'll take /that/)

Kotthoff (1993) notes that, as agreements are dispreferred within arguments, concessions always involve a change of footing out of an argumentative frame. This consensual frame is emphasized by the parallel rhythm of the two clauses in turn 23 (underlined in the above extract) and repetition of *to do it* with the pronouns *I* and *you*, which seems to align the two participants symbolically: *You want me to do it? I'll be happy to do it.* Andy then reciprocates with a concession of his own in 24, by offering to do the task himself.

Having apparently just come to an agreement, Don re-opens the discussion in 26 marking the discourse shift with high key (arrow up: ↑).[7]

Example 6.12

26 Don   ↑I don't know *why* ... we don't start entering them like they are.
27 Andy   'Cause I don't want to have to go into– all of 'em twice, and ... I have
          all the complete over here and once I enter 'em I put 'em over here, [1]
          and we'd have to look *he:re* and look *there*, I mean–
28 Don   Okay.
29 Andy   [Is moving away] /??????/
30 Don   You're the boss.

However, Don does not pursue his point, but concedes to Andy in turn 28, by saying *okay*, followed up by a tongue-in-cheek idiomatic formulation *you're the boss* (turn 30), thus ending the encounter on a light-hearted note. This comment seems to indicate that Don is only conceding on formal grounds, not because he is really convinced. However, the use of an idiomatic cultural allusion means that any implied criticism is indirect, and therefore 'off-record' and deniable.

The above analysis shows that despite their disagreement, the discussion is essentially resolution-oriented, and Don and Andy therefore argue in a co-operative manner; each trying to persuade the other of his position. In arguing their case, each tends to adopt a different strategy. The argument proceeds in such a way that Don negatively evaluates the way Andy wants to do the task, for example:

6   [...] I don't think it pays to do it any more often than that.
16   [...] I honestly don't even think it's worth it.
18   I don't think you're gonna ... come up with enough to make it worth–
          the ti–

Andy, on the other hand, uses accounts to justify his proposed actions, for example in turn 7 (Example 6.9 above), and also later in turn 27:

26 Don   ↑I don't know *why* ... we don't start entering them like they are.
27 Andy   'Cause I don't want to have to go into– all of 'em twice, and ... I have
          all the complete over here and once I enter 'em I put 'em over here, [1]
          and we'd have to look *he:re* and look *there*, I mean–

Accounts can be useful strategies in joint problem resolution, as Firth (1995b) found in examining business negotiations. Because accounts emphasize the reason for disagreement, they reduce the negative effects of disagreement, and thus 'provide a "bridge" between "conflict" and its potential "resolution"' (ibid: 222).

One interesting aspect of these differing strategies employed by the two speakers is that they do not seem to match their relative status within the office: Andy is Don's superior (as Don explicitly states at the end of the encounter), but evaluating is what one would expect from a person in a position of power, and accounting from someone who must 'account for' their actions *to* a superior.

There are other ways in which the discourse of the participants seems at odds with their institutional roles. While Don's language is quite forceful and direct (he interrupts, uses intensifiers and explicit language, as shown in Example 6.10 above), Andy's language is less argumentative, more indirect and at times even hesitant and vague, e.g.:

9   Andy   Ah ... *no.* but we wan'– but–

Even after Don produces his polemic metapragmatic comment (*Well then we'll check 'em at the end of this week or at the beginning of* **next** *week. that's what I'm* **saying**), Andy responds with a non-committal epistemic modal (*might*), a vague tag (*or something*) and a hedge (*just*):

13 Andy   I <u>might</u> check 'em tomorrow <u>or something</u> <u>just</u> to–
14 Don   Okay,
15 Andy   <u>just</u> to have more–

Andy seems to try to opt out of the argument fairly early on by offering to do the task himself, as shown in the above example (turn 13). His language displays characteristics of the type found by O'Donnell (1990) in the language of less powerful speakers in putting forward arguments in business meetings: the use of modality and hedges as negative politeness strategies.

As triangulation of the data was not possible in this case, it is not apparent why such a 'role reversal' seems to occur here. But, as we have already seen on a number of occasions, other factors besides hierarchical status can influence speakers' roles in the discourse. Here, it may play a role that Don is older than Andy and has been working in the office longer; and the fact that Don feels free to express his disagreement directly may also be a reflection of a close, informal working relationship. The nature of the genre itself comes into play: as a collaborative genre, decision-making typically contains more direct forms of expression and evaluative language than unidirectional genres. Whatever other factors are involved, this conversation provides a good illustration of the way in which the relative roles of discourse participants are not necessarily predetermined by their workplace roles, but are negotiated in the course of the encounter. Other workplace studies (e.g., Gavruseva 1995) have also shown how status does not play a static role in workplace interaction, but is negotiated.

6.3.2 Conflictual discourse

Although the encounter analysed in the previous section involved a certain amount of disagreement, the participants were nevertheless communicating co-operatively and working towards a joint resolution. However, one particular longer encounter in the ABOT corpus, which we will call 'Problem with an order' (Examples 6.13–15), has a distinctly argumentative flavour: it is clear to the outside observer that tempers flare up in the course of the conversation. How does this manifest itself linguistically, and what particular devices do speakers use in such conflictual discourse? Also, how is the language of such an encounter distinct from other discourse of the same genre?

The encounter is from the office of a British printer, and involves Sid, the managing director, and Val, the office administrator, discussing how to solve a particular problem they have with one of their customers. They have printed some labels for a customer according to a quotation. The customer, however, says the labels are the wrong size and claims these changes were discussed in various telephone conversations with Sid and with the platemaker. The customer therefore does not want to pay for this work.

One thing that is immediately striking about this conversation is the presence of a number of exclamations or expletives, such as *Oh God help us* or *damn*, whereas in the rest of the corpus very little strong language occurs. There are also quite a number of fixed expressions and idioms which seem to express an argumentative posture, e.g.: *I'm not going to waste my time*; *that's neither here nor there*.

Emphatic markers of subjective stance

A closer examination of the interpersonal markers used by both speakers in this encounter shows that there is a proportionally large number of what one could call strong or emphatic markers of subjective stance. In the analysis of modality in Chapter 5, it was found that decision-making conversations typically have relatively high frequencies of markers of subjective stance – that is modal items which express speakers' judgements and opinions. This may involve fairly moderate or mild judgements and opinions expressed using epistemic modals, e.g., *I think*, *I would*. Stronger and more forceful expressions of subjective stance include the following types of interpersonal marker:

- deontic modals expressing obligation and necessity (e.g., *have to* or *should*)
- epistemic modals expressing strong commitment (*must, surely, obviously*)
- intensifiers, exclamations and expletives
- evaluative lexis and idioms.[8]

In addition, any items that make the discourse more explicit, removing any vagueness or ambiguity, also contribute to a forceful and unhedged mode of expression. One device speakers use in order to clarify or emphasize their communicative purpose is the use of metalanguage and explicit performatives e.g., *I'm just saying … *or* I don't accept all this.*

In order to determine whether the incidence of such emphatic markers of subjective stance in this particular encounter is higher than in more 'normal' co-operative types of discourse, their density[9] in this encounter was compared to two other encounters from the same genre of decision-making (one from the same company involving one of the same speakers, and the other from the American publisher). The density of these emphatic markers was then compared to that of all other interpersonal markers: deontic modals expressing permission, inclination and opinion (e.g., *can, want, think*), epistemic and possibility modality, hedges and vague language. It was found that emphatic markers of subjective stance are indeed proportionally more frequent in the encounter 'Problem with an order' (Examples 6.13–15), whereas other interpersonal markers are less frequent than in the other two encounters ('Co-operative decision-making' 1 and 2). The results of the comparative analysis are summarized in Figure 6.1.

These results show that the overall density of interpersonal markers is higher in 'Problems with an order' than in the other two encounters, which can be attributed to the much higher density of emphatic markers here: 12.7 per cent, compared to only 3.9 per cent and 7.2 per cent in the other conversations. Other

Figure 6.1 Density of emphatic markers compared to other markers (%)

Density	'Problems with an order'	Co-operative decision-making 1 (British printer)	Co-operative decision-making 2 (American publisher)
Total interpersonal markers	19.0	12.0	14.7
Emphatic markers of subjective stance	12.7	3.9	7.2
Other interpersonal markers	6.2	8.2	7.5

interpersonal markers are less frequent, accounting for only 6.2 per cent of the total number of words, compared to 8.2 per cent and 7.5 per cent in the other two conversations. It seems, therefore, that one of the ways in which conflictual discourse is marked linguistically in relation to non-conflictual discourse, is by the increased use of emphatic markers of subjective stance and the simultaneous reduction of indirectness and hedging devices.

Let us now look in more detail at some of the devices used in the encounter 'Problem with an order'. Example 6.13 shows the beginning of the conversation:.

Example 6.13 'Problem with an order'

1	Sid	Can I just discuss with you about this *da:mn* label, <u>where do you think we ought to go</u>.
2	Val	↑Uhm … (<u>Oh my god</u>) I don't– I don't– … See the <u>difficulty</u> is, we quoted a: size, didn't we, which is what you *said you* quoted it, an' that's what you were *work*ing to. An' if it had been any different, they <u>should've</u> *told* us.
3	Sid	But then the <u>obligation</u>, <u>must</u> be NPL's <u>mustn't</u> it, well how do I word it to them. [3]
4	Val	↑Well, … the hu– the other side of it, is that … you know, you told
5	Sid	⌊I mean this is– I mean this is not–
6	Val	NPL the size, a mill <u>normally</u> isn't … <u>sort of</u> that much a <u>problem</u>, is it? [2]
7	Val	↓ Mind you, I <u>suppose</u> Gary <u>would</u> say, this is <u>slightly</u> different, what do you want us to do:, They <u>should've</u> said something,

From the outset, Val and Sid's discourse contains a fairly high concentration of emphatic markers of subjective stance (underlined with a solid line), including deontic modals of obligation and necessity (*ought to, should, must, mustn't*), evaluative lexis referring to problems (*difficulty, problem*) and other 'conflictual' themes (*obligation*), as well as exclamations or expletives (*damn, Oh my god*). Sid also uses a metaphor of movement in initiating the discussion: *where do you think we ought to go*. Movement as a metaphor for solving the problem is repeated throughout the ensuing conversation, e.g.:

- See if you can <u>get anywhere</u> …
- but you'd <u>been through</u> all this

Sid's discourse is aggressive and conflictual from the start (e.g., his use of *damn* in the very first turn), whereas Val's is more measured, containing some emphatic markers, but also some epistemic modals and hedges (underlined with a dotted line). This measured tone is emphasized by her use of the discourse organizer *the other side of it is* … in turn 4. By asking Val to propose a solution to the problem, Sid essentially puts her in the role of conflict resolver. As the conversation progresses, and Sid responds negatively to all Val's suggestions, she herself becomes increasingly irritated, as can be seen in her use of more forceful language (underlined) much later in the discussion (turn numbers are from the full transcript of the encounter):

Example 6.14

109 Sid   Well where does that leave the other one, a hundred an— and forty *one*. which was reduced to *forty*. ↓ 'cause /she's <u>deceptive</u>/. ↑I mean see— <u>you can't— you can't have— you can't—</u>

110 Val   ⌊I don't know. I don't know Sid. I haven't— I haven't been onto that size. ↑ She's— *she's* <u>actually</u> *say*ing, .hh that all of them. as far as she was concerned, all of the artwork sizes *changed* slightly, an' I said well it *can't* be that way, because … we had cutters made to the *sizes*.

111 Sid   No I'm sorry, <u>I don't accept all this</u>. If you give somebody an order, you give a— you give them an order with the sizes on it.

112 Val   ⌊↑ Well Sid, <u>it's no good talking to me</u> about it then.

113 Sid   What?

114 Val   'Cause <u>she's gonna stand her ground</u>. So …

115 Sid   ⌊And I'm standing mine, too.
        [1.5]

116 Val   Well y— you probably won't get *paid* then. So *then* what.
        [1]

117 Val   ↑Si— <u>You gotta— you gotta</u> go to [name of company], … <u>*surely*</u>,

In addition to using emphatic markers, both speakers show their irritation through frequent repetition (*you can't— you can't*; *you gotta— you gotta*), and interruptions (turns 110 and 112). Lack of movement is also used as a metaphor for the hardening of positions and the inability to reach an agreement in turns 114 and 115, where Val and Sid use the same metaphorical idiom to represent the two conflicting positions:

114 Val   'Cause she's gonna <u>stand her ground</u>. So …

115 Sid   ⌊And I'm standing mine, too.

It is interesting that such echoing of the other speaker's words, which is often a sign of convergence and agreement (see Zhang 1998), should be used here with the opposite effect: divergence and disagreement. In fact, such echoing, referred to as 'contrastively matched counter' (Coulter 1990) or 'format tying' (M.H. Goodwin 1990) in the literature on argumentative discourse, seems to be quite a typical feature of arguments (see also McCarthy 1998: 112–14). By using such a device, speakers 'subvert' their interlocutor's words in order to strengthen their own arguments (Kotthof 1993), and it allows them to simultaneously rebut a prior assertion and advance an alternative position (Coulter 1990).

Throughout the discussion, both speakers also use idioms and metaphors as argumentative devices, in particular spatial and motion metaphors (*stand your ground* is used six times), which provide the speakers with powerful images to argue their positions. According to Low (1988: 128), one of the functions of metaphor is to 'compel attention by positively or negatively dramatizing' something; and in this encounter participants pick up on one another's metaphors, with their compelling images of movement or stagnation, in order to further their own arguments.

The above extract shows a critical point in the encounter, when the conflict comes to a head. In addition to all the markers of conflict already mentioned, both speakers produce 'metapragmatic acts' – explicit performatives or metalanguage – which unambiguously state the intent of the utterance (see Thomas 1984) and, as we saw in the encounter 'Discussing applications', signal a conflictual form of discourse. Sid takes the lead by saying *I don't accept all this* (turn 111) in response to Val clarifying the customer's point of view, and thus rejects it outright. Val responds to this with a metapragmatic comment of her own, *it's no good talking to me about it then* (turn 112), essentially disengaging from the discussion and giving up her efforts to find a solution. The situation has come to an impasse, with both parties 'standing their ground'.

Explicit performatives and metalanguage of the type shown above are in fact quite rare in naturally occurring discourse (see Stubbs 1986, McCarthy 1998, Koester 2002). Even then, they are not usually employed to perform metapragmatic acts, but can be used for clarification, as framing devices (see Section 2.5) or for speech reporting, e.g.:

Example 6.15

86 Val   No, the only– the only possibility is, ... u:h ... which <u>I'd said I would discuss is</u> ... .hh *if:*, they consider the thirty-*nine* mill label, still isn't small e– ↓ <u>as you suggested</u>

There are many such examples in this encounter of metalanguage and performatives used in speech reporting, and also to refer to hypothetical or future discourse. But quite a number of such devices are used to refer to the speaker's own or their interlocutor's discursive action in the current speech event, for example:

- Can I just <u>discuss</u> with you ...
- you're both <u>standing your ground</u> (two instances)
- Why is it every time we <u>have a conflict</u> ...
- I'm just <u>saying</u> ...

There are 11 such explicit performatives (or metalinguistic devices) referring to the current speech event, which is quite high compared to the other two decision-making conversations, where there are no such items. A closer examination of these 11 instances shows that almost all of them occur at conflictual moments of the discourse, and are examples of metapragmatic acts which involve explicit 'on-record' performance of speech acts and therefore are highly face-threatening or even face-aggravating. This can be seen quite clearly in the part of the encounter just examined (Example 6.14 above) where a number of these items cluster together.

Despite another attempt by Val after the 'stand-off' (shown in Example 6.14) to reach some kind of compromise with Sid, the discussion ends in a stalemate, and the problem remains unresolved. Furthermore, in a subsequent interview, Val indicated that she did not believe it was likely an amicable agreement would be reached, and predicted that Sid would have another argument with the customer and possibly take the matter to court. Unlike the conversation between Andy and Don analysed earlier, this is an example of unsuccessful conflict resolution.

6.3.3 Dealing with conflict – summary and conclusion

The analysis of the above two encounters shows that argumentative discourse is characterized by a number of structural and linguistic features. Within argumentative sequences, disagreements become the preferred type of response, intrusive interruptions are frequent, and speakers use emphatic markers of subjective stance: modals expressing strong commitment or obligation, evaluative devices such as descriptive adjectives, idioms and metaphors, and metalanguage and performatives. The increased use of such devices corresponds to the simultaneous reduction of interpersonal markers that contribute to indirectness, such as vague language, hedges and modals of possibility, permission or inclination.

The first conversation analysed, 'Discussing applications', was essentially resolution-oriented, with the discourse moving from conflict back to consensus (even if total agreement is not achieved). In arguing their point, both speakers use persuasive devices such as accounts to justify disagreement or evaluative language. The second encounter, 'Problem with an order', is an example of a much more conflictual encounter, as displayed in the increased use of emphatic markers of subjective stance, especially more face-threatening and aggressive ones such as explicit performatives and expletives. Despite the persuasive efforts of one of the speakers, the conflict ends in a stand-off and the problem is not resolved. One reason for heightened conflict in this encounter is no doubt the greater severity of the problem faced; however, triangulation of the data suggests that personality may also play an important role.

It is particularly interesting that, in both encounters, the participants negotiate roles in the discourse which do not correspond to their institutional roles. In 'Discussing applications', Don, the institutional subordinate, behaves discursively more like the dominant participant by expressing himself more directly and using evaluative language, whereas Andy, his superior, uses more vague language and hedging. Similarly, in 'Problem with an order', Val, the subordinate, is the one who takes the lead in suggesting possible solutions to the problem, and her boss appeals to her for help. These examples illustrate, once again, that discursive roles are negotiated, and not necessarily determined by institutional roles. Of course, this is not to suggest that institutional roles do not matter. Sid's aggressive, uncooperative mode of expression throughout the discussion can also be seen as a sign of his institutional superiority – it is his company, so in the end he can say (and do) what he wants. In both encounters, the decision is ultimately up to the person who wields institutional power, not to the person who argues best, as Don's closing remark, *you're the boss*, so succinctly sums up.

6.4 Conclusion

The encounters examined in this chapter have served to illustrate some of the complex ways in which speakers' transactional goals in accomplishing workplace tasks interact with their goals in building and maintaining workplace relationships, as well as with their institutional roles and the power relationships associated with these. As we have seen, a number of factors influencing linguistic choice and discursive strategies need to be taken into account: the discursive relationship resulting from the generic goal, the institutional relationship and the identities negotiated locally in the course of the encounter. Discursive identities are not static, but negotiated through talk, and speakers may invoke their institutional identities or play them down.

The analysis of a variety of workplace conversations has shown that, regardless of the power relationship, discourse participants orient to relational as well as transactional goals, employing both politeness and solidarity strategies, frequently in very similar ways, as we saw for example in the use of solidarity strategies in procedural discourse. But the power relationship may also mean that the onus is on one of the participants to do *more* relationship work, as illustrated in the meeting between the supplier and the customer, where the supplier used more politeness strategies, and the customer more direct, unmitigated language.

The complex interplay between the different roles and identities can be explored particularly revealingly by looking at different encounters from the same genre. Thus we found that in procedural discourse, both discursive and institutional dominance tend to be mitigated and played down, but power can be also invoked in certain cases by the institutionally dominant speaker. Collaborative genres like decision-making entail a discursively equal relationship, and therefore opinions can be expressed more freely, even leading to arguments in some cases. Discourse participants may also negotiate discursive identities which do not correspond to their institutional roles: in the two conflictual encounters examined, we saw the institutional subordinate negotiate a dominant position in taking the lead in attempting to reach a resolution.

Finally, we should not forget that the specific nature of the relationship between speakers and individual personality and style are also important factors influencing the shape and characteristics of each encounter. While corpus-based analysis of the kind described in Chapter 5 gives insights into the general characteristics and the common features of a particular genre, in-depth qualitative analysis of individual encounters, as focused on in this chapter, reveals the great variety of strategies available to speakers in pursuing transactional and relational goals in workplace talk.

7 Relational talk in workplace interactions[1]

7.1 Introduction

The importance of taking into account speakers' relational goals in understanding talk at work has been a recurring theme throughout this book. In this chapter, we turn our attention specifically to relational talk at work. As outlined in Chapter 4, relational talk, or elements of talk, in workplace discourse can occur at various levels from entire encounters consisting of small talk or office gossip down to individual interpersonal markers within transactional talk:

1   non-transactional conversations: office gossip and small talk
2   phatic communion: small talk at the beginning or end of transactional encounters
3   relational episodes: small talk or office gossip occurring during the performance of a transactional task
4   relational sequences and turns: non-obligatory task-related talk with a relational focus
5   interpersonal markers: the use of modals, vague language, and so forth, in transactional genres.

Examples of each of these were given in Section 4.4, and the frequency and function of a variety of interpersonal markers within different genres were discussed in detail in Chapter 5. Taking once more a genre-based approach, this chapter investigates some of the factors affecting the occurrence, placement and function of relational talk at work.[2] The investigation is based on approximately 30 hours of British and American office conversations (described in Section 2.6), part of which was transcribed for the ABOT Corpus, as well as interview data with many of the discourse participants. The chapter will begin with an overview of relational talk in the different office settings, and then examine in more detail the different types of relational talk listed above – in particular relational sequences occurring during transactional talk.

Non-transactional talk occurred in *all* the office settings in the study, but the frequency varied from office to office and speaker to speaker. Two factors which seem to influence whether and to what extent relational talk occurs in a workplace encounter are the relationship between the speakers and the physical setting. Such talk was more likely to occur if there was a prior relationship between the participants. Only a few encounters in the corpus are between complete strangers, and in these relational elements are sparse. Relational talk seems to occur particularly frequently between co-workers who have developed a close relationship, for example some colleagues have a customary joking relationship (see Norrick 1993: 43–81) and engage in frequent banter. Other studies confirm this link between small talk and the speakers' relationship: Ylänne-McEwen (1996) found that in travel agency encounters, the level of acquaintance between server and client played a role in the occurrence of relational talk.[3]

In the offices where data for the ABOT Corpus were collected, the physical setting itself played an important role. Large open-plan offices, where a number of co-workers share the same physical space, are conducive to the occurrence of relational talk, as people can engage in small talk or banter without too much disruption of their work. One of the interviewees working in the cramped open-plan office of an American food co-operative even remarked that small talk played a role in helping people work together amicably while sharing a small physical space. This is similar to McCarthy's (2000) finding that relational talk is frequent in close-contact service encounters, for example at the hairdresser's or during a driving lesson, where client and server are obliged to spend a certain amount of time in each other's company in close proximity. Non-transactional talk was also particularly prevalent in the two university offices in the study, where there was a great deal of coming and going of visitors and colleagues from other offices. Here the role of the office as meeting point for members of the department and gateway to the department for outsiders seems to foster the occurrence of relational talk.[4]

Linked to such contextual and temporal constraints on task performance is the question of whether the occurrence or non-occurrence of relational talk is a systematic component of genre. McCarthy (2000) found that differences in the occurrence and distribution of relational talk in the two types of close-contact service encounter examined (the hairdresser's and a driving lesson) could be explained in terms of important differences between the two genres. Unlike at the hairdresser's (or in other service encounters), however, the physical and institutional context of the office does not narrowly constrain the type of talk that can occur. Can systematic links between genre and the occurrence and distribution of relational talk nevertheless be found in the data? This chapter attempts to answer this question, as well as investigate some of the functions of the different types of relational talk at work.

7.2 Non-transactional conversations: office gossip and small talk

As we saw in the overview of relational talk in Section 4.4.1, the labels 'small talk' and 'office gossip' are used for conversations, covering a variety of genres, which are not transactional: participants either discuss topics outside work (in the case of small talk), or talk about some aspect of the workplace, without actually engaging in a workplace task (in the case of office gossip). Non-transactional discourse is thus fairly heterogeneous, but nevertheless some common features can also be identified. First of all, similar topics occurred in the different office settings. Office gossip tended to be about colleagues or other people in the trade/business, and about events in the office or within the profession (e.g., talking about a conference). The most frequent small talk topics were the weekend and holidays, family and friends, personal experiences, food, the weather and current events. Narrative is a particularly frequent genre in office gossip and small talk, as illustrated in Section 4.4.1, Examples 4.2 and 4.3). Small talk in all the offices involved varying degrees of joking, banter and teasing; however it was noticeable that in some offices, there was more of a 'joking culture' than in others.

We saw in Section 5.5 that intensifiers occur significantly more frequently in non-transactional than in transactional discourse, and there is also some evidence that evaluative lexis is more frequent here. The following encounter, which occurred in an American university office, provides a good example of how speakers involved in relational talk use such interpersonal markers, combined with other devices expressing affect and involvement, in order to build solidarity and common ground.

This encounter is between three speakers, Don, Andy and Helga, and involves the discussion of the best way to eat French chestnut butter – *crème de marrons* – (Don has brought Andy a jar back from Paris); this then leads on to the discussion of another French speciality: *crème fraîche*. The discourse consists of a variety of genres: information provision, observation–comment, narrative and instructions, and is characterized by the frequent use of evaluative lexis and intensifiers, especially in the observation–comment segments. The following intensifiers and evaluative lexis occur in this conversation, a number of them more than once:

- intensifiers: *very, real, really, so, all*
- evaluative lexis: *funny, (you're) joking, hilarious, great, delicious, horrible, the best, (I) love (it)*.

The extract below shows the end of the conversation (turn numbers are from the full transcript in order to reflect this), where the discussion has turned to *crème fraîche*:

Example 7.1

69 Helga ⌊They also have that as ice cream ...
70 Andy   ⌊Crème fraîche?
71 Don   Crème fraîche. yeah.
72 Helga (Right.) ↑ *Oh!* ↓(Crème fraîche.) =
73 Andy   It's <u>great</u> =
74 Helga = *That* is <u>the *best*</u>. =
75 Andy   = Yeah =
76 Don   ⌊I *love* it. I *love* it.
77 Helga   ⌊<u>I could kill</u> /??/
78 Andy   ⌊Yeah,
79 Andy   Yeah, =
80 Helga = <u>I could kill</u> /for/ that
81 Andy   ⌊Heheh
82 Andy   ↑ *<u>Wow</u>*! ↓ Okay? heheheh=
83 Don   =Now you know.
84 Helga ⌊↑ You know what that is? ↓ Triple by-pass.
84 Don   Heheh

(See also Example 5.21 for a narrative extract from the same conversation.)

The genre here can be described as observation–comment, where one speaker makes an observation (*They also have that as ice cream*, which is misheard by another speaker as *crème fraîche*, thus in fact shifting the topic), which is responded to by a series of comments (e.g., *It's great*, *That is the best*).[5] Besides evaluative adjectives (*great*, *the best*), a number of other evaluative and emphatic devices are used. *I love it, I love it* in turn 76 is an explicit marker of affect (as defined by Biber and Finegan 1989), of which there are only a few in the whole corpus (this is the only instance of the verb *love*). Other similar devices used are exclamations (*Oh! Wow!*), hyperbole (*I could kill for that*) and humour (the comment that eating such things will cause a *triple by-pass*). All these are emphatic markers of subjective stance, devices which were also frequent in conflictual discourse (see Section 6.3.2), the difference being that here they are used for positive evaluation and agreement.

In addition to such emphatic markers of subjective stance (underlined), the discourse is characterized by frequent overlaps and latching, emphatic stress and high key pitch (arrow up: ↑), as well as a great deal of laughter, all of which create a highly involved form of interaction. Speakers also repeat their own and each other's words (e.g., the repetition of *crème fraîche* in turns 71 and 72), which are solidarity strategies showing involvement and convergence (see Tannen 1989 and Zhang 1998).

As exemplified in this encounter, non-transactional genres characteristically show a particularly strong relational orientation of the speakers towards solidarity through the use of such markers and devices expressing affect and involvement. But in addition to building solidarity, relational discourse like this also gives participants the opportunity for self-presentation. The hilarity in this encounter is produced by the information that the French eat chestnut butter (very sweet and high in calories) together with whipped cream – a preposterous notion in a fat-conscious North American society. By laughing together about this strange foreign custom the participants bond and invoke common ground; but at the same time, they are able to display their knowledge of French food, thereby building up identities of themselves as cosmopolitan and knowledgeable of European culture.

It is also interesting to examine where relational stretches of talk occur in relation to other genres. Relational talk and relational episodes occur in the course of all sorts of generic activities (e.g., briefing, decision-making, service encounters). However, making arrangements does seem to be followed particularly frequently by relational talk, often at or towards the end of a longer encounter in which a series of tasks have been dealt with. This may be because making arrangements, with its orientation towards the future, is a task that is typically done last, as observed by Schegloff and Sacks (1973: 317), who note that making arrangements is often a component of closing sequences. Once participants have accomplished this final task, they may feel more at liberty to engage in small talk, which is a typical encounter-final element (see Section 7.3.1 below on phatic communion).

7.3 Relational talk in transactional discourse

In addition to entire conversations or independent segments of talk which consist entirely of office gossip or small talk, non-transactional talk sometimes occurs in the middle of transactional business, thus involving a temporary switch out of that genre. Such 'relational episodes', which occur during transactional talk, can be distinguished from 'phatic communion' – the ritual small talk which frequently occurs at the beginning and/or end of an encounter.

7.3.1 *Phatic communion*

As observed by Holmes and Stubbe (2003: 90), small talk in workplace discourse typically occurs as phatic communion 'at the boundaries of interaction'. Nevertheless, as Laver (1975) points out, such phatic exchanges do not necessarily occur in every encounter. The presence or absence of phatic communion depends on a number of factors, for example whether or not the participants have already spoken to each other that day. In the course of a day, co-workers may have frequent contact with one another, for example if they work in the same office. Phatic exchanges are more likely if one of the speakers has to enter and leave the other's workspace in order to engage in conversation. Co-workers who share the same physical space do not necessarily need to open up or close down conversations, but may remain in a constant state of potential engagement, for example speaking to each other in single adjacency pairs or short sequences separated by silences. The day of the week or the time of year also seems to influence the presence of phatic elements, for example upcoming or past weekends or public holidays may be brought into the conversation. This phenomenon illustrates the highly deictic nature of phatic communion (see Laver 1975: 222–3), as evident in the topics chosen by speakers in the phatic phases, which involve deictic reference to the physical environment (e.g., the weather), to time (the time of day and the recent past or near future) and to self or other (e.g., health and well-being). Some of these characteristics of phatic communion are illustrated in Examples 4.4 and 4.5.

Laver (ibid.) proposes that speakers *do* engage in phatic communion when the roles they will play in the encounter are not clearly defined in advance. Data from the ABOT Corpus provide evidence that phatic communion is most likely to occur when the speakers' *relational* roles are not well established. In the few encounters between strangers (all service encounters) there are no phatic exchanges, as the participants rely on their pre-established transactional roles (server and servee) and do not attempt to build a relationship. Co-workers who have contact on a daily basis do not need to preface all encounters with small talk, as they already have an established relationship. On the other hand, people who do not work together on a regular basis need to spend more time on relationship-building in their occasional encounters, and it is in conversations between people in this group that phatic communion occurs most. A good example of this in the corpus can be found in a meeting between a supplier and a customer, who rarely see each other face to face. While the phatic phases of most encounters consist of short sequences, sometimes just a single adjacency pair, in this meeting the initial small talk takes up 18 turns (the longest in the corpus) and the closing phase 8 turns. This reflects a greater effort on the part of the participants to establish a relationship, and is evidence of the high value placed on good relationships for the achievement of transactional goals.

7.3.2 Relational episodes

Relational episodes are defined as short sequences of non-transactional talk occurring in the middle of (rather than before or after) a transactional encounter, and thus involve a temporary switch out of the transactional genre being performed. This is often occasioned through interruption by a third party, but may also be initiated by the speakers involved in the performance of a workplace task. Why should speakers choose to engage in relational talk in the middle of performing a workplace task? While there may be many reasons for this, analysis of a number of such episodes shows that they do not necessarily have a purely relational or social function, but can also play a role in the performance of the task at hand.

A good example of this occurs in an American advertising company in which two colleagues, Chris and Amy, both senior managers, are trying to come up with a solution to a problem with their accounting, for which Amy is responsible. There is a longer interruption towards the beginning of the encounter which is caused by a colleague, Becky, entering the office to inform Amy of some urgent arrangements to do with UPS coming to pick something up. This then leads onto a story about a mix-up between a UPS and a Federal Express parcel. At the end of the story Becky produces the following comment which is echoed by Amy:

Example 7.2

Becky	Everybody's been having these rough days in the past couple o' (/days/)
Amy	⌊It's been a … rough day.
	(It's been a rough day)

It seems that Becky's summarizing remark gives Amy the opportunity to general-ize and broaden the issue of problems temporarily away from her own particular problem which they have been discussing. After repeating *it's been a rough day*, she then says to Becky:

Example 7.3

Will you close on your freakin' house? I think *that's* been hangin' over all of our heads!

Here Amy refers to a completely unrelated issue – the fact that Becky has been experiencing some problems buying a new house – and humorously implies that this is somehow responsible for her (and others') current problems at work. In this way Amy minimizes her own particular problem by placing it within the context of other problems, and is thereby able to detract attention from her pre-dicament by bringing some small talk into the conversation. The next 15 turns are taken up with small talk about Becky's house, and interestingly, when Amy and Chris resume their discussion of the accounting problem, they enter a new phase of the discourse: Amy now begins to talk about possible solutions. It is as if the interruption and ensuing relational talk provided a catalyst for a turning point in the discussion.

This example shows that relational episodes can serve a particular purpose in the performance of a transactional genre, and that such episodes cannot be consid-ered irrelevant for the workplace task. Other discourse studies of relational talk in institutional contexts have also shown that such talk can play an important role in the achievement of task goals (Iacobucci 1990, N. Coupland and Ylänne-McEwen 2000, Ragan 2000, Holmes and Stubbe 2003). This does not mean, however, that these episodes do not also serve more general relational goals, such as creating involvement and affiliation. The interplay between transactional and relational goals can be multi-layered and complex; as Coupland (2000: 6) remarks 'small talk … cannot be segregated from the "mainstream" concerns of talk at work. It is an intrinsic part of the talk at work complex.'

7.4 Relational sequences and turns

'Relational sequences' or 'relational turns' address some aspect of the task but are not obligatory for the accomplishment of the task. This kind of talk frequently occurred in the corpus in the course of various workplace tasks, and involved discourse units of varying lengths: individual turns (or parts of turns), adjacency pairs or short side sequences. Most frequently they consisted of comments of some kind about the task, usually a positive evaluation, for example:

Example 7.4

| Carol | Okay, Okay, Well it sounds like uh … everything's gone very well. |
| Beth | Yes. The fort has been held down. Hehehehehe |

These comments are made at the end of a meeting after the second speaker, Beth, has finished briefing her boss, Carol, about activities in the office during her absence on a business trip (see also Example 5.15).

Speakers also frequently make humorous remarks such as the second speaker's repartee in the example below:

Example 7.5

Amy	So even if I see you at the marketing task force, and don't have my
	things you won't … have to embarrass me.
Chris	⌊Forgive you anyway yes.

7.4.1 Relational sequences and genre

Relational sequences or turns occur in all transactional genres; in fact there are very few conversations which do not have at least one such turn. They occur particularly frequently in making arrangements, often involving comments on the importance of accomplishing the task, as we shall see in the analysis below of two (out of ten) conversations involving arrangements. This, as well as the fact that making arrangements is often followed by extended small talk (as we saw earlier), provides some evidence that speakers are more relationally oriented when making arrangements than when performing some other transactional genres.

Besides arrangements, no other genres stand out as having comparatively more relational sequences; however, particular types of relational element can be observed in certain genres. A specific type of relational turn or turn unit occurs in some procedural, and most requesting discourse. In these genres, the participants being given instructions or being granted a request frequently show their appreciation with comments such as

- *Great!*
- *Oh wonderful!*
- *Super!*

These all involve the use of evaluative adjectives, which are often markers of interpersonal involvement and solidarity. As such comments are always the second part of an adjacency pair (that is they involve reacting or responding to a previous utterance), the 'slot' in which they occur is not optional. In procedural discourse, acknowledging that instructions have been understood can be considered an obligatory element of this genre. However, as the corpus evidence shows, it is optional for speakers to produce such interpersonal markers in this slot rather than simple tokens of acknowledgement. Compare, for example, the following two extracts (acknowledging turns are underlined):

Example 7.6 (a)

1   Ann   Uh:m ... *that* is for the Save the Earth stuff, and ... I will– it will
             eventually probably get thrown awa:y, but ... if you haven't come
             across a packing list for Save the Earth products? =
2   Meg   = <u>Okay,</u>
3   Ann   = hang onto it.
4   Meg   <u>Okay.</u>

Example 7.6 (b)

1   Beth   you can order them, and they'll come by the van, in about a week.
2   Judy   [<u>That's how you *do* it</u>
3   Judy   <u>O::h. Not ba:d. I should know how to do this.</u>

(Example 7.6 b from the Cambridge International Corpus
© Cambridge University Press)

In Example 7.6a, the instructions are acknowledged with the repetition of the minimal response token *okay* (see Gardner 1997); whereas in Example 7.6b, the response is much more elaborate. In addition to an evaluative adjective, spoken with emphatic stress (*not **ba:d***), Judy shows her appreciation in summarizing the instructions in turn 2 (overlapping with Beth's turn) with emphatic stress (*that's how you **do** it*) and makes a self-evaluative comment in turn 3 (*I should know how to do this*). These observations are consistent with McCarthy's and Carter's (2000) and McCarthy's (2003) findings that non-minimal response tokens often serve interactive and affective discourse functions.

However, such markers of appreciation only occur in procedural discourse where the person receiving instructions or directives is higher in the institutional hierarchy or, if lower, is nevertheless a senior member of staff (e.g., a manager). Junior members of staff or trainees do not respond to instructions in this way, but merely acknowledge them with a back-channel signal like *okay* (as in Example 7.6a). This is probably because instruction-giving is what is expected of supervisors or superiors. It is part of their job to train new employees and tell their subordinates what to do, and this does not warrant any special appreciation.

In the case of the instruction-giver being a superior, relational sequences pertaining to the understanding of the instructions occasionally occur, e.g.:

Example 7.7 (a)

Ben   Alright, but you're sort of– getting the … getting the drift of it yeah,

Example 7.7 (b)

Meg   Yeah. an' I immediately forgot everything you told me about–
Ann   ⌊That's okay.

The first example is a closing remark made by a manager to his junior employee at the end of a training session and its function seems to be to check not only the new employee's understanding of the immediate task, but also whether he is coping in general. The second example consists of an adjacency pair, which can be analysed as apology–acceptance (Meg, who is being trained for a new task, effectively apologizes for not remembering some instructions she has already been given). Similar to the other examples above, turns/adjacency pairs like this seem to perform primarily a relational function: to reassure the trainee in coping with a new task.

7.4.2 The place of relational sequences in transactional genres

But how do such relational sequences and turns fit together with the transactional elements of the genre being performed, and where do they occur? This section provides an analysis of three encounters and tries to answer the question of how and where relational sequences occur during task-oriented talk, as well as proposing some initial observations about the role of such talk within transactional encounters.

Requesting

The first extract is from a longer one-to-one meeting which takes place in the editorial offices of an American publisher. The two speakers, Beth and Judy, are editors who work together on a regular basis. Judy has a more senior position than Beth, but is not her immediate boss. Judy has recently returned from a posting in Tokyo, a circumstance which is frequently referred to in this and other encounters (see Example 6.6). The genre is requesting action, as here Beth asks Judy to sign some reprint forms. The whole requesting episode, which involves two separate requests, takes up 38 turns, but the transactional elements of the genre (making the requests, giving details and background information regarding the actions requested, performing the actions) only make up the bare bones of the talk exchanged (20 turns), and are 'fleshed out' with relational talk. This is illustrated in Example 7.8 below, which shows the first half of the conversation (the different phases of the discourse are labelled, and the transactional phases highlighted in bold):

Example 7.8 'Requesting a signature'

Request	1	Beth	Oh you know what. While you're here, can you sign off on the reprint card?
Accept	2	Judy	⌊Yeah.
Relational	3	Beth	Because that would certainly help.
sequence	4	Judy	⌊I hope what I'm /saying ?/ makes sense I mean hehehe
	5	Beth	⌊Hmm?
	6	Judy	For a couple of months, I feel like I just *started* this *job*?
	7	Beth	⌊No. I know, I know, Well Judy, you're in a comp*le*tely different country now,
	8	Judy	⌊I *know*.
	9	Beth	And ...
	10	Judy	⌊I feel like this is a brand new job though. I was like Oh yeah reprints.
	11	Beth	⌊Yeah.

	12	Beth	Well in a way it doesn't get like o:ld you know
	13	Judy	⌊Hehehehe
	14	Beth	like *o:ld* same old thing because it's something *new.*
	15	Judy	⌊Ri::ght ⌊I kno:w
Details/	16	Beth	Okay. so let's see. This is for the student's book, a:nd you
background			know, it was funny, Carol signed off on it? But we didn't
information			even know what qual– quantity /we wanted to have/?
	17	Judy	⌊O:h okay,
	18	Beth	So I mean I wouldn't pay that much attention to that.
Performing	19	Judy	⌊/I'll just sign/
action	20	Beth	You wanna sign right over there, ⌊Judy: Yeah⌋ and I'll
			put in twenty … uh twenty-six thousand will do.
	21	Judy	And today is seven …
	22	Beth	Today is seven fifteen, … ninety-seven.
	23	Judy	⌊seven
	24	Beth	Yeah.
	25	Judy	Okay,

(from the Cambridge International Corpus © Cambridge University Press)

Dividing up the discourse in this way shows that the relational talk is fitted in-between the transactional phases of the genre. The same pattern is repeated again with a second request. Almost half of the discourse is taken up with relational talk which has some relevance for the task, but is certainly not obligatory for its accomplishment. Nevertheless, relational sequences must be seen by the participants to be relevant to the task at hand. Beth's comment in turn 3, *because that would certainly help*, has a relational orientation, as it shows appreciation for Judy's role in the task, but it is also of immediate relevance for the activity they are engaged in, and in fact provides an account for the request. However, when Judy responds in turn 4 *I hope what I'm /saying ?/ makes sense* … Beth does not immediately understand the relevance of this remark and queries it with *Hmm?* in turn 5. Judy then explains what she means in the next turn: *for a couple of months, I feel like I just started this job*, which leads to an extended relational sequence. The relevance of Judy's remarks in turns 4 and 6 at this point in the encounter, when she has just been asked to perform a task, seems to be to express concern about her ability to perform this (and other) tasks adequately after her long absence. She thereby provides an account for any potential problems prior to carrying out the requested task, and Beth responds with affiliation:

6	Judy	For a couple of months, I feel like I just *star*ted this *job?*
7	Beth	⌊No. I know, I know,
		Well Judy, you're in a com*ple*tely different country now,

Beth repeatedly shows affiliation and solidarity in both relational sequences by sympathizing and reassuring her, for example by emphasizing the positive aspect of feeling unused to the job:

12/14   Well in a way it doesn't get like o:ld you know like *o:ld* same old
            thing because it's something *new*.

Later in the conversation, she also expresses her appreciation of Judy as a colleague by remarking that this task is easier now that Judy is back:

It's so nice that you can sign off on these now because hehehe in the past it was– it was harder

With this remark, Beth also emphasizes the important role Judy fulfils in performing the task, and thus she highlights the significance of the activity in which they are engaged. As we have already seen in Example 6.6, Judy's long absence probably explains the unusually high incidence of relational talk in this and other encounters.

Making arrangements

The next two encounters involve arrangements, a genre in which relational sequences are particularly frequent. The first encounter is from the American university data and shows two speakers, Don, who works in the office of a graduate school, and John, a maintenance man, making arrangements about some cleaning. As with the last example, the transactional and relational phases of the encounter are labeled, the former in bold:

Example 7.9 'Arranging cleaning'

Greeting:	1	Don	Hi.
phatic	2	John	Hi.
			[1]
Pre-	3	John	Uhm ... just checking out the: uh ... / ? steps/ for–
arrangement			tomorrow
	4	Don	⌊Yea:h. That– that's still the current schedule,
			although it's gonna change over the– /?/ over the next
			couple of weeks (before school starts again)
	5	John	Yeah (Uhu that's /???/)
Making	6	John	Okay. I just need to: ... uh you know tomorrow
arrangement			night, do the ... dining hall and the small dining room
			to clean the carpet .(/so ?? for that./)

	7	Don	I don't think you got a problem there, an' there's nothing in the book?
	8	John	Nothing in here, =
	9	Don	= Then you're all set
	10	John	(/with that/)

Finalizing arrangement

Pre-	11	Don	But I'd like to mark it for you =
finalizing	12	John	⌊/I'll uh–/
Relational	13	John	= I was gonna say–
sequence	14	Don	⌊so that nothing … *goes* in
	15	John	⌊Yeah
	16	John	Yeah we're thinking together on that. I just … considered it.

Finalizing/	17	John	So Tuesday night Don, it's– when I need to be in there,
specifying	18	Don	After what time.
arrange-	19	John	I would say after five o'clock?
ment	20	Don	five … on?
	21	John	five on yup,
	22	Don	And then uh … refectory.
	23	John	Yes sir.
			[1.5]
Relational	24	Don	That– that uh … (is like a little insurance)
sequence	25	John	Yeah. /Oh yeah it's easy /to get all these–
	26	Don	(Keep it straight) Yeah.
	27	John	(/Yeah/)
			[1: John moves towards door]
Pre-closing:	28	John	You get confused enough around here.
Relational	29	Don	Heheheh [1] Especially this stuff. [1] This– you know … this *job*. Of all the *jobs*. This is the one where the *least* little error will come back to haunt you.
sequence			
Closing	30	John	Uh-huh?
	31	Don	(/Yeah/)

The relational sequences all involve positive evaluations of the task, which are not obligatory for the accomplishment of this genre. Whereas in the last encounter analysed, such sequences were fitted in between the transactional phases, here the first one (turns 13–16) occurs during the phase of finalizing arrangements. Clearly this has to do with the sequential nature of talk: after Don's announcement (turn 11) that he would like to confirm the arrangements in writing, an agreement by John that this is a good idea (turns 13 and 16) is a relevant next action, even if it is not obligatory. Don's preliminary remark includes an account of why the finalizing phase is important (*so that nothing goes in*), and John's ensuing relational turns involve affiliating with this account (*we're thinking together on that*). This is similar to the pattern of account-affiliation observed in the relational sequence in Example 7.8 above. In conversation analytical terms, turns 11–16 can be analysed as a pre-sequence: a sequence which is preliminary to some subsequent discursive action, in this case finalizing the arrangements (see Schegloff 1980 and Levinson 1983: 345–64). Here John uses this structural 'slot' (the presequence) for relational purposes.

The other two relational sequences occur towards the end of the encounter: the first one (turns 24–7) immediately after finalizing the task, and the next one, after a brief pause as John walks towards the door, as a pre-closing sequence (28–9) before the closing exchange (30–1). In both these sequences the speakers summarize and positively evaluate the task just accomplished[6] using idioms:

26　　　　(Keep it straight) Yeah.
29　　　　the *least* little error <u>will come back to haunt you</u>.

Schegloff and Sacks (1973) note that proverbial formulations can be used as topic-bounding techniques to close down conversations, especially 'monotopical' ones like this. As we saw in Section 5.6, idioms are frequently used as summarizing devices at the end of a segment of discourse. By summarizing and positively evaluating the whole encounter, the speakers can bring the encounter to a mutually satisfactory conclusion; thus such sequences perform a function very similar to encounter-final phatic communion – ritual small talk occurring at the end of an encounter. One place, therefore, where relational sequences are likely to occur is after the accomplishment of a task, as the last phase of the genre, especially if it is also the end of the encounter.

The second conversation involving arrangements is from a British university office and occurs towards the end of an encounter between Liz, the department secretary, and Jim, a professor. Here, Jim wants to arrange a meeting with Liz about a journal for which he is editor. The same obligatory phases for making arrangements occur as in the last encounter analysed, but the relational sequences do not all occur in the same place, as can be seen in the extract below of the first part of the conversation:

Example 7.10 'Journal meeting'

Making	1	Jim I was wondering if … you an' I could *possibly* this
arrangement		week, at about eleven o'clock on Thursday morning,
(proposing)		*rei*nforce each other half an hour on– just to *look*
		through [name of journal] and see where we are.

Relational	2	Liz ⌊Yes it's— it's on my mind *terribly*, in fact
sequence	3	Jim ⌊yeah
	4	Liz I've been dreaming about it all night.
	5	Jim Well *I* had a dream about it as *well*.
	6	Liz ⌊So—
	7	Liz I've got to get i— because it's on my mind so much I—
	8	Jim ⌊It's funny ⌊a really guilty conscience
		about it =
	9	Liz = Yes, I am, so I *must* … get on and do it.
Making	10	Liz So yes, Thursday at eleven will be fine.
arrangement	11	Jim ⌊Heheheh
(accepting)		
Finalizing/	12	Jim Ok, we'll just review where we are: an' …
specifying		what's … urgent and what's um …
arrangement	13	Liz ⌊yeah um
	14	Jim perhaps not so urgent to do.
	15	Liz Ok. […]

Here the two parts of the core phase in this genre – making the arrangement – are interrupted by a relational sequence: Jim proposes a meeting in turn 1, but Liz does not agree to this proposal until turn 10. From turns 2–9, the two speakers remark on how this matter has been on their minds so much that they have been dreaming about it. This can be analysed as a side sequence (see Jefferson 1972 and Schegloff 1972), where the second pair part of an adjacency pair is delayed by intervening turns. The function of this side sequence seems to be for the participants to demonstrate how urgent they both feel the proposed meeting is. Thus, prior to responding to Jim's proposal, Liz demonstrates in turn 2 (*it's on my mind terribly*) that she has understood something *implied* in his initial utterance which is not obvious from the actual wording – that is, the urgency of the meeting.

Again, the relational sequence follows a pattern similar to previous examples: the urgency of the meeting, which is the theme of the side sequence, provides an account – a justification for arranging the meeting, which is followed by affiliation. In commenting (in turn 2) on how this matter has been on her mind, Liz shows that she understands the meeting is urgent (and even overdue, thereby providing an account); by remarking that he feels the same, Jim shows affiliation with her, which is reflected in the manner in which he mirrors her utterances (key phrases are underlined):

4	Liz	I've been dreaming about it all night
5	Jim	Well I had a dream about it as *well*

7   Liz   I've got to get i– because <u>it's on my mind so much</u> I–
8   Jim   It's funny   <u>a really guilty conscience about it</u>

Jim uses echoing and repetition as an involvement strategy that communicates solidarity: in turn 5 he uses almost the same wording as Liz, and then in turn 8 he produces a synonymous expression.

The conversation between Liz and Jim then moves on to a few other workplace matters, but the arrangements are returned to at the end:

Example 7.11

Pre-closing: 24 Jim [...] Yeah um– let's let's come up to date and uh ... um ...
Transactional 25 Liz By Thursday.
(summarizing) 26 Jim By Thursday.
                27 Liz Thursday at eleven. Brilliant =
                28 Jim = Let's see where we are and what's doing ... an' ... you know what needs ... urgent attention
                29 Liz Yes. /?/ smashing.
Relational   30 Jim I– it's funny, *I* dreamt about it as well last night yeah
(commenting)

As in the other arrangement-making encounter, there are relational elements in the pre-closing phase of the encounter (there is no closing exchange here, as Jim does not immediately leave the room): Liz uses two adjectives which positively evaluate the task accomplished (*brilliant, smashing*), embedded within the transactional summarizing phase, where the arrangements made are reiterated (turns 24–9); and Jim then produces a relational turn (30) which echoes the dream theme of the earlier relational sequence. In summarizing the arrangements, Jim makes explicit reference to the urgency of the meeting by using the words *urgent attention* which seems to confirm that the function of the relational side sequence is to highlight this urgency. As in the two previous encounters, relational sequences not only provide an opportunity to express solidarity and so contribute to a positive working relationship, but more specifically allow participants to demonstrate why the task is important, thereby ascribing meaning to their activity.

The above examples show that *where* relational sequences occur within transactional genres is extremely flexible. One place where relational sequences do tend to occur is towards the end of an encounter, and here they perform a function similar to phatic communion: bringing the encounter to a felicitous conclusion. But in these examples, relational sequences also occurred in other parts of the encounter: in 'Requesting a signature' (Example 7.8), they were placed in between the transactional phases, but in the other two encounters, which involve arrangements (Examples 7.9–11), some also occurred in the middle of a phase. In these encounters, relational talk occurred in pre-sequences and side sequences, which indicates that these may be conversational structures that lend themselves to the development of relational talk (but more conversations would need to be investigated). Furthermore, in all the encounters, and in a number of others in the corpus, relational sequences involve the production of accounts, followed by affiliation from the interlocutor. This is perhaps not so surprising, as the literature on accounts shows they are frequently used for relational purposes (see Iacobucci 1990: 87).

The interweaving of relational talk into transactional genres confirms two opposing characteristics of spoken discourse. The fact that relational sequences can occur seemingly at any time is evidence for the sequential organization of talk: as conversation analysts have frequently pointed out, the immediate talk-intrinsic context of an utterance is relevant for the 'next action'. Thus, a relational turn or sequence can occur at virtually any point in the discourse, as long as it is seen as relevant in some way to the task at hand. On the other hand, the fact that participants find their way through the phases of the genre and do not leave out any of the obligatory features, in spite of the diversions of relational sequences, shows that they are following some kind of global script and are orienting to generic structure.

However, it would be a mistake to see such relational sequences as mere diversions: as we have seen, they perform important relational functions relative to the immediate task as well as in terms of the working relationship in general. Some of the functions of relational talk in task-oriented workplace talk will now be explored in some more detail.

7.4.3 The functions of relational talk in transactional genres

Relational sequences and accounts

As observed in the relational sequences analysed so far, accounts seem to occur frequently within or as triggers of relational talk. Scott and Lyman (1968: 46) define accounts as 'statements made to explain untoward behavior and bridge the gap between actions and expectations'. In the extracts examined so far, the 'untoward behaviour' justified in accounts is fairly mild: in 'Requesting a signature' (Example 7.8), the fact that Judith feels unused to the duties of her job after a long absence (*I feel like I just started this job*), and in 'Journal meeting' (Examples 7.10–11) that the meeting was not arranged sooner. In 'Arranging cleaning' (Example 7.9) and 'Journal meeting' (Examples 7.10–11) the accounts also explain why the task is important, thereby validating its performance. However, there are some examples of relational sequences in the data where accounts *are* used to justify or excuse the failure to meet expectations. One such example occurs in a meeting between the president of a small American advertising company, Chris, and his sales manager, Joe, in which Joe reports to Chris about activities in his department during the week. This particular stretch of talk begins with a critical remark from Chris about poor sales this week:

Example 7.12

1 Chris Haven't seen much in the way of *sales* the last half of the week.
2 Joe   .hh Well, a lot of the media, the— the orders have been *very* difficult getting out. Stuff is— is jammed.
3 Chris Oh they didn't go out?
4 Joe   *Yeah.* Jane's orders are *clog*ged. And … trying to get out heheh
5 Chris   ⌊Heheh   ⌊clogged orders!
6 Joe   Clogged orders! .hh they can't get out o' the system.
7 Chris ⌊Oh no!

Joe produces an account to justify the low level of sales in turns 2 and 4 by describing orders they have been unable to process as *jammed* and *clogged*. This leads to a relational sequence in which both speakers quip and laugh about this description of orders as *clogged*. As in the other examples, Chris honours Joe's account by showing affiliation and alignment with him in a relational sequence.

In Example 7.12, as well as in other examples in the data, the account and subsequent affiliation are done in a non-serious, joking frame. Why should this be so? Here Joe has to deal with a potentially problematic situation: he has to defend himself against a fairly serious criticism – that his department has not delivered the expected number of sales. Doing an account seriously and 'on-record' in situations like this can be face-threatening or even 'job-threatening' (in the case of Joe). Humour and relational talk (like idioms – see Section 6.2) provide speakers with an opportunity of dealing with a difficult or awkward situation without losing face. As humorous claims are deniable (Eggins and Slade 1997: 156), they can be used by speakers to express meaning indirectly in order to protect their own and their interlocutors' face.

Identity negotiation

Relational sequences can also be used by participants for identity negotiation. The following example is again from the American advertising company and involves a meeting between Chris, the president, and Mike, his circulation manager responsible for the company's publications. The genre is procedural/directive discourse, with Chris giving Mike some guidelines for a procedure to keep a record of how quickly he deals with requests (see also Examples 3.13–15). A number of relational turns or sequences occur from turns 6–14 while Chris and Mike are discussing the details of the procedure:

Example 7.13

1 Mike   So what if the request comes ... uh ... by e-mail at the end of a day, on Monday, and I don't even see it until ...

2 Chris   I don't know how were you– how were you gonna keep this before.

3 Mike   (Uh that's a good point) Okay. So I'll ... so I'll just– ignore time ... between ... me leaving and– hehehe an' me coming in. [3] ↓Okay.

4 Chris   /??/ Like-   ⌊So– yeah. /???/.

5 Mike   ⌊So– so a request at five p.m. an'and an' I– complete it at nine the next day that's one hour

6 Chris   Right. Hahahahahahahahah .hh No I think hehehehehhehehehe

7 Mike   ⌊Right

8 Mike   What? [2] What?

9 Chris   Yes correct. That's not a– that's not a: uh twenty-hour waiter. Yes heheh yes

10 Mike   [mock-whiny voice] I'm sorry but I had to sleep first and eat breakfast

11 Chris   ⌊Heheheh

12 Chris   [mock-whiny voice] ↑ I do– I do that almost every day!

13 Mike   ⌊Hehehehe

14 Chris   (Heheheh)

15 Mike   Okay. An' we decided [...]

At this point in the discussion (turns 1–5), Mike is trying to establish what he should enter in his log if he receives a request in the evening and does not deal with it until the next morning – he is trying to make sure he does not need to count the time in between. But instead of replying 'seriously' to the query, Chris starts laughing in turn 6, which marks a shift into a relational mode via an abrupt frame switch that disorients Mike (turn 8: *What?* [2] *What?*), as he does not immediately interpret this response as relevant to his query. Chris then returns to a serious transactional frame in turn 9 to confirm that this would indeed not be considered *a 20-hour waiter* (meaning a 20-hour waiting period or interval). Mike then joins in the joke, and both speakers engage in a brief relational sequence from turns 10–14, signalled by a clear frame switch: a mock-whiny tone of voice and laughter. The reason for Chris's laughter at this point seems to be that he sees as ludicrous the implication of what Mike says in turns 1–5: that if he does not deal with a request that comes in the evening until the next morning, this might be counted as a delay. By suggesting this, Mike seems to assign Chris the identity of an authoritarian, unreasonable boss. Chris's laughter may be due to his not feeling comfortable with such an identity. By switching to a relational, joking frame, he apparently attempts to reduce this asymmetry and establish a more equal relationship. The fact that he adopts the same mock-whiny voice as Mike is an indication that he is trying to align himself on a more equal footing with his employee.

The function of the relational sequence thus seems to be identity negotiation. Schenkein (1978) discusses the use of side sequences by insurance salesmen to delay responding to a first formulation in order to negotiate some aspect of their identity. Notice that a similar delay occurs here when Chris starts laughing in turn 6 instead of responding to Mike's query. The identities negotiated here are clearly associated with the genre being performed – procedural/directive discourse. Not only is Chris Mike's boss, but within this discourse frame, his role is to give Mike directives. The relational sequence arises out of this frame and the corresponding discursive (as well as institutional) identities, and in fact involves joking *about* these. It plays an important role in balancing conflicting transactional and relational goals in a particularly delicate situation – the evaluation of a subordinate by his boss.

Relational sequences can also reinforce, rather than challenge, institutional roles, for example when a manager checks whether the new employee he is training is coping (see Example 7.7 above):

Ben   Alright, but you're sort of– getting the … getting the drift of it yeah,

By expressing concern for how the employee is coping, Ben underlines his responsibility as manager and trainer for the well-being of new staff.

The analysis of the above extracts has shown that relational sequences can have important, quite specific functions for the performance of a transactional genre. Coupland (2000: 18–22) also identifies such a function of relational talk for transactional goals in showing that 'small talk' in doctor–geriatric patient consultations plays a significant role in informing the judgements the doctor makes during the consultation.

The specific functions of relational sequences identified in the extracts analysed can be summarized as follows:

- contributing to a positive working relationship by showing affiliation and solidarity
- demonstrating why the task is important, and thereby validating its performance
- performing a discursive action (e.g., an account) indirectly and thus avoiding or defusing awkward or conflictual situations
- negotiating institutional and discursive identities.

These are of course not the only functions that such relational sequences can perform in transactional workplace talk. Holmes and Stubbe (2003: 87–107), for example, show that small talk may also be used in workplace discourse to exercise or resist power in subtle ways.

7.5 Conclusion

The analysis has shown that relational talk cannot be neatly separated from transactional talk, but is found at all levels of workplace discourse, and can occur virtually at any time. Although there were notable differences from office to office in the amount of office gossip and small talk engaged in, there were no venues in which some longer stretches of non-transactional talk did not occur. Although there are few longer deviations from task goals, at least some relational elements are present in nearly every encounter, and the analysis shows that relational talk can potentially occur in each of the genres investigated.

It was more difficult to establish systematic links between genre and relational talk. There does seem to be a close association between making arrangements and relational talk, both in terms of the frequent sequential proximity of arrangements and small talk, as well as in the particularly high frequency of relational episodes and sequences in making arrangements. Particular types of relational sequence or turn were also found in certain genres, for example appreciative remarks in procedural and requesting discourse.

A recurring pattern of relational sequences across a range of genre types was that of account followed by affiliation. It seems that accounts, as evaluative comments on the task either in terms of its significance or as an excuse for some shortcoming, do frequently have a relational function and lend themselves to the development of relational talk. In the data, relational sequences were also found in pre-sequences, prefiguring an obligatory phase of the genre, and in side sequences which are both micro-structures identified by conversation analysts as typical features of talk. Whereas the CA literature has concentrated, for example, on misapprehension sequences, which occur because clarification of some kind is needed before a second pair part can be produced, the evidence in the data examined here suggests that the primary function of some side sequences may be relational. In a larger corpus more such regularities might well be discovered.

Certain regularities were also observed in the placement of relational elements: relational sequences, like phatic communion, frequently occurred after the completion of a task and towards the end of an encounter. However, the most important conclusion to be drawn from the analysis may be that because of participants' constant attention to relational goals, relational elements may occur at almost any time when they are sequentially relevant to the task being performed.

The interviews conducted in the offices showed that participants themselves were aware of the role of relational talk in their work. All the interviewees felt that small talk *did* have a function and was not just trivial, from very general remarks that it 'humanizes the enterprise' to more sophisticated ideas about the role it performed in relation to their work. For example, one speaker felt that small talk was a way of getting informal feedback from co-workers, and another remarked that it was sometimes possible to come up with a solution to a problem during small talk. Such participant input provides important validation for the claims made here regarding the importance of relational talk within workplace discourse.

8 Conclusion

This book has had two main aims: (1) to propose and develop a set of approaches for the analysis of spoken workplace discourse; and (2) to contribute to the description of institutional talk in general, and office talk in particular, in terms of lexico-grammar, genre, and discursive practices.

Throughout this book, an integrated approach to the analysis of workplace discourse has been advocated, and it is my hope that such an approach has also been demonstrated in the analysis of a corpus of office conversations. Two approaches which have been particularly highlighted in this book are genre analysis and corpus-based analysis. Starting with the premise that examining both macro and micro features of interaction provides clues to generic activity, corpus-based methods are a powerful and effective method of examining micro-features of genre at the level of lexico-grammar and phraseology. So, for example, the investigation of interpersonal markers (Chapter 5) showed that different instances of the same genre share similar linguistic characteristic at the local level. Some of the key differences between the different workplace genres investigated were identified by this method. Genre is therefore shown to be a significant factor influencing linguistic choice (see McCarthy 1998 and Biber *et al.* 1999), in addition to other factors, such as social distance and power, which have generally been given more prominence in studies of institutional discourse.

The illustrative study carried out using the ABOT Corpus also demonstrates that valuable insights into language use can be gleaned from a relatively small corpus. Many of the high-frequency items examined in the corpus analysis exhibited similar patterns and tendencies as in larger corpora (e.g., CANCODE, CANBEC and the LSWE Corpus).

But genre analysis and corpus-based analysis should also be combined with a fine-grained analysis of individual interactions. Qualitative methods, such as conversation analysis and interactional sociolinguistics, which focus on the turn-by-turn development of talk, provide useful tools for the analysis of spoken genre, for instance the identification of 'contextualization cues' as signals of generic activity (Chapters 2 and 3). As demonstrated in the two final chapters through the analysis of different interactions, the application of such methods is essential in order to gain an understanding of the strategies used by people working together to pursue both their transactional and their relational goals.

The qualitative analysis of a variety of encounters throughout the book explored the many devices used in the management of discourse participants' sometimes conflicting transactional goals (associated with specific institutional roles) and their goals in building and maintaining relationships with their interlocutors. While institutional role and relative power were certainly shown to be important factors, we saw that the roles and identities taken up in the discourse are also negotiated, and may or may not correspond to the speakers' institutional roles. For example, in the two conflictual encounters analysed in Chapter 6, we saw that speakers' discursive roles were largely at odds with their institutional roles. Furthermore, speakers sometimes invoke identities related to their relational goals which are less asymmetrical than their institutional roles. Relational side sequences, which involve a shift in footing and alignment, are evidence of such identity negotiation.

Using a genre-based approach enabled us to identify a further type of dominance in addition to institutional dominance or asymmetry: discursive dominance. There seemed to be a tendency for dominant speakers in unidirectional genres to try to reduce discursive asymmetry through the use of politeness and solidarity strategies. One might want to speculate that this may indicate some kind of general impetus towards interactional symmetry in dialogic discourse. Perhaps this has something to do with invoking and building 'intersubjectivity', which is the assumption of discourse participants that they 'share a co-conception of the world' (Overstreet and Yule 1997b). Schiffrin (1990) and Schegloff (1992c) have suggested that intersubjectivity is not static but interactively managed, which means that it necessitates the involvement of both discourse participants. Perhaps the efforts of dominant speakers to reduce asymmetry can be seen as an attempt to achieve intersubjectivity.

One of the central themes in this book regarding the nature of workplace interaction, is that we do not find a sharp distinction between 'on-task' transactional talk and relational talk or small talk. As we have seen, not all talk occurring at the workplace is task-focused and speakers do not always orient to their institutional roles. Even when they do focus on task goals, certain aspects of the discourse cannot be explained with reference to the transactional task, but are evidence of their attention to relational goals. Nevertheless, relational talk in workplace contexts is not the same thing as in social contexts. While building solidarity and common ground is often the primary function of relational talk at work, it can also reflect institutional concerns linked for example to power (e.g., in the case of politeness), and may play an important role in terms of the speakers' task goals.

While earlier studies of workplace discourse have usually assumed a fairly sharp distinction between work-oriented talk and 'social talk', more recent studies (e.g., Holmes and Stubbe 2003 and many of the studies in Coupland 2000), have recognized the permeability of this distinction, and have taken an interest in the role of relationally oriented talk at work. This is an encouraging trend, as the interface between transactional and relational talk is an area of enquiry into workplace discourse that promises to be particularly fascinating in terms of the socio-linguistic insights to be gained. Naturally occurring talk at work provides a rich resource for the investigation of interpersonal meaning and of linguistic practices linked to relational goals on the one hand, and transactional goals on the other. As already indicated, another direction for future studies of workplace discourse which promises to yield a more complete description of the data is supplementing more traditional methods, such as genre analysis and conversation analysis, with a corpus-based approach.

Finally, it is fitting to end with at least some discussion of any practical applications that work of the kind reported in this book may have. With the current emphasis on 'soft skills', i.e. on effective communication in the workplace, insights gained from a close analysis of workplace interactions are certainly of practical relevance to the practitioners themselves. Some researchers advocate a collaborative approach, where insights from the research are fed back to the organization which is being studied (see Sarangi and Roberts 1999 and Holmes and Stubbe 2003). In addition to providing feedback to specific organizations as part of the research process, research results from discourse-based studies could also usefully inform staff development training in general. As Cameron (2000: 44) points out, most training in communication skills is based on 'an over-simple understanding of the relation of form and function, coupled with a disregard for the principles of politeness'.

With many years of experience as an ELT practitioner, my own interest is particularly in the applications of research of the kind conducted in this book for language pedagogy, in particular Business English. The interpersonal dimension of language has been largely neglected in the teaching of General and Business English. Even the so-called 'communicative approach' has tended to view communication as a simple exchange of ideational content. As demonstrated time and again in this book, and in a number of other recent studies, the relational dimension of language is an extremely important aspect of spoken interaction, even in business communication. Although some attention is given to small talk and socializing in Business English courses, this tends to be seen as entirely separate from the business side of communication. The pervasiveness of relational elements of talk within all kinds of task-oriented interaction needs to recognized and built into the language teaching syllabus. Furthermore, the emphasis in language courses tends, understandably, to be on clear communication; but, as we have seen, vagueness is a normal feature of consensual talk, even when the focus is on conveying information.

While detailed suggestions for improving language pedagogy are beyond the scope of this book, I would like to suggest that there are four broad areas of interpersonal meaning which are particularly relevant to the language of work, and could therefore usefully be integrated into a General or Business English syllabus:

1 Expressing stance

This involves evaluating, making judgements and expressing opinions, using such linguistic devices as modals, conditionals, idioms and evaluative adjectives, e.g.:

> I think it looks better without, but I'd rather it was on.

As evaluating is central to much transactional workplace talk, especially decision-making, a good repertoire of such language is essential for learners.

2 Hedging and politeness

Here the emphasis is on the relational function of devices like modals, adverbs, vague language and past tense for mitigating and face-saving, e.g.:

> Uh just wanted to come and chat to you a little bit about the company.

3 Showing solidarity

Specific functions here are expressing agreement and positive evaluation (e.g., through evaluative adjectives and idioms) and expressing emotions (e.g., through emotive verbs, such as *like, love*), e.g.:

> You know what Debbie, that's a very good idea.

Solidarity and convergence are also expressed through positive feedback signals (e.g., *Great!*), colloquialisms, slang and humour. While some attention is given to 'politeness' in most language courses, language which expresses relational solidarity does not usually feature in any systematic way in most teaching. It is hoped that the description and analysis of naturally occurring workplace interactions in this book will make some small contribution to teaching and to research on workplace discourse.

Notes

2 Approaches to analysing workplace discourse

1 Labov does not use the term 'genre', but others working within genre analysis have used his model (see Christie 1986, Eggins and Slade 1997).
2 Some of the data now form part of the Cambridge International Corpus (copyright Cambridge University Press). Where such data are quoted, the corpus is acknowledged at the end of the data extract.

3 Pursuing transactional goals

1 See also McCarthy and Handford (2004) on the central role of speculating and hypothesizing in collaborative business talk in general.
2 Reprinted from J. Holmes and M. Stubbe, *Power and Politeness in the Workplace*, London: Pearson Education, 2003: 66, with permission from Pearson Education.
3 Charles and Charles (1999) use the following transcription conventions:
   ...   a recognizable pause
   /   a longer pause
   {}   overlapping speech
   S   seller
   B   buyer
   S2   subordinate negotiator on seller side.
4 Reprinted from M. Charles and D. Charles, 'Sales negotiation: bargaining through tactical summaries', in M. Hewings and C. Nickerson (eds), *Business English: Research into Practice*, Harlow: Longman, 1999: 75–6.
5 *I don't know why this is large*: refers to the question on the list (Figure 3.1) – *You don't mail nationally do you?* – which should not be in bold, as it is another question, not a heading.
6 The *'I was wondering'* approach: Chris means that beginning a sales talk with *I was wondering ...* should be added to the list of 'Conversation stoppers'.

4 Relational goals

1 Poncini (2002) uses the following transcription conventions:
   (.)   short pause under 0.3 seconds
   (+)   pause of about 0.4–0.7 seconds
   (++)   pause of about 0.8–1.7 seconds

(( )) contextual information.

2 Reprinted from G. Poncini, 'Investigating discourse at business meetings with multi-cultural participation', *International Review of Applied Linguistics* 40 (2002): 361.

5 A corpus-based comparison of workplace genres

1 Unless otherwise indicated, the canonical form refers to all lemmas of the verb, e.g., *will* refers to *will, 'll* and *won't*.

2 For a discussion of how to distinguish between lexical and modal uses of *think* and *know* see Halliday (1994: 354) and Koester 2001, Chapter 4.

3 See McCarthy and Handford (2004) for results for *need (to)* in the CANBEC (Business) Corpus.

4 Although grammatically speaking, *want* is a lexical verb and *want to* a quasi-modal. These two forms were not examined separately as they express the same range of modal meanings.

5 Similar uses of *can* in directives in institutional discourse were found by Farr (2005, Chapter 7) and Pufahl Bax (1986).

6 For a more detailed discussion of the types of items included in the category of 'vague language' see Koester 2001.

7 Note that the indirect formulation of the supplier's intention as an idiom (*get your troops to give us a shot*) also functions as a mitigator (see Chapter 6).

8 However, there is some overlap here with research on metaphor in discourse, for example Bargiela-Chiappini and Harris 1997a have looked at metaphors used in business meetings (see also Koller 2004 for work on metaphor in written business discourse, and L. Cameron 2002 and 2003, and L. Cameron and Low 2004 on metaphor in educational discourse).

9 See also McCarthy (1991: 82–4) for further examples of idioms in problem-solution patterns.

6 Negotiating consensus and conflict in workplace talk

1 Other studies of blue-collar contexts also have found imperatives to be the preferred form of instructional discourse (see Weigel and Weigel 1985, Bernsten 1998).

2 McCarthy and Handford (2004) also found that *we* was frequently used with a relational face-saving function in directives and requests in the one-million-word CANBEC Corpus (see Chapter 2).

3 As Jefferson (1972) and other conversation analysts have shown, side sequences represent breaks from, but not termination of, a current activity: the expectation that a second pair part will be produced to match the initial first pair part holds throughout the side sequence. Thus Paul becomes more and more frustrated that the second pair part (Sam admitting to his mistake) is not forthcoming.

4 Ervin-Tripp (1976: 36) and Holmes and Stubbe (2003: 37–8) also found that more indirect language occurred in directives to new employees.

5 *Well* often prefaces a disagreement because, as Schiffrin (1987) observes, it is used when a response is not fully consonant with prior discourse. *I mean* signals some kind of modification in speaker intention and can therefore be used, as here, to change the frame of the discourse (ibid.).

6 Muntigl and Turnbull (1998) call this type of disagreement an 'irrelevancy claim', as it challenges the relevancy of the other speaker's claim; they propose that it is the most 'face-aggravating' type of disagreement.

7 Switching to high key (or higher pitch) marks the utterance as contrastive to what came before (Coulthard and Brazil 1981), and therefore often signals a new discourse phase.

8 Although idioms may be used for the purpose of expressing opinions more indirectly, they can nevertheless be considered to be emphatic markers of subjective stance, because of their evaluative function in discourse, and the fact they are marked items which draw attention to themselves (see Section 5.6). It clearly also depends on the idiom chosen.

9 Density shows the proportion of the text made up of emphatic markers. This is calculated by dividing the number of emphatic markers by the total number of words in the text, and expressing this as a percentage.

7 Relational talk in workplace interactions

1 Parts of this chapter are reprinted from A. Koester, 'Relational sequences in workplace genres', *Journal of Pragmatics* 36 (2004): 1405–28, with permission from Elsevier.

2 See also Holmes and Stubbe's (2003, Chapter 5) examination of the distribution and function of small talk in the New Zealand Language in the Workplace (LWP) database.

3 See also King and Sereno (1984) on the effect of relationship history on communication.

4 Although it does not address the issue of relational talk, Goodwin's (1995) comparative study of 'front regions' (where servers are in contact with the public) and 'back regions' shows the important influence of the physical environment on the discourse.

5 See McCarthy (1998: 140–3) for other examples of observation–comment genre in conversation.

6 Such 'encounter evaluations' were also found by N. Coupland (1983: 472) in travel agency discourse.

Bibliography

Adolphs, S. and Carter, R. (2003) 'And she's like "it's terrible like": spoken discourse, grammar and corpus analysis', *International Journal of English Studies* 3, 1: 45–56.

Aijmer, K. (1985) 'Just', in S. Bäckman and G. Kjellmer (eds), *Papers on Language and Literature*, Göteborg: Acta Universita Gothoburgensis: 1–10.

Aston, G. (1988) *Learning Comity: An Approach to the Description and Pedagogy of Interactional Speech*, Bologna: Cooperativa Libraria Universitaria Editrice Bologna.

—— (1995) 'Say "Thank you": some pragmatic constraints in conversational closings', *Applied Linguistics* 16, 1: 57–86.

Atkinson, J.M. (1992) 'Displaying neutrality: formal aspects of informal court proceedings', in P. Drew and J. Heritage (eds): 199–211.

Atkinson, J.M. and Drew, P. (1979) *Order in Court*, London: Macmillan.

Atkinson, P. (1999) 'Medical discourse, evidentiality and the construction of professional responsibility', in S. Sarangi and C. Roberts (eds): 75–107.

Bakhtin, M.M. (1986) 'The problem of speech genres', in C. Emersen and M. Holquist (eds), *Speech Genres and Other Late Essays*, Austin, TX: University of Texas Press: 60–102.

Bargiela-Chiappini, F. and Harris, S.J. (1995) 'Towards the generic structure of meetings in British and Italian managements', *Text* 15, 4: 531–60.

—— (1997a) *Managing Language: The Discourse of Corporate Meetings*, Amsterdam: John Benjamins.

—— (eds) (1997b) *The Language of Business: An International Perspective*, Edinburgh: Edinburgh University Press.

Bargiela-Chiappini, F. and Nickerson, C. (eds) (1999) *Writing Business: Genres, Media and Discourses*, Harlow: Longman.

Bernsten, J. (1998) 'Marked vs unmarked choices on the auto factory floor', in C. Myers-Scotton (ed.), *Codes and Consequences*, Oxford: Oxford University Press: 178–91.

Bettyruth, W. (1988) *The Jury Summation as Speech Genre*, Amsterdam: John Benjamins.

Bhatia, V.K. (1993) *Analysing Genre: Language Use in Professional Settings*, London: Longman.

Biber, D. (1988) *Variation across Speech and Writing*, Cambridge: Cambridge University Press.

—— (1990) 'Methodological issues regarding corpus-based analyses of linguistic variation', *Literary and Linguistic Computing* 5, 4: 257–69.

—— (1993) 'Representativeness in corpus design', *Literary and Linguistic Computing* 8, 4: 243–57.

Biber, D. and Finegan, E. (1989) 'Styles of stance in English: lexical and grammatical marking of evidentiality and affect', *Text* 9, 1: 93–124.

Biber, D., Johansson, S., Leech, G., Conrad, S. and Finegan, E. (1999) *Longman Grammar of Spoken and Written English*, Harlow: Pearson Education.

Bilbow, G.T. (1997) 'Cross-cultural impression management in the multicultural workplace: the special case of Hong Kong', *Journal of Pragmatics* 28: 461–87.

Bilmes, J. (1995) 'Negotiation and compromise: a microanalysis of a discussion in the United States Federal Trade Commission', in A. Firth (ed.): 61–81.

BNC, The Spoken Component of the BNC, January 2005: http://www.natcorp.ox.ac. uk/what/spok_design.html: (accessed 16 October 2005).

Boden, D. (1994) *The Business of Talk: Organizations in Action*, Cambridge: Polity Press.

——(1995) 'Agendas and arrangements: everyday negotiations in meetings', in A. Firth (ed.): 83–99.

Brazil, D. (1997) *The Communicative Value of Intonation in English*, Cambridge: Cambridge University Press.

Brown, P. and Levinson. S. (1978/1987) 'Universals in language usage: politeness phenomena', in E.N. Goody (ed.), *Questions and Politeness*, Cambridge: Cambridge University Press: 56–289; reissued as *Politeness: Some Universals in Language Usage*, Cambridge: Cambridge University Press, 1987.

Bryman, A. and Cramer, C. (1990) *Quantitative Data Analysis for Social Scientists*, London and New York: Routledge.

Button, G. and Sharrok, W. (1995) 'Practices in the work of ordering software development', in A. Firth (ed.): 159–81.

Cameron, D. (2000) *Good to Talk? Living and Working a Communication Culture*, London: Sage.

Cameron, L. (2002) 'Metaphor in science education: a discourse focus', *British Educational Research Journal* 28, 5: 637–74.

——(2003) *Metaphor in Educational Discourse*, London: Continuum.

Cameron, L. and Low, G.D. (2004) 'Figurative variation in episodes of educational talk and text', *European Journal of English Studies* 8, 3: 355–73.

Carter, R. (1987) *Vocabulary*, London: Allen and Unwin.

Carter, R. and McCarthy, M.J. (2004) 'Talking, creating: interactional language, creativity and context', *Applied Linguistics*, 25, 1: 62–88.

——(2006) *The Cambridge Grammar of English*, Cambridge: Cambridge University Press.

Carter, R., Hudson, J. and McCarthy, M. (1997) 'Spoken genres: CANCODE work in progress', paper presented at the annual meeting of the British Association for Applied Linguistics held at the University of Birmingham, Birmingham, September 1997.

Chafe, W. (1982) 'Integration and involvement in speaking, writing and oral literature', in D. Tannen (ed.), *Spoken and Written Language: Exploring Orality and Literacy*, Norwood, NJ: Ablex Publishing Corporation: 35–53.

——(1986) 'Evidentiality in English conversation and academic writing', in W. Chafe and J. Nichols (eds), *Evidentiality: The Linguistic Coding of Epistemology*, Norwood, NJ: Ablex Publishing Corporation: 261–72.

Channell, J. (1994) *Vague Language*, Oxford: Oxford University Press.

—— (2000) 'Corpus-based analysis of lexis', in S. Hunston and G. Thompson (eds): 38–55.

Charles, M. (1996) 'Business negotiations: interdependence between discourse and business relationship', *English for Specific Purposes* 15: 19–36.

Charles, M. and Charles, D. (1999) 'Sales negotiations: bargaining through tactical summaries', in M. Hewings and C. Nickerson (eds): 71–82.

Cheepen, C. (2000) 'Small talk in service dialogues: the conversational aspects of transactional telephone talk', in J. Coupland (ed.): 288–311.

Christie, F. (1986) 'Writing in schools: generic structures as ways of meaning', in B. Couture (ed.), *Functional Approaches to Writing Research Perspectives*, London: Frances Pinter: 221–40.

—— (2002) *Classroom Discourse Analysis: A Functional Perspective*, Sydney: Continuum.

Cicourel, A. (1987) 'The interpenetration of communicative contexts: examples from medical encounters', *Social Psychology Quarterly* 50, 2: 217–26.

—— (1999) 'The interaction of cognitive and cultural models in health care delivery', in S. Sarangi and C. Roberts (eds): 183–224.

Coates, J. (1983) *The Semantics of the Modal Auxiliaries*, London: Croom Helm.

Conrad, S. and Biber, D. (2000) 'Adverbial marking of stance in speech and writing', in S. Hunston and G. Thompson (eds): 56–73.

Corsaro, W. and Rizzo, T. (1990) 'Disputes in the peer culture of American and Italian nursery-school children', in A.D. Grimshaw (ed.): 21–66.

Cotterill, J. (2000) 'Multiple voices: monologue and dialogue in the O.J. Simpson criminal courtroom', in M. Coulthard, J. Cotterill and F. Rock (eds): 403–15.

Coulter, J. (1990) 'Elementary properties of argument sequences', in G. Psathas (ed.): 181–203.

Coulthard, M. (ed.) (1994) *Advances in Written Text Analysis*, London: Routledge.

—— (2000) 'Suppressed dialogue in a confession statement', in M. Coulthard, J. Cotterill and F. Rock (eds): 417–24.

Coulthard, M. and Ashby, M.C. (1976) 'A linguistic description of doctor–patient interviews', in M. Wadsworth and D. Robinson (eds), *Studies in Everyday Medical Life*, London: Martin Robertson: 69–88.

Coulthard, M. and Brazil, D. (1981) 'Exchange structure', in M. Coulthard and M. Montgomery (eds): 82–106.

Coulthard, M. and Montgomery M. (eds) (1981) *Studies in Discourse Analysis*, London: Routledge and Kegan Paul.

Coulthard, M., Cotterill, J. and Rock, F. (eds) *Dialogue Analysis VII: Working with Dialogue. Selected papers from the 7th IADA Conference, Birmingham 1999*, Tübingen: Max Niemeyer Verlag.

Coupland, J. (ed.) (2000) *Small Talk*, Harlow: Pearson Education.

Coupland, J., Robinson, J. and Coupland, N. (1994) 'Frame negotiation in doctor–elderly patient consultations', *Discourse and Society* 5, 1: 89–124.

Coupland, N. (1983) 'Patterns of encounter management: further arguments for discourse variables', *Language in Society* 12: 459–76.

Coupland, N. and Ylänne-McEwen, V. (2000) 'Talk about the weather: small talk, leisure talk and the travel industry', in J. Coupland (ed.): 163–82.

Cutting, J. (1999) 'The grammar of the in-group code', *Applied Linguistics* 20, 2: 179–202.

——(2000) *Analysing the Language of Discourse Communities*, Oxford: Elsevier Science.

Delin, J. (1998) 'Facework and instructor goals in the step aerobics workout', in S. Hunston (ed.): 56–71.

Devitt, A. (1991) 'Intertextuality in tax accounting: generic, referential and functional', in C. Bazerman and J. Paradis (eds), *Textual Dynamics of the Professions*, Madison, WI: The University of Wisconsin Press.

Dow, E. (1999) 'Negotiation comes of age: research into non-native contexts and implications for today's business English materials', in M. Hewings and C. Nickerson (eds): 83–99.

Drew, P. (1992) 'Contested evidence in courtroom cross-examination: the case of a trial for rape', in P. Drew and J. Heritage (eds): 470–520.

Drew, P. and Heritage, J. (eds) (1992) *Talk at Work*, Cambridge: Cambridge University Press.

Drew, P. and Holt, E. (1998) 'Figures of speech: figurative expressions and the management of topic transition in conversation', *Language in Society* 27, 4: 495–522.

Dudley-Evans, T. (1994) 'Genre analysis: An approach to text analysis for ESP', in M. Coulthard (ed.): 219–28.

Duranti, A. and Goodwin, C. (eds) (1992) *Rethinking Context: Language as an Interactive Phenomenon*, Cambridge: Cambridge University Press.

Edwards, A. and Westgate, D. (1994) *Investigating Classroom Talk*, London: Falmer.

Eggins, S. and Slade, D. (1997) *Analysing Casual Conversation*, London: Cassell.

Ehrman, M. (1966) *The Meanings of the Modals in Present-day American English*, The Hague: Mouton.

Ervin-Tripp, S.M. (1976) '"Is Sybil there?" The structure of some American English directives', *Language in Society* 5: 25–66.

Fairclough, N. (1992) *Discourse and Social Change*, Cambridge: Polity Press.

——(1995a) *Media Discourse*, London: Arnold.

——(1995b) *Critical Discourse Analysis*, London: Longman.

Farr, F. (2005) 'Reflecting on reflections: a corpus-based analysis of spoken post-teaching practice interactions in an English language teaching academic environment', unpublished PhD thesis, University of Limerick, College of Humanities.

Firth, A. (ed.) (1995a) *The Discourse of Negotiation: Studies of Language in the Workplace*, Oxford: Pergamon.

——(1995b) '"Accounts" in negotiation discourse: a single-case analysis', *Journal of Pragmatics* 23: 199–226.

Francis, D.W. (1986) 'Some structures of negotiation talk', *Language in Society* 15: 53–80.

Freedman, A. and Medway, P. (eds) (1994) *Genre and the New Rhetoric*, London: Taylor and Francis.

Garcez, P. de M. (1993) 'Point-making styles in cross-cultural business negotiation: a microethnographic study', *English for Specific Purposes* 12, 2: 103–20.

Gardner, R. (1997) 'The listener and minimal responses in conversational interaction', *Prospect* 12, 2: 12–31.

Gavruseva, L. (1995) 'Positioning and framing: constructing interactional asymmetry in employer–employee discourse', *Discourse Processes* 20: 325–45.

Gibbons, J. (ed.) (1994) *Language and the Law*, London and New York: Longman.

Goffman, E. (1967) *Interaction Ritual: Essays on Face to Face Behaviour*, New York: Anchor Books.

—— (1972) 'On face-work: an analysis of ritual elements in social interaction', in J. Laver and S. Hutcheson (eds), *Communication in Face to Face Interaction*, Harmondsworth: Penguin.

——(1974) *Frame Analysis*, New York: Harper and Row.

——(1981) *Forms of Talk*, Philadelphia, PA: University of Pennsylvania Press.

Goodwin, C. and Duranti, A. (1992) 'Rethinking context: an introduction', in A. Duranti and C. Goodwin (eds): 1–42.

Goodwin, C. and Goodwin, M.J. (1992) 'Assessments and the construction of context', in A. Duranti and C. Goodwin (eds): 147–82.

Goodwin, M.H. (1990) *He-said-she-said: Talk as Social Organization among Black Children*, Bloomington, IN: Indiana University Press.

——(1995) 'Assembling a response: setting and collaboratively constructed work talk', in P. ten Have and G. Psathas (eds), *Situated Order: Studies in the Social Organization of Talk and Embodied Activities*, Washington, DC: International Institute for Ethnomethodology and Conversation Analysis and University Press of America: 173–85.

Graham, J.L. (1983) 'Brazilian, Japanese and American business negotiations', *Journal of International Business Studies* 14: 47–61.

Greatbatch, D. and Dingwall, R. (1997) 'Argumentative talk in divorce mediation sessions', *American Sociological Review* 62: 151–70.

——(1998) 'Talk and identity in divorce mediation', in C. Antaki and S. Widdicombe (eds), *Identities in Talk*, London: Sage: 121–32.

——(1999) 'Professional neutralism in family mediation', in S. Sarangi and C. Roberts (eds): 271–92.

Grimshaw, A.D. (ed.) (1990) *Conflict Talk: Sociolinguistic Investigations of Arguments in Conversations*, Cambridge: Cambridge University Press.

Gumperz, J.J. (1982) *Discourse Strategies*, Cambridge: Cambridge University Press.

—— (1992) 'Contextualization and understanding', in A. Duranti and C. Goodwin (eds): 229–52.

—— (1999) 'On interactional sociolinguistic method', in S. Sarangi and C. Roberts (eds): 453–71.

Gunnarsson, B., Linell, P. and Nordberg, B. (eds) (1997) *The Construction of Professional Discourse*, Harlow: Addison Wesley Longman.

Halliday, M.A.K. (1970) 'Functional diversity in language as seen from a consideration of modality and mood in English', *Foundations of Language* 6: 322–61.

——(1978) *Language as Social Semiotic*, London: Edward Arnold.

—— (1985; 2nd edn 1994) *An Introduction to Functional Grammar*, London: Edward Arnold.

Halmari, H. (1983) 'Intercultural business telephone conversations: a case of Finns vs. Anglo-Americans', *Applied Linguistics* 14, 4: 408–30.

Handford, M. (2004) 'A pragmatic interpretation of a corpus of spoken Business English', paper presented at the annual conference of the International Association of Teachers of English as a Foreign Language, Liverpool, April 2004.

Hasan, R. (1985) 'The structure of a text', in M.A.K. Halliday and R. Hasan, *Language, Context and Text: Aspects of Language in a Social-semiotic Perspective*, Cambridge: Cambridge University Press: 52–69.

Heath, C. (1992) 'The delivery and reception of diagnosis in the general-practice consultation', in P. Drew and J. Heritage (eds): 235–67.

Heritage, J. (1997) 'Conversation analysis and institutional talk', in D. Silverman (ed.), *Qualitative Research: Theory, Method and Practice*, London: Sage: 161–82.

Heritage, J. and Sefi, S. (1992) 'Dilemmas of advice: aspects of delivery and reception of advice in interactions between health visitors and first-time mothers', in P. Drew, and J. Heritage (eds): 359–417.

Heritage, J. and Watson, D. (1979) 'Formulations as conversational objects', in G. Psathas (ed.): 123–62.

Hewings, M. and Nickerson, C. (eds) (1999) *Business English: Research into Practice*, Harlow: Pearson Education.

Hoey, M. (1983) *On the Surface of Discourse*, London: Allen and Unwin.

——(1994) 'Signalling in discourse: a functional analysis of a common discourse pattern in written and spoken English', in M. Coulthard (ed.): 26–45.

Holmes, J. (1983) 'Speaking English with the appropriate degree of conviction', in C. Brumfit (ed.), *Learning and Teaching Languages for Communication*, London: Centre for Information on Language Teaching and Research: 100–13.

——(2000a) 'Politeness, power and provocation: how humour functions in the workplace', *Discourse Studies* 2, 2: 159–85.

——(2000b) 'Doing collegiality and keeping control at work: small talk in government departments', in J. Coupland (ed.): 32–61.

——(2001) 'Managing conflict at work', paper presented at the annual convention of the American Association for Applied Linguistics, St Louis, Missouri, February 2001.

Holmes, J. and Stubbe, M. (2003) *Power and Politeness in the Workplace*, London: Pearson Education.

Holmes, J., Stubbe, M. and Vine, B. (1999) 'Constructing professional identity: "Doing power" in policy units', in S. Sarangi and C. Roberts (eds): 351–85.

Hundsnurscher, F. (1986) 'Dialogmuster und authentischer Text', in F. Hundsnurscher and E. Weigand (eds), *Dialoganalyse: Referate der 1. Arbeitstagung in Münster*, Tübingen: Niemeyer: 35–49.

Hunston, S. (ed.) (1998) *Language at Work: Selected Papers from the Annual Meeting of the British Association for Applied Linguistics held at the University of Birmingham, September 1997*, Clevedon: Multilingual Matters.

——(2002) *Corpora in Applied Linguistics*, Cambridge: Cambridge University Press.

Hunston, S. and Thompson, G. (eds) (2000) *Evaluation in Text*, Oxford: Oxford University Press.

Hutchby, I. (1996) *Confrontation Talk: Arguments, Asymmetries and Power on Talk Radio*, Hillsdale, NJ: Lawrence Erlbaum Associates.

Hutchby, I. and Wooffitt, R. (eds) (1998) *Conversation Analysis*, Cambridge: Cambridge University Press.

Hyland, K. (1996) 'Writing without conviction? Hedging in science research articles', *Applied Linguistics* 17, 4: 433–54.

Hyon, S. (1996) 'Genre in three traditions: implications for ESL', *TESOL Quarterly* 30, 4: 693–722.

Iacobucci, C. (1990) 'Accounts, formulations and goal attainment strategies in service encounters', in K. Tracy. and N. Coupland (eds): 85–99.

Jarvis, J. and Robinson, M. (1997) 'Analyzing educational discourse: an exploratory study of teacher response and support to pupils' learning', *Applied Linguistics* 18, 2: 212–18.

Jefferson, G. (1972) 'Side sequences', in D. Sudnow (ed.): 294–338.

—— (1988) 'On the sequential organization of troubles-talk in ordinary conversation', *Social Problems* 35, 4: 418–41.

Johnson, K.E. (1995) *Understanding Communication in Second Language Classrooms*, Cambridge: Cambridge University Press.

Kennedy, G. (2000) 'Using a corpus: applications of language as probability', paper presented at the annual convention of the American Association for Applied Linguistics, Vancouver, March 2000.

King, S.W. and Sereno, K.K. (1984) 'Conversational appropriateness as a conversational imperative', *Quarterly Journal of Speech* 70: 264–73.

Kniffka, H. (ed.) (1996) *Recent Developments in Forensic Linguistics*, Frankfurt am Main: Peter Lang.

Koester, A. (2001) 'Interpersonal markers in workplace genres: pursuing transactional and relational goals in office talk', unpublished PhD thesis, University of Nottingham, School of English Studies.

—— (2002) 'The performance of speech acts in workplace conversations and the teaching of communicative functions', *System* 30, 2: 167–84.

—— (2004) 'Relational sequences in workplace genres', *Journal of Pragmatics* 36: 1405–28.

Koller, V. (2004) *Metaphor and Gender in Business Media Discourse: A Critical Cognitive Study*, Basingstoke: Palgrave Macmillan.

Kotthoff, H. (1993) 'Disagreement and concession in disputes: on the context sensitivity of preference structures', *Language in Society* 22: 193–216.

Kuiper, K. and Flindall, M. (2000) 'Social rituals, formulaic speech and small talk at the supermarket checkout', in J. Coupland (ed.): 183–207.

Kumaravadivelu, B. (1999) 'Critical classroom discourse analysis', *TESOL Quarterly* 33, 3: 453–84.

Labov, W. (1972) *Language in the Inner City*, Oxford: Basil Blackwell.

Lakoff, R. (1973) 'The logic of politeness; or minding your p's and q's', *Papers from the 9th Regional Meeting of the Chicago Linguistics Society*, Chicago: Chicago Linguistic Society: 292–305.

Lampi, M. (1986) *Linguistic Components of Strategy in Business Negotiations*, Helsinki: Helsinki School of Economics.

Laver, J. (1975) 'Communicative functions of phatic communion', in A. Kendon, R. Harris and M. Key (eds), *The Organization of Behaviour in Face-to-face Interaction*, The Hague: Mouton: 215–38.

Leech, G. (1969) *Towards a Semantic Description of English*, London: Longman.

——(1971) *Meaning and the English Verb*, London: Longman.

Levinson, S.C. (1983) *Pragmatics*, Cambridge: Cambridge University Press.

Linde, C. (1997) 'Evaluation as linguistic structure and social practice', in B.L. Gunnarsson, P. Linell and B. Nordberg (eds): 151–72.

Longacre, R.E. (1983) *The Grammar of Discourse*, New York and London: Plenum Press.

Low, G. (1988) 'On teaching metaphor', *Applied Linguistics* 9, 2: 125–47.

Lyons, J. (1977) *Semantics*, vol. II, Cambridge: Cambridge University Press.

McCarthy, M. (1991) *Discourse Analysis for Language Teachers*, Cambridge: Cambridge University Press.

——(1998) *Spoken Language and Applied Linguistics*, Cambridge: Cambridge University Press.

——(2000) 'Mutually captive audiences: small talk and close contact service encounters', in J. Coupland (ed.): 84–109.

——(2003) 'Talking back: "small" interactional response tokens in everyday conversation', *Research on Language in Social Interaction*, special issue on Small Talk, edited by J. Coupland, 36, 1: 33–63.

McCarthy, M. and Carter, R. (1994) *Language as Discourse*, London: Longman.

——(2000) 'Feeding back: non-minimal response tokens in everyday English conversation', in C. Heffer and H. Sauntson (eds), *Words in Context: A Tribute to John Sinclair on his Retirement*, Birmingham: Department of English, University of Birmingham.

——(2004) '"There's millions of them": Hyperbole in everyday conversation', *Journal of Pragmatics* 36: 149–84.

McCarthy, M.J. and Handford, M. (2004) '"Invisible to us": a preliminary corpus-based study of spoken business English', in U. Connor. and T. Upton (eds), *Discourse in the Professions. Perspectives from Corpus Linguistics*, Amsterdam: John Benjamins: 167–201.

McEnery, T. and Wilson, A. (1996) *Corpus Linguistics*, Edinburgh: Edinburgh University Press.

Malinowski, B. (1923) 'The problem of meaning in primitive languages', in C.K. Ogden and I.A. Richards (eds), *The Meaning of Meaning*, London: Routledge and Kegan Paul; excerpt reprinted as 'Phatic communion', in J. Laver and S. Hutcheson (eds) (1972) *Communication in Face to Face Interaction*, Harmondsworth: Penguin: 146–52.

Mandala, S. (1998) 'The pragmatics of advice in natural talk and textbook dialogue', unpublished PhD thesis, University of Cambridge Research Centre for English and Applied Linguistics.

Mandelbaum, J. (1990/91) 'Beyond mundane reason: conversation analysis and context', *Research on Language and Social Interaction* 24: 333–50.

Marriott, H.E. (1995) '"Deviations" in an intercultural business negotiation', in A. Firth (ed.): 247–69.

Martin, J.R. (1989) *Factual Writing: Exploring and Challenging Social Reality*, Oxford: Oxford University Press.

—— (2000) 'Beyond exchange: appraisal systems in English', in S. Hunston and G. Thompson (eds): 142–75.

Martin, J.R. and Rothery, J. (1986), *Writing Project Report No. 4* (Working Papers in Linguistics), Sydney: Linguistics Department, University of Sydney.

Maynard, D.W. (1989) 'On the ethnography and analysis of discourse in institutional settings', in J.A. Holstein and G. Miller (eds), *Perspectives on Social Problems*, vol. I, London: JAI Press: 127–46.

——(1992) 'On clinicians co-implicating recipients' perspective in the delivery of diagnostic news', in P. Drew and J. Heritage (eds): 331–58.

Mayr, A. (2004) *Prison Discourse: Language as a Means of Control and Resistance*, Basingstoke: Palgrave Macmillan.

Merritt, M. (1976) 'On questions following questions in service encounters', *Language in Society* 5: 315–57.

Miller, C.R. (1984) 'Genre as social action', *Quarterly Journal of Speech* 70, 2: 151–67.

Mitchell, T.F. (1957) 'The language of buying and selling in Cyrenaica: a situational statement', *Hésperis* 44: 31–71; reprinted in T.F. Mitchell (ed.) (1975) *Principles of Firthian Linguistics*, London: Longman: 167–200.

Moon, R. (1992) 'Textual aspects of fixed expressions in learners' dictionaries', in P. Arnaud and H. Béjoint (eds), *Vocabulary and Applied Linguistics*, London: Macmillan: 13–27.

——(1997) 'Vocabulary connections: multi-word items in English', in N. Schmitt and M. McCarthy (eds), *Vocabulary: Description, Acquisition and Pedagogy*, Cambridge: Cambridge University Press: 40–63.

—— (1998) *Fixed Expressions and Idioms in English: A Corpus-based Approach*, Oxford: Clarendon Press.

Muntigl, P. and Turnbull, W. (1998) 'Conversational structure and facework in arguing', *Journal of Pragmatics* 29: 225–56.

Nelson, M. (2000) 'A corpus-base study of business English and business English teaching materials', unpublished PhD thesis, University of Manchester.

Neu, J. (1998) 'Conversation structure: an explanation of bargaining behaviors in negotiation', *Management Communication Quarterly* 2, 1: 23–45.

Norrick, N.R. (1985) *How Proverbs Mean: Semantic Studies in English Proverbs*, Berlin: Mouton de Gruyter.

——(1993) *Conversational Joking*, Bloomington: Indiana University Press.

O'Donnell, K. (1990) 'Difference and dominance: how labor and management talk conflict', in A.D. Grimshaw (ed.): 193–216.

O'Keeffe, A. (2006) *Investigating Media Discourse*, London: Routledge.

Oertli, P. (1991) 'The language of business meetings: teaching materials in the light of one reality', unpublished MA dissertation, CELS, University of Birmingham.

Overstreet, M. and Yule, G. (1997a) 'On being explicit and stuff in contemporary American English', *Journal of Pragmatics* 25, 3: 250–8.

—— (1997b) 'Locally contingent categorization in discourse', *Discourse Processes* 23: 83–97.

Palmer, F.R. (1979, 2nd edn 1990) *Modality and the English Modals*, London: Longman.

Paltridge, B. (1996) 'Genre, text type and the language learning classroom', *ELT Journal* 50, 3: 237–43.

Perkins, M. (1982) 'The core meaning of the English modals', *Journal of Linguistics* 18: 245–73.

Pomerantz, A. (1984) 'Agreeing and disagreeing with assessments: some features of preferred/dispreferred turn shapes', in J.M. Atkinson and J. Heritage (eds) *Structures of Social Action*, Cambridge: Cambridge University Press: 57–102.

—— (1998) 'Multiple interpretations of "context": How are they useful?' *Research on Language and Social Interaction* 3, 1: 123–32.

Poncini, G. (2002) 'Investigating discourse at business meetings with multicultural participation', *International Review of Applied Linguistics* 40: 345–73.

—— (2004) *Discursive Strategies in Multicultural Business Meetings*, Bern: Peter Lang.

Powell, M.J. (1992) 'Semantic/pragmatic regularities in informal lexis: British speakers in spontaneous conversational settings', *Text* 12, 1: 19–58.

Prince, E.F., Frader, J. and Bosk, C. (1982) 'On hedging in physician–physician discourse', in R.J. Di Pietro (ed.), *Linguistics and the Professions: Proceedings of the 2nd Annual Delaware Symposium on Language Studies*, Norwood, NJ: Ablex: 83–97.

Psathas, G. (ed.) (1979) *Everyday Language: Situations in Ethnomethodology*, New York: Irvington Publishers.

Pufahl Bax, I. (1986) 'How to assign work in an office: a comparison of spoken and written directives in American English', *Journal of Pragmatics* 10: 673–92.

Ragan, S.L. (2000) 'Sociable talk in women's health care contexts: two forms of non-medical talk', in J. Coupland (ed.): 269–87.

Roberts, C. and Sarangi, S. (1999a) 'Introduction: negotiating and legitimating roles and identities', in S. Sarangi and C. Roberts (eds): 227–36.

Roberts, C. and Sarangi, S. (1999b) 'Hybridity in gate-keeping discourse: issues of practical relevance for the researcher', in S. Sarangi and C. Roberts (eds): 473–503.

Rogerson-Revell, P. (1999) 'Meeting talk: a stylistic approach to teaching meeting skills', in M. Hewings and C. Nickerson (eds): 55–70.

Rumelhart, D.E. (1975) 'Notes on a schema for stories', in D.G. Bobrow and A.M. Collins (eds), *Representations and Understanding*, New York: Academic Press: 211–36.

Sacks, H. (1987) 'On the preferences for agreement and contiguity in sequences in conversation', in G. Button and J.R.E. Lee (eds), *Talk in Social Organization*, Clevedon: Multilingual Matters: 54–69.

Sadock, J.M. (1977) 'Truth and approximation', *Berkeley Linguistic Society Papers* 3: 430–9.

Sarangi, S. and Roberts, C. (eds) (1999) *Talk Work and Institutional Order: Discourse in Medical, Mediation and Management Settings*, Berlin: Mouton de Gruyter.

Schank, R.C. and Abelson, R.P. (1977) *Scripts, Plans, Goals, and Understanding: An Inquiry into Human Knowledge Structures*, Hillsdale, NJ: Lawrence Erlbaum Associates.

Schegloff, E.A. (1972) 'Notes on conversational practice: formulating place', in D. Sudnow (ed.): 75–119.

—— (1980) 'Preliminaries to preliminaries: can I ask you a question?' *Sociological Inquiry* 50: 104–52.

——(1992a) 'On talk and its institutional occasions', in P. Drew and J. Heritage (eds): 101–34.

——(1992b) 'In another context', in A. Duranti and C. Goodwin (eds): 191–227.

——(1992c) 'Repair after next turn: the last structurally provided defense of intersubjectivity in conversation', *American Journal of Sociology* 97, 5: 1295–345.

Schegloff, E. and Sacks, H. (1973) 'Opening up closings', *Semiotica* 8, 4: 289–327.

Schenkein, J. (1978) 'Identity negotiations in conversation' in J. Schenkein (ed.), *Studies in the Organization of Conversational Interaction*, New York: Academic Press: 57–78.

Schiffrin, D. (1987) *Discourse Markers*, Cambridge: Cambridge University Press.

——(1990) 'The principle of intersubjectivity in communication and conversation', *Semiotica* 80, 1/2: 121–51.

Schneider, K. (1989) 'The art of talking about nothing: zur Beschreibung phatischer Dialoge', in E. Weigand and F. Hundsnurscher (eds), *Dialoganalyse II: Referate der 2. Arbeitstagung Bochum 1988, I and II*, Tübingen: Niemeyer: 437–49.

Scott, M. (1999) *Wordsmith Tools*, Version 3 (corpus analytical software suite), Oxford: Oxford University Press.

Scott, M. and Lyman, S. (1968) 'Accounts', *American Sociological Review* 33: 46–62.

Silverman, D. (1999) 'Warriors or collaborators: reworking methodological controversies in the study of institutional interaction', in S. Sarangi and C. Roberts (eds): 401–25.

Sinclair, J.M. (1987) 'Mirror for a text', MS, University of Birmingham.

Sinclair, J.M. and Coulthard, M. (1975) *Towards an Analysis of Discourse*, Oxford: Oxford University Press.

Spencer-Oatey, H. and Xing, J. (1998) 'Relational management in Chinese–British business meetings', in S. Hunston (ed.): 31–46.

Stenström, A.-B. (1990) 'Lexical items peculiar to spoken discourse', in J. Svartvik (ed.), *The London–Lund Corpus of Spoken English: Description and Research*, Lund: Lund University Press: 137–75.

Strässler, J. (1982) *Idioms in English: A Pragmatic Analysis*, Tübingen: Günther-Narr-Verlag.

Stubbs, M. (1986) 'A matter of prolonged fieldwork: notes towards a modal grammar of English', *Applied Linguistics* 7, 1: 1–25.

Sudnow, D. (ed.) (1972) *Studies in Social Interaction*, New York: Free Press.

Swales, J.M. (1990) *Genre Analysis: English in Academic and Research Settings*, Cambridge: Cambridge University Press.

Tannen, D. (1989) *Talking Voices: Repetition, Dialogue, and Imagery in Conversational Discourse*, Cambridge: Cambridge University Press.

——(ed.) (1993a) *Framing in Discourse*, Oxford: Oxford University Press.

—— (1993b) 'What's in a frame? Surface evidence for underlying expectations', in D. Tannen (ed.): 14–56.

——(1994) *Talking from 9 to 5*, New York: William and Morrow Company.

—— (1998) 'The power of talk: who gets heard and why', *Harvard Business Review*, Sept.–Oct. 1995, reprinted in D.D. Oaks (ed.), *Linguistics at Work*, Fort Worth, TX: Harcourt Brace College Publishers: 242–59.

Tannen, D. and Wallat, C. (1987) 'Interactive frames and knowledge schemas in interaction: examples from a medical examination/interview', *Social Psychology Quarterly* 50: 205–16; reprinted in D. Tannen, (ed.) (1993): 57–76.

ten Have, P. (1991) 'Talk and institution: a reconsideration of the "asymmetry" of doctor–patient interaction', in D. Boden and D.H. Zimmerman (eds), *Talk and Social Structure*, Cambridge: Polity Press: 138–63.

——(1995) 'Medical ethnomethodology: an overview', *Human Studies* 18: 245–61.

Thomas, J. (1984) 'Cross-cultural discourse as "unequal encounter": towards a pragmatic analysis', *Applied Linguistics* 5, 3: 226–35.

Thornborrow, J. (2001) *Power Talk: Language and Interaction in Institutional Discourse*, London: Pearson Education.

Threadgold, T. (1989) 'Talking about genre: ideologies and incompatible discourses', *Cultural Studies* 3, 1: 101–27.

Tottie, G. (1991) 'Conversational style in British and American English: the case of back-channels', in K. Aijmer and B. Altenberg (eds), *English Corpus Linguistics*, London: Longman: 254–71.

Tracy, K. and Coupland, N. (eds) (1990) *Multiple Goals in Discourse*, Clevedon: Multi-lingual Matters.

Tsui, A.B.M. (1994) *English Conversation*, Oxford: Oxford University Press.

van Dijk, T.A. (1993) 'Principles of critical discourse analysis', *Discourse and Society* 4, 2: 249–83.

Ventola, E. (1979) 'The structure of casual conversation in English', *Journal of Pragmatics* 3: 267–8.

——(1983) 'Contrasting schematic structures in service encounters', *Applied Linguistics* 4: 242–58.

——(1987) *The Structure of Social Action. A Systematic Approach to the Semiotics of Service Encounters*, London: Frances Pinter.

Vuchinich, S. (1990) 'The sequential organization of closing in verbal family dispute', in A.D. Grimshaw (ed.): 118–38.

Wagner, J. (1995), '"Negotiating activity" in technical problem solving', in A. Firth (ed.): 223–45.

Walsh, S. (2006) *Investigating Classroom Discourse*, London: Routledge.

Weigel, M.M. and Weigel, R.M. (1985) 'Directive use in a migrant agricultural community', *Language in Society* 14, 1: 63–79.

Williams, M. (1988) 'Language taught for meetings and language used in meetings: is there anything in common?' *Applied Linguistics* 9, 1: 45–58.

Willing. K. (1992) 'Problem-solving discourse in professional work', *Prospect* 7, 2: 57–65.

——(1997) 'Modality in task-oriented discourse: the role of subjectivity in "getting the job done"', *Prospect* 12, 2: 33–42.

Yamada, H. (1990) 'Topic management and turn distribution in business meetings: American vs Japanese strategies', *Text* 10, 3: 271–95.

Ylänne-McEwen, V.T. (1996) 'Relational processes within a transactional setting: An investigation of travel agency discourse', unpublished PhD thesis, University of Wales, Cardiff.

Zhang, X. (1998) 'Echoing in English conversation: a corpus-based study', unpublished PhD thesis, University of Nottingham.

Index

Related titles from Routledge

An Introduction to Discourse Analysis: Theory and Method, 2nd edition

James Paul Gee

'If you only read one book on discourse analysis, this is the one to read. Gee shows us that discourse analysis is about a lot more than linguistic study; it's about how to keep from, as he says, "getting physically, socially, culturally, or morally 'bitten' by the world".'

Ron Scollon, Georgetown University, USA

James Paul Gee presents here his unique, integrated approach to discourse analysis: the analysis of spoken and written language as it is used to enact social and cultural perspectives and identities.

Assuming no prior knowledge of linguistics, the book presents both a theory of language-in-use, as well as a method of research. This method is made up of 'tools of inquiry' and strategies for using them.

Perspectives from a variety of approaches and disciplines, including applied linguistics, education, psychology, anthropology, and communication, are incorporated to help students and scholars from a range of backgrounds formulate their own views and engage in their own discourse analyses.

ISBN10: 0–415–32860–8 (pbk)
ISBN10: 0–415–32861–6 (hbk)

ISBN13: 978–0–415–32860–9 (pbk)
ISBN13: 978–0–415–32861–6 (hbk)

Available at all good bookshops
For ordering and further information please visit www.routledge.com

Discourses in Place: Language in the Material World

Ron Scollon and Suzie Wong Scollon

'Written with directness and charm, and an abundance of persuasive examples, this book locates meaning not just in language but in the richness and complexity of the lived world ... its insights will start a generation of new thinking, and research. It marks a turning point in linguistics and semiotics alike.'

Gunther Kress, *Institute of Education, University of London, UK*

Discourses in Place develops the first systematic analysis of the ways we interpret language as it is materially placed in the world. It argues that we can only interpret the meaning of public texts like road signs, notices and brand logos by considering the social and physical world that surrounds them. Drawing on a wide range of real examples, from signs in the Chinese mountains to urban centres in Austria, France, North America and Hong Kong, this textbook equips students with the methodology and models they need to undertake their own research in 'geosemiotics', and is essential reading for anyone with an interest in language and the ways in which we communicate.

ISBN10: 0–415–29048–1 (hbk)
ISBN10: 0–415–29049–X (pbk)
ISBN10: 0–203–42272–4 (ebk)

ISBN13: 978–0–415–290487 (hbk)
ISBN13: 978–0–415–290494 (pbk)
ISBN13: 978–0–203–422724 (ebk)

Available at all good bookshops
For ordering and further information please visit www.routledge.com

The Language of Work

Intertext Series
Almut Koester

'*The Language of Work* is, without doubt, a valuable addition to the excellent Intertext series. Almut Koester combines intellectual rigour with accessibility and provides readers with an authoritative and coherent overview of language in the workplace. It is a skilful combination of essential knowledge and engaging and thought-provoking activities.'

Steve Cooper, Principal Examiner *AS/A2 English Language*

'This book will provide students with a clear and useful introduction to the study of language in the world of work. It includes lots of appropriate examples and helpful self-study activities. It even ends on a practical note, with the last unit providing students with some linguistic insights into the job advertisements they are likely to deal with.'

Neil Mercer, *The Open University*

The Language of Work

- examines how language is used in business and the workplace, looking at a range of situations and data: from meetings to negotiations, official reports to emails between colleagues
- explores representations of work in job adverts, TV programmes and advertising
- looks at the way people in business interact through small talk, politeness, customer care and management—employee relationships
- is illustrated with lively examples taken from the real world and includes a full glossary
- features a useful section on entering the world of work, including advice on CV writing, job interviews and developing 'transferable skills'.

ISBN10: 0–415–30729–5 (hbk)
ISBN10: 0–415–30730–9 (pbk)

ISBN13: 978–0–415–30729–1 (hbk)
ISBN13: 978–0–415–30730–7 (pbk)

Available at all good bookshops
For ordering and further information on the Intertext series please visit:
www.routledge.com/rcenters/linguistics/series/intertext.html

eBooks – at www.eBookstore.tandf.co.uk

A library at your fingertips!

eBooks are electronic versions of printed books. You can store them on your PC/laptop or browse them online.

They have advantages for anyone needing rapid access to a wide variety of published, copyright information.

eBooks can help your research by enabling you to bookmark chapters, annotate text and use instant searches to find specific words or phrases. Several eBook files would fit on even a small laptop or PDA.

NEW: Save money by eSubscribing: cheap, online access to any eBook for as long as you need it.

Annual subscription packages

We now offer special low-cost bulk subscriptions to packages of eBooks in certain subject areas. These are available to libraries or to individuals.

For more information please contact webmaster.ebooks@tandf.co.uk

We're continually developing the eBook concept, so keep up to date by visiting the website.

www.eBookstore.tandf.co.uk

DISCARDED
CONCORDIA UNIV. LIBRARY

CONCORDIA UNIVERSITY LIBRARIES
SIR GEORGE WILLIAMS CAMPUS
WEBSTER LIBRARY